EYEWITNESS

*The Case of the Carefully Crafted
Central Coast Rapist*

by
Lori Carangelo

Access Press

COVER IMAGE-
LEFT: 1989 photo of Joseph Belarde Garcia;
MIDDLE: 10-18-1989 composite created by Darrell R. Klasey according to
Jacqueline Brooks' description of her attacker;
RIGHT: 1989 mugshot of new suspect discovered December 2020

Printed in the United States of America
ISBN 978-0-942605-61-7

Contents

PREFACE - 5

Chapter 1:
(1989) THE ARREST – 7

Chapter 2:
(1989) ACCUSERS and ALIBIS – 17

Chapter 3:
(1991) TRIAL of the CAREFULLY CRAFTED
CENTRAL COAST RAPIST – 41
The Troublesome DNA – 48; Surprise Witness – 51

Chapter 4
(2004-2013) INNOCENCE PROJECTS,
MISSING DNA, and GOVERNOR JERRY BROWN –73

Chapter 5
(2015) A BITTERLY BIASED PAROLE HEARING – 89

Chapter 6:
(2019) INNOCENCE: A TOUGH SELL:
LOYOLA and LARRY HOBSON- 107

Chapter 7:
(2020) GOVERNOR GAVIN NEWSON,
WARDENS, MURDERS and COVID-19 – 117

Chapter 8:
(2021) IT WASN'T JOE – 143

Chapter 9:
"EYEWITNESS" – A BANNED BOOK – 151

Chapter 10:
(2021) GOVERNOR NEWSOM and CALIFORNIA ROARS BACK-
D.A. DAN DOW REMAINS SILENT, PAROLE REVISITED
and CONTINUING EFFORTS TO FREE JOE GARCIA – 153

PHOTO: JOE GARCIA'S DUNGEON-LIKE CELL

BIBLIOGRAPHY – 167

INDEX – 173

PHOTOS (JOE GARCIA, 1989-2022) - CONTACT JOE – 179

ABOUT THE AUTHOR – 181

MORE BOOKS BY THE AUTHOR - 182

ADDENDUM - 183

JOE'S 2025 PAROLE HEARING
"EYEWITNESS" TO BE INVESTIGATED

PREFACE

I was raped. It happened decades ago, but I know the pain and anguish suffered by Rape victims even as they move on with their lives. I had also seen how women who honestly claim they were sexually assaulted by powerful, wealthy men – celebrities, Supreme Court justices, even presidents – are disbelieved, mocked and intimidated. And I certainly have no sympathy for rapists.

When I received Joe Garcia's first letter in 2009, he was merely seeking information about his Native American tribal roots via my organization, Americans For Open Records (AmFOR). His letter also informed me he had been incarcerated since 1989 on charges of *Rape*, but added *"PS: Just so your know, I'm innocent and was wrongfully convicted."* What I "knew," from researching and writing true crime stories, was that lots of prisoners who are undoubtedly guilty *claim* innocence. But eventually I read the police reports and thousands of pages of Joe Garcia's trial transcripts, and interviewed those involved with his case and those who were close to him and not only believe him to be innocent but also have *proven* it.

It's time for the truth to be told about how an innocent man has had 32 years of his life stolen as result of a wrongful conviction. It's time to free Joe Garcia.

-The Author

DEDICATION

This book is dedicated to more than 3,233 exonerees
on the National Registry of Exonerations since 1989
(when Joe Garcia was wrongfully convicted)
and to those who (like Joe Garcia) still wait for justice.

> *"The law does not expect a man to be prepared
> to defend every act of his life which may be suddenly
> and without notice alleged against him."*
> -Chief Justice John Marshall

Chapter 1:
(1989) THE ARREST

In 1989, Joe Garcia was unquestionably the "poster child" for a life turned around. And he was reaping the rewards. **Fred "Mike" Raike** had just upgraded Joe's job description from Office Manager to Account Executive for "Homes and Land" magazine at Mike's real estate office in Atascadero, California. Joe and his wife, **Judy**, married in 1982 while he was in prison, having met via a Christian dating service. By 1989, they were living the good life in the small college town of Atascadero in the middle of San Luis Obispo County California's beautiful wine country. Judy was a schoolteacher and four months pregnant with their first child.

Joe began motivational public speaking at local churches, schools and business groups on how he had turned his life around ten years before, September 2, 1978, while in a holding cell on a Robbery charge – when he stole to feed his heroin addition. Joe said that's the night he allowed God to come into his life and that's how he stayed off drugs since, and was helping others struggling with drug addiction. He also volunteered his services at Atascadero State Hospital when his friend, Doris Bieg, convinced the hospital's Director to hire him to conduct groups with the patients, some of whom he knew from the different prisons when he, too, was incarcerated.

Mike Raike was an exceptional employer who mentored Joe and became his good friend, while Joe became Mike's "right hand" as he learned the business. Short in stature at 5'5," Mike had a larger than life, friendly, outgoing personality, ideal for sales. A workaholic, he was married with three children. Mike knew all about Joe's past, but it did not overly concern him, as he and his wife had begun attending Joe and Judy's Bible Study class where he observed Joe's ease at interacting with people and making them feel comfortable. By mid-year, Mike was confident that Joe was ready for more responsibility by handling magazine sales. Concurrently, Joe was mentoring local youth to help them quit the drug-related lifestyle that he had quit. Joe felt that Mike's confidence in him saved him from repeating his "past mistakes."

1982-89 had been happiest years for Joe and his wife,
Judith ("Judy") Emily Garcia –
Photos: first meeting, wedding, honeymoon

Mike Raike, CEO/Owner, and Joe Garcia, Account Executive,
Homes and Land magazine and Real Estate, Atascadero, California, 1989

If only Joe could similarly save his mother, Rose.

Rose Carmel Belarde Garcia, once a stunning Italian, German, Native American beauty, grew up in Los Angeles during the 1930s Depression Era with strict Catholic parents. A typical rebellious teenager in 1941 at Emerson Junior High, she befriended Norma Jean Mortenson Baker who became Marilyn Monroe. The two teenage girls had shared their aspirations about becoming Hollywood movie stars. But in 1942, at 17, Rose, too, lost her identity, by marrying 30-year old **Raymond Apodaca Garcia**, a Native American registered with the Pueblo tribe.

Rose and Raymond Garcia, 1942

Rose was 21 when Joe was born on July 20, 1948, in Culver City, California. Angelina, Ray Jr., and Michael completed the family. Ray Sr. was a chef at the popular Beverly Hills restaurant on Wilshire, Armstrong Schroeder Cafe, known as "Schroeder's" by the movie stars who hung out there. The job enabled Raymond to purchase home in the upper Wilshire district of West Los Angeles, off Bundy, near the home of then-football great, O.J. Simpson. The Garcia children lacked for nothing – there were toys galore, pony rides, weekends at Santa Monica Beach.

But in 1955, Rose and Ray divorced. Rose then went through a succession of men and the neighborhood women accused her of sleeping with their husbands or boyfriends. Rose didn't view herself as a prostitute but as a single parent who had to keep food on the table for her children. The reality of her lifestyle, after Raymond, was clouded by her alcoholism and eventually heroin addiction. It led to poverty, domestic violence and Joe's painful childhood memories, including his mother's unwanted

9

inappropriate sexual advances toward him when he was between 10 and 11 years old, which she said was to "make him a man." Her addictions and behaviors led to Joe's own heroin addiction by age 15. Up until then, his arrests had been for petty thefts, starting at age 10 when a storeowner caught him stealing a 10-cent bag of balloons. A judge sent him to Juvenile Hall Detention– "juvie" – where he witnessed a young boy being raped. At 11, Joe planned on becoming an altar boy at St. Sebastian's Church where he was baptized and had his First Communion. But that plan ended when the priest caught him breaking into the collection box.

Rose was a loving mother when sober, but when she was intoxicated, she abused him. When he was 8, she hung him in a closet for wetting his bed; her boyfriend cut him down. At 10 and 11, after that experience, he attempted suicide by hanging himself and again by overdosing on pills. When he was 11, Rose punished him for stealing $1.50 from her bowl of coins by burning his hands on a hot plate. She also sometimes choked, slapped or hit him with a stick or wire. Yet he always tried to "save" her and continued to steal to help support her and his siblings.

Joe's father died in 1987 and Rose continued to go through men, most of whom mistreated her, and she ended up on the streets. Heroin became Joe's downfall and he graduated to adult prison at age 18. At 19, he was sent to Deuel Vocational Institution for Men at Tracy. At Tracy, he trained as a 158-bound welter weight boxer until he was good enough to participate in prison-authorized boxing matches, partly to defend himself from the hardened criminals he then lived with, and partly to avoid succumbing to peer pressure from prison gangs wanting to recruit him. From there, his repeat offenses – stealing for drugs – landed him in California Institution for Men (CIM) and eventually he was sent to the toughest prison of all - San Quentin.

In 1988, Joe was a free man who, with Judy's support, now dedicated himself to "serving God instead of serving time." That's when he searched out and found Rose. He and his brothers tried an intervention, hoping Rose would let them take her to the Women's Home of Victory Outreach in La Puente where she could have a roof and "get clean." Rose said she appreciated the offer but *Maybe later*," as she left to resume her addictions and homeless existence.

Rose died at the Women's Drug Treatment and Recovery Center in Englewood, California on March 1, 2003.

Joe thanked God for Judy. She didn't smother him, just enabled him to develop his potential which made him feel good about himself. After two years together, she felt secure enough that he was not only a good husband but also would be a good father, so they were now happily expecting a baby. Judy smiled as she remembered the Saturday when they drove to Salinas Mall "just for the ride" and to wander around the shops:

> *"We bought a new television, new work clothes for Joe, and had dinner at Sbarro's, a pizza restaurant at the Mall, and finally drove back home very late... close to 9:30 PM. By the time we arrived home, it was after midnight, but Joe, thinking about his 'big day' ahead, had to try on his new shirts before coming to bed."*

The next morning, Thursday, October 19, 1989, began like any other day, except that Joe laid in bed a bit longer this day, envisioning landing the contract with a Century 21 broker who Mike Raike had been trying to sign up for the past two years. As usual, Judy had already been awake and up at 4:15 AM, even though she had plenty of time to get ready for school. When Joe awoke about half an hour later, they exchanged their usual "*Good Mornings*" and their usual agreement about breakfast. As usual, Judy was reading her Daily Devotion when Joe finally got up, lost in thought as he headed for the shower without interrupting his wife's prayer. As usual, by quarter to six, the couple was enjoying their morning coffee with a slice of wheat bread on which precisely one teaspoon of peanut butter was spread, as they chatted about their weekend plans over breakfast. As usual, their dog, "Mister," reminded Joe it was time to let him out to do his business. And, as usual, Joe and Mister got in some playtime before Joe was ready to leave for work. Even Mister appeared to be smiling. As usual, at 7:00 am, Joe walked Judy to her car, the sky was overcast over the California coastal community, but the light fog would probably burn off by Noon. As usual, Joe opened her car door for her. As usual, they shared a quick goodbye kiss and "I love yous." As she started to drive off, Joe called out to her that he would phone her around Noon. It was going to be a good day indeed. All was right with the world.

Joe had driven only a couple blocks from their home in his brand new Ford Probe when he noticed *two* cars were speeding up to him. One was obviously a police car. Joe didn't think they were after him until he saw flashing red lights of the Atascadero Police car in his rear view mirror. As he promptly pulled over to the side of the road, *three* cars then surrounded his. When Officers **Patrick Louis Zuchelli** and **Thomas R. De Priest** got out of their car and approached him, Joe didn't think he had

11

committed any infraction, certainly nothing to warrant this, but he automatically began to reach for his wallet in expectation of having to show his driver's license. Instead, the officer instructed him *"Sir, would you mind stepping out of the car?"*

Puzzled, Joe asked, *"What's the problem, officer?"* Now *four* men had stepped out of their cars and Joe immediately recognized one of them, which gave him a disturbing feeling in the pit of his stomach. It was **Detective Gary Simms** who he had met ten days before.

The uniformed officer told Joe, *"These gentlemen would like to speak with you. Could you please get out of your car?"*

The detectives had been staking out Joe's home for the past hour. They waited until Judy had gone to work and Joe left the house. They did it that way because they wanted to search his car for possible "evidence." Detective Simms then walked over to Joe.

"How's it going Mr. Garcia? Sorry for the inconvenience but after our talk at Denny's, you left me and my partner thinking we needed to speak with you again."

About ten days before, Detective Simms had phoned Joe at his office stating that he and his partner had been investigating a report that Cyndi Wittmeyer's 15-year old daughter, Tyra, had been assaulted, and they needed to talk to him. So Joe suggested they meet away from his office, at Denny's restaurant, where he often had breakfast, depending on his and Judy's schedule.

The detectives had questioned Joe at Denny's for close to an hour while he had breakfast. One of the things they wanted to know was how he had become acquainted with the Wittmeyer family. Joe explained that Cyndi worked for Mike Raike at the same office with Joe, and so she was aware of Joe's Christian ministering. She was worried about her son, Travis, and hoped Joe might help him get off drugs. The detectives also asked about a video that the Wittmeyers said Joe had made for patients at Atascadero Hospital, because, in the video, Joe shared "his past prison experience." But when Simms asked what he had been convicted for, Joe said only that he had been convicted "for Burglary." Joe did not volunteer that he had also been convicted in 1979 for Rape, fearing that the actual circumstances would not have mattered to the detectives, only that he had been convicted.

12

Now, surrounded by cops and cars, Joe looked bewildered at first, but then ventured to ask, *"Am I under arrest or something?"*

"No, we just want to talk with you, and, if you don't mind, we'd like to search your car," was the response.

"I don't mind, but why would you need to search my car?" Joe asked. *"We just want to clear you of having any weapons,"* Simms explained. As the other detective searched Joe's car, Simms had the other officer place Joe in the back seat of the squad car, saying he was being *"detained for questioning."*

Joe again asked *"Am I being arrested?"* and was again told *"No."* So when asked if he wanted an attorney present, Joe wanted to know *"Why?"* Simms said *"Because the interview will be taped and we don't want you to feel alarmed by not having an attorney present."*

Since no one read him his Miranda Rights, Joe believed he was not being arrested and did not need an attorney, so he cooperated.

At first, Joe believed he may have come to Simms' attention from his association with Travis Wittmeyer and Travis' link to drugs. At the police station, Simms asked Joe if he had any idea who could have molested Tyra Wittmeyer, and who did Travis hang out with? And what kind of problems was Travis having with his parents? And how long Joe had known the Wittmeyer family and how he interacted with them?

After establishing that the last time Joe had been to the Wittmeyers was three days after the attack on Tyra, they asked Joe what he knew about *other* unsolved crimes – and his whereabouts on the specific days of each of those crimes. Although Joe offered his alibis in each instance, the detectives tried to confuse him by misquoting his responses.

Joe then twice offered to take a polygraph test but was twice ignored. By then, Joe was well aware that the interview was actually an interrogation and he strongly objected, as flashbacks of all he had endured during incarcerations flooded his memory. After three hours of questioning, Joe stated it was time for him to leave. The detectives then left the room for about fifteen minutes.

When they returned, Simms stated that they *"had a gut feeling that he was involved in one way or another, or covering up for someone."*

One of the detectives told Joe he was being arrested, handcuffed him, and only then read him his Miranda Rights at the police station where he was booked, processed into the jail, and finally permitted to call his boss and his wife. Mike assured Joe he would still have a job when released. In fact, Mike was one of many who believed Joe had to be innocent of any crimes for which he was now being arrested.

Judy remembers *"It was close to lunchtime and I was at work at school when the office called and told me I had a visitor. When the detective walked into my classroom, I wasn't totally surprised because Joe had been working with professionals and various authorities by using his past as a tool for counseling young people who were headed on a similar path. The detective asked me if I knew where my husband was. I thought I knew exactly where he was and told him he's probably in his car."*

There were no cell phones then, so Judy couldn't call him. The detective then just came right out with it. *"Joe has been arrested."*

Judy went on, *"To say I went into shock would be an understatement. My life as I knew it ended at that moment. I even said it aloud. I was immediately led to the Principal's office. The Principal and a close co-worker at first just sat with me in silence, my thoughts raging. My Principal suddenly knelt down and prayed for me and our situation. It was one of many surreal moments in a sea of heartaches and indescribable pain."*

A friend of Judy's drove her home since she could not do so in such a state of upset. As she entered her home, Judy was even more devastated. The police had ransacked the home during their search. On some level, Judy believed the search had been planned for when she was away from home in order to "protect" her and the baby.

She sat by the phone waiting for Joe's next call. Details of his arrest, and the crimes he was suspected of, were all over the TV news, which she could not bear to watch. Much later, when a judge ordered release of the car and Judy went to pick it up, she was told the car was "gone."

Joe told her to pack up her things and stay with her parents in New Jersey, temporarily, until the matter is resolved, promising her it would be. He couldn't envision it could turn out any other way, assuring her *"After all, I'm innocent."*

After Joe's arrest, several of the alleged victims who saw Joe's photo in newspapers throughout San Luis Obispo County, and on TV, phoned police "confirming" that Joe was their perpetrator, even those who had previously described their attackers as being under 20 years old, White, or Black or Hispanic - which did not match 42-year old Joe, a Native American.

At the County jail, while Joe was in leg restraints and handcuffs, someone yelled out *"Hey, that's the Rapist!"* which triggered several inmates who had seen him on TV for several months, to assault him. A larger inmate interceded, saving Joe from more serious injury. No one was ever charged.

Two weeks after Joe's arrest, Judy, who was then three thousand miles away from her husband, and pregnant, was still in such depths of sorrow, shock and despair, that she locked herself in her parents' bathroom, intent on committing suicide. She recalled *"I told the Lord I could not live through this and begged him to please end my life. But then the thought of ending my child's life, or having him survive without parents, is what saved us. Thereafter, I prayed God to please help me raise an emotionally stable child, since I knew I was not."*

In January 1990, while eight months pregnant, Judy managed to land a job and maintain a work schedule as a teacher at Head Start. She got a ride to work every morning and walked home each afternoon, sure she would not give birth while Joe was still in prison, as God would make sure they were reunited.

In February 1990, in New Jersey, Judy gave birth to their beautiful, healthy son, Jordan. Although she had full support of her church-going family, there was an emptiness without Joe. She spent the year after Jordan's birth on the couch, holding her baby and sleeping, afraid to go to work again, in case someone should take their son as they had taken Joe.

Judy's sisters and brothers tried, in many ways, to get her off the couch. They would sometimes use their lunch breaks to bring her lunch and would encourage her to at least sit out in the backyard in the sunshine. But she couldn't let herself think of others' lives going on "out there" while hers had "ended." Eventually, she ventured out to the yard, with Jordan in his carriage. Still in pain, she began to walk back and forth, pushing the carriage, forcing herself to get up every day to take care of her son. Even if it took all day to muster enough energy to take a daily shower and dress, each activity was another milestone. For the next milestone, she "did her nails," as a step of faith that she would eventually feel better. She had no therapist, no magic pill to numb her depression. By summer, she began sitting *in front* of the house with her family where she was forced to see life around her. One day, her parents brought home a stroller and she began taking Jordan on strolls through the neighborhood in the early morning or late afternoon when all was quiet, while contemplating her life, realizing not only Joe but also her car, furniture and clothes were three thousand miles away in California. She wasn't overly concerned for Joe's problems. As Judy put it, *"I guess priorities make one realize what's important and our baby was the priority."* As their son grew, the chubby baby acquired a happy personality of his own that was now fun, not just an awesome responsibility. And Joe received lots of photos – of Judy holding their newborn baby, Jordan in his PJs, Jordan on his first birthday, Jordan with piles of Christmas presents and taking his first steps around a six foot tree trimmed with silvery garlands and twinkling lights. The pain of not being able to be with his wife when she gave birth, and not being able to hold hi son in his arms, was more than he could bear.

But the nightmare had just begun.

Judy and Jordan Garcia - without Joe - 1991

"The rape of justice violates justice everywhere."
-Colin Tegerdine

Chapter 2:
(1989) ACCUSERS and ALIBIS

In 1989, a rash of unsolved Rapes and residential Break-ins terrorized the tranquil communities of San Luis Obispo County, California. Initially, a suspect had been arrested and *positively identified by three women* as being their attacker, but DNA testing, as yet unproven as a forensic tool in criminal cases, allegedly cleared him.

Police then focused on Joe because he had a record and they knew he had been somehow involved with the family of one of the victims, 15-year old Tyra Wittmeyer. Tyra said her assailant was **17 to 20 years old and named "Steve," a friend of her brother Travis.** None of the victims described Joe, a 42-year old 6'1" Native American who had distinctive tattoos all over his body. At the time, the U.S. Department of Justice crime statistics "by race" categorized people as only "Black" or "White," identifying most Hispanics as "White." An interesting statistic by the FBI showed that in *93% of rapes the rapist and victim were the same color*, and that victims have a difficult time identifying suspects of a different race. And in a study by Eugene Kamin, "out of 109 reported rapes in a small western town, *41% were false accusations*."

In 1989, police believed they had a sufficient *circumstantial* case to charge Joe Garcia with more a dozen crimes, including Burglaries, Rape and Attempted Rape, at first involving *eleven* female victims. One of the women, **GLORIA L. JOHNSON**, who passed away in 2010, had refused to testify against Joe when pressured to do so, and that case was thrown out (Trial Transcript page 00154, 00173).

Gloria L. Johnson

MICKIE J. ALLEMAN picked Joe from a news photo, claiming he was "The Naked Man" she had seen streaking through the neighborhood on a bicycle, just a couple of blocks from where there had been an incident in which Joe became suspect, and so was also suspected as being "The Naked Man" further described as either having brown hair or red hair or wearing a red head covering or beanie cap. Alleman was certain "The Naked Man" had *NO tattoos*. At trial, Joe's attorney had him take off his shirt in front of the jurors who were shocked to see the huge gorilla tattooed on Joe's back, among his several other tattoos all over his body.

Unable to refute Alleman's "no tattoos" misidentification, Teresa Estrada-Mullaney, the prosecuting attorney, tried to convince the jury that Alleman *"probably didn't notice all the tattoos, because her eyes were more focused on his semi-erect penis"* (Trial Transcript page 5567). But in San Luis Obispo Police Report #89290021, when Alleman was asked if "The Naked Man" was *circumcised,* Alleman stated that, although he had been under a porch light and only 7 feet away from her, she *didn't know* if he was circumcised because, she said, she had focused on his *face*. Alleman's "Naked Man" incident was thrown out.

The prosecuting attorney persisted in accusing Joe of raping **MARGARITA LUCILLE SMITH** despite that Joe was never charged, Smith never testified, and no crime was committed. But that still left **eight women** who allegedly identified Joe at his 1991 trial... or did they? -

- Beverly Joan Brian
- Stacia Michele Deane (Tayrien)
- Carrie Suzanne Dorgan
- Tyra Dawn Wittmeyer
- Jacqueline Denise Brooks
- Tracey Denise Archer (Stearns)
- Cheryl Ann Picco
- Catherine Terese Pinard (Owen)

The women, the allegations, and the facts in each of the eight cases, in chronological order according to dates of the incidents, were as follows.

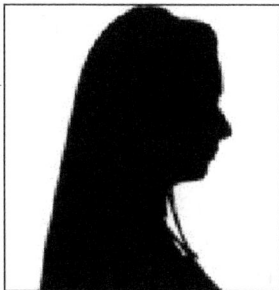

BEVERLY JOAN BRIAN
(Trial Transcript pages 00067-00102, 1723, 1743, 1751)

JULY 12, 1988, at 7:00 PM to 9:00 PM, Beverly Brian, 53, White, about 5'7," 130 pounds, with long mixed brown and gray hair down to the middle of her back, had been a medical transcriptionist in Santa Margarita and, in 1982, ran as a Democrat candidate for the 29th State Assembly seat but did not wage a heavy campaign and lost. When Joe encountered her in 1988, her ranch in Santa Margarita was in foreclosure and she was homeless. She had recently been hospitalized for a head injury and a badly bruised eye which she said was caused by two men who had assaulted her.

At Joe's trial, Brian seemed distracted when she claimed Joe attempted to rape her. **Bert Robinson**, Joe's friend of four years, had been staying at Brian's ranch in exchange for his maintenance work there because Brian could not pay anyone. Bert, together with Joe and Brian, drove to Brian's ranch in Bert's truck filled with some hay, to help feed the animals still on the ranch and to help with maintenance. The trio worked for about four hours there that day before taking a break. That's when, out of the blue, Brian told Joe and Bert that she felt *"Someone is going to kill me."*

Judy, was away at a teacher's convention, so Joe, always willing to help others, offered to have Brian rest up from her injury at his condo on Tiberon and El Camino, the main street in Atasacadero. Bert Robinson then also stayed at Joe's condo for several days in an upstairs bedroom while Brian gladly accepted the sofabed downstairs.

In the trial transcripts, Brian claimed that she was on the sofa reading a book when Joe assaulted her, trying to undress her, and that she prevented both men from raping her by claiming that she had cystitis. She also testified she asked Joe to phone her father who lived out of state. According to Joe, when he made that call, her father loudly and angrily warned Joe that his daughter was *"crazy"* and that Joe needed to *"get her*

19

out of the house," then abruptly hung up on Joe. Hearing what her father had said, Brian became extremely irrational, yelling that "things" were attacking her.

Joe and Bert were both used to evangelizing, so did the only thing they could think of at the time – they prayed over her in hope of calming her down. When Brian did calm down, both men went upstairs to sleep, leaving Brian quietly settled on the sofa. Bert testified in Joe's behalf that no inappropriate behaviors by the men had occurred.

But at some time during the night, Brian ran from the condo and hid underneath a desk at a Shell gas station across the street. There, she told the station attendant that she was being chased, so the attendant called 911. **Officers Cynthia P. Reid and William D. Tilley** logged the matter as "5150" – meaning Brian was "mentally ill" and determined "no crime had occurred." (Trial Transcript pages 1735-1736 – Officer Cynthia Reid testimony).

On April 25, 1990, Investigator **John H. Pierce** faxed the following to Joe's attorney, **Jon Gudmunds**:

> *"Regarding the Beverly Brian case, I have located 16 case numbers wherein she was the plaintiff in small claims actions and two where she was as a defendant. There are five criminal cases where she was charged with various crimes, two for 242 PC."* ["242 PC is **Assault and Battery**."]

But Gudmunds failed to follow-up and obtain Brian's records. Neither was the police officer, Cynthia P. Reid, asked to confirm that Brian had told her *"It was Joe who was afraid of Brian"* and that *"no crime was committed.*

Bert Robinson was not charged with anything and neither the police nor District Attorney had any evidence that Joe had done anything to Beverly Brian.

AND YET JOE WAS CHARGED WITH
ASSAULT AND INTENT TO RAPE BEVERLY JOAN BRIAN.

STACIA MICHELE DEANE (TAYRIEN)
(Trial Transcript pages 1921, 1943-44)

JULY 14, 1989, at 4:00 AM, in San Luis Obispo, Stacy Deane, described as 28, White, about 5 ft, 140 pounds, with short dark hair, told police an intruder had walked into her bedroom through a sliding glass door that had been left ajar. She said he had a gun, and that he told her to *"put on her robe."* **William B. Deane** heard his daughter scream and entered the bedroom. The intruder then said he was "looking for his sister." Then he took out a screwdriver and re-hung the screen on the slider door before fleeing. The Deanes described the undisguised intruder as "Mexican, early 30s, 5'10," 185 pounds, with brown hair, brandishing a 9mm gray metal gun in his right hand, wearing a red t-shirt, bluejeans and white sneakers." Bill Deane further described the man as having facial whisker stubble (Trial Transcript pages 2094, 2106-7,-20,-24-6,28-9, 4043,-46-7).

At the time of the break-in, Joe had proof that he was in San Luis Obispo Jail, 17 miles away, having been stopped the day before on suspicion of Driving Under the Influence (DUI) and his car, containing his belongings and his dog, "Mister," had been searched, as well as his home. No weapon found. **Officers De Priest and Zuchelli** confirmed seeing the dog in the car and that Joe did not score on either the breath test or urinalysis for alcohol or drugs. He was not released until 3:50 AM, only 10 minutes before Deane's intruder entered her home, and over an hour before Joe reached his car on foot where police had left it parked because he did not have the minimum ten dollars that the taxi company required released prisoners to have before they would pick up and transport them from the jail. Joe's alibi was supported by jail employee's testimony and jail records.

AND YET JOE WAS CHARGED WITH
BURGLARY AND INTENT TO RAPE STACIA MICHELE DEANE.

21

CARRIE SUZANNE DORGAN
(SLO Police Report 89-15980; Transcript pages 00135,-73 L28, 1628-84)

SEPTEMBER 9, 1989, at 3:00 PM in San Luis Obispo, Carrie Dorgan, 27, said a man wearing a ski mask forced his way into her home, pushed her into her bedroom, but then *"changed his mind about raping her."* She described her attacker as having an Oriental tattoo, an aqua t-shirt, red fanny pack, driving a bluish gray Volkswagon Sirocco. She even identified her attacker as **"Terry"** and later said she lied to the Sheriff when first questioned because her boyfriend was present.

Earlier that day, Joe had gone to Frank Loure's house, next door to Carrie's residence. Dorgan noticed Joe did not find the man at home and they struck up a conversation. Joe's attorney, Gudmunds, unfortunately advised Joe *"not to admit ever meeting Dorgan, since no crime has actually been committed."* When Dorgan took the stand, she truthfully told the Court how she met Joe and that he paid her for her assistance which consisted of driving him around Los Osos to locate homes that he needed to photograph for his company's "Homes and Land" magazine, because Joe had avoided driving that week after injuring his foot. When they were done locating and photographing the homes, Joe did pay her. Because she alleged to Joe that her boyfriend had been beating her, Joe gave her his business card with his phone number – *which would be odd if Joe intended to rape her.* On September 6, 1989, records show that Joe was admitted to Twin Cities Hospital in Atascadero with an ankle injury and was on crutches at the time of the alleged break-in and attack. Phone bills further evidenced that Joe was making calls from his office at the time of the attack

AND YET JOE WAS CHARGED WITH
ASSAULT WITH INTENT TO RAPE CARRIE S. DORGAN

TYRA DAWN WITTMEYER
(Police Report 89-2807;
Transcript pages 00174-0196, 2171,-97,2213,-15,-18,2220)

SEPTEMBER 17, 1989, at 12:30 AM, Tyra Wittmeyer, 15, described her attacker, a short time after she was sexually assaulted in her own bed. She described her assailant as *"White, although dark skinned, **17 to 20 years old**, 5'9," to 5'11,' unknown hair color, skinny but heavy with broad shoulders and hips, wearing a ski mask, black jacket, gray sweatpants,"* and that he had *"bad breath like stale marijuana and an unusual body odor."*

    Two days after the incident, when Joe was at the Wittmeyer home, Tyra ran up to him and gave him a hug – no marijuana odor, no recognition of him from such close physical contact as being her assailant, …because he wasn't. Yet Tyra stated in court that Joe "smelled like marijuana" *after* **Detective Gary Simms** alleged Joe "smelled like marijuana" when he placed Joe in his squad car, despite that Joe didn't use marijuana and was not found to be using it when arrested. Tyra stated her assailant had a 6-inch blue steel handgun (no gun was found during a search of Joe's car and home and none was admitted as evidence at trial) and that her assailant was possibly driving an orange Volkswagon bus…Joe owned a gray Ford Probe coupe. She said her assailant kept painfully poking her arm and head with his gun and that she *"knew her attacker's voice"*… She told police ***"It wasn't Joe."***

    Tyra's assailant had asked her where her brother, **Travis,** was, so he knew the family. Cyndi and Tyra told police ***"It was Steve"*** (9-17-89 Atascadero Police Report). **Police Officer Mario Atkins** stated *"We found* ***Steve Bolt,*** *tested his blood, and it wasn't him."* (Trial Transcript page 5569)… yet no written report about this prime suspect was found.

While Tyra Wittmeyer was being assaulted, her friend, **Karla Gearhart,** 21, (misspelled "Carla Gearheart" in police reports), was asleep in the next bedroom. Tyra said *"The guy pointed to Karla's bedroom and told me 'My friends tied her up.'"* Gearhart said she had been asleep and unaware the whole time. *So she was not called to testify at Joe's trial.*

Karla Gearhart (Knuckles)

Travis Wittmeyer (Tyra's brother) and their mother, Cynthia Wittemeyer

Joe said he had known the Wittmeyer family "for about 16 months before the incident," and had visited their home "at least thirty to sixty times." Cyndi and Joe both worked as account executives for **Fred "Mike" Raike** at "Homes and Land" magazine.

Joe had seen the young man known as **"Steve"** at the Wittmeyer home on three or four occasions and described him as being in his early 20s at most. Cyndi had also seen and voiced her disapproval of **Steve Bolt**, who apparently was living out of his vehicle.

Joe described Steve and five other friends of **Travis Wittmeyer,** 17, as *"all looking like surfers... they looked like Travis, rather than drug addicts... although most of them were into drugs."* And Joe noticed that they would only show up at the Wittmeyer home on weekdays when Travis' father, **Bill Wittmeyer**, was not at home.

Joe had been trying to help Travis kick drugs by keeping him occupied with body building exercises and other healthy activities, because, according to Joe, *"Cyndi's husband did not want to get involved."*

Steve Bolt was never subpoenaed to testify when Tyra was questioned at trial, and Joe's attorney never asked Tyra *why* she identified Steve, her brother's friend who she would have known, as her assailant.

Jane Kulick, RN, upon examining Tyra Wittmeyer, noted that rape kit findings were consistent with recent genital injury, including vaginal abrasions and laceration. Tyra reported that her attacker *"kissed and licked my chest, put his hand between my legs and tried to force his finger into my vagina, but when I told him it was hurting me, he tried to insert his penis. He almost got it in when it slipped down and he stopped."* He then forced her to masturbate him between her breasts. After he ejaculated, he cleaned her chest with her own clothing, pointed his gun toward the ceiling and made it "click" as he told her to *"Wait five minutes before calling for help."*

On the evening of the day of the incident, Cyndi phoned Joe and asked him to come by to talk with Tyra and Travis. Cyndi told Joe *"Thank God she wasn't raped,"* but said Tyra had been *"touched all over her body,"* when describing details to Joe. Yet at trial, Tyra Wittmeyer alleged she had been *"raped three times,"* perhaps not knowing whether the legal determination, when there is not penetration, was Sexual Assault or Attempted Rape.

Gudmunds' process server, **Samuel Deluca**, was unable to serve either Tyra or Cyndi Wittmeyer with subpoenas to testify for Joe's defense. Joe's two investigators, **Michael Scott** and **Conrad Feirabend** of Atascadero, who were hired by Gudmunds, located Cyndi Wittmeyer at a motel where, according to Joe, the Prosecution team had kept her in hiding for about three months to prevent her from being subpoenaed by the Defense counsel (Transcript pages 3372–3372). The investigator's report stated that, during an attempt to serve the subpoena, a "big guy" came to the door of the motel stating she *"wasn't there."* When the investigators told the man they had observed the woman through the window, the man closed the door. Having seen Cyndi was inside, it is not known why they they didn't toss the subpoena inside the motel room when the door was open, which is an acceptable tactic used by process servers.

Detective Gary Simms stated *"Based on the information I had obtained, along with the fact that the physical description of Joe Garcia was a very close match to that provided by the victims, and that Joe had knowledge about the victim and her family, and knew details abut the Assault, which he had no access to, I obtained his criminal history from our files. I found Garcia had been convicted for Rape in Simi Valley in 1979."* **Simms did not state whether he had checked for any other known sex offenders in the area at the time.**

At the time that Tyra Wittmeyer was assaulted, Joe and Judy had just returned home from an all-day shopping trip in Salinas that Saturday, verified by time-stamped sales receipts and witnesses working at Salinas Mall. They had dinner at Sbarro's pizza restaurant as it was closing at 9:25 PM. **Sbarro's manager was subpoenaed and testified that he remembered the couple.** They didn't get home until 12:25 AM the next morning. Exhausted from their day, they went to sleep by 12:40 AM. **Judy testified to this for three days.**

Joe's description, semen and hair samples **did not match** those found on Tyra Wittmeyer, nor at the crime scene, and the DNA control sample for ethnicity alone was **inconclusive and flawed** (the problems with the DNA are cited in the section of this book captioned "The Troublesome DNA" quoting the DNA experts with Transcript page numbers.)

At trial, when Tyra Wittmeyer was asked to identify her attacker, *she never accused Joe.* On the stand, under oath, she stated only that, during the time that the District Attorney's investigator had visited her home multiple times, *he had told her that they "thought it could be Joe"* and she was led to believe there was a *"DNA match."*

**AND YET JOE WAS CHARGED WITH
BURGLARY AND SEXUAL ASSAULT
OF TYRA DAWN WITTMEYER.**

Statements by Cyndi Wittmeyer, in 9-17-89 Atascadero Police report.

CASE NUMBER		PAGE
89-2807		2

☐ INJURY   ☐ PROPERTY LOSS   ☒ NARRATIVE   Check one or more

NARRATIVE:

On 9-17-89, at approx. 1228hrs., Mrs. Wittmeyer telephoned ATPD and provided possible suspect info. She said she obtained info that a subject known only as "Steve" might be the suspect. She described Steve as a WM, 21yrs., 6-2, wide build, and drives an orange VW bus that has a rainbow decal in the rear window, possible plate of 1BN546, Ca. Mrs. Wittmeyer said Steve was an acquaintance of her son, Travis. Steve had been given permission by Travis to spend the night, referring to 9-16-89, at the Azucena address. She said Steve would have prior knowledge that the door was going to be unlocked and that the Victim and Ms. Gearhart would be alone. Mrs. Wittmeyer said Steve is a transient type and has no formal address. She said Travis met Steve at Kevin Pernod's home, in Morro Bay. The residence is near the area of Main and Anchorage, however, didn't know the street numbers.

Mrs. Wittmeyer said, at the moment, Steve was at or near Morro Rock. At approx. 1240hrs., Morro Bay PD was contacted and were requested to search the area. A short time later they called back and

REPORTING OFFICER	ID NO	APPROVING SUPERVISOR	48 PROPERTY ENTERED APS
M.P. toll			Y ☐ N ☐ N/A ☐

27

JACQUELINE DENISE BROOKS
(Police Report 89-5944; Transcript pages 00037-00066, 1844,-69,1908,-15)

OCTOBER 11, 1989, at 4:00 PM in Morro Bay, Jacqueline Brooks, 18, White, about 5'5," 125 pounds, light brown blonde-highlighted hair past her shoulders, said she was attacked by a man she described as a **"light skinned Negro with a Southern accent,"** age 30 to 40, 5' 9," 185 to 200 pounds, perhaps with a moustache, bad breath, a JC Penney shopping bag as a mask, leather fur-lined slippers, navy blue zippered hoodie jacket and mauve pants and simulated having a handgun. On October 18, 1989, San Luis Obispo Police Fingerprint Tech, Darrell R. Klasey, created **a composite image of the suspect with obvious African American facial features**.

Joe believes Jacqueline's mother, Jan Brooks, 41, a City Councilwoman, pressured District Attorney Barry T. LaBarbera to prosecute Joe. The police report indicates her assailant drove a silver Ford Probe (Joe had a gray Ford Probe). Prosecuting Attorney Teresa Estrada-Mullaney knew the license plate number Brooks offered was **not** Joe's plate number, so, at trial, she told the jury that *"five of the seven license plate characters were correct – just not in the correct order."* Phone records proved Joe was talking by phone with Carrie Dorgan at the time of the Brooks incident, but Joe's lawyer, Jon Gudmunds, failed to introduce that report at trial. A semen sample (rape kit) from Brooks, two hairs, as well as Joe's blood and saliva, were tested. There was **no match** and the control sample for ethnicity was flawed. Brooks admitted that she and her boyfriend, **Donald A. Burson**, had consensual sex just hours before the alleged rape. Asked WHY she later picked *Joe* after describing her attacker as *"Negro,"* Brooks replied *"His eyes reminded me somehow of the man who raped me."* Not a positive identification.

AND YET JOE WAS CHARGED WITH
INTENT TO RAPE JACQUELINE D. BROOKS

(LEFT): 10-18-89 Composite Image of the Suspect
drawn by Darrell R. Klasey,
as described by Jacqueline Brooks who said her
attacker was "Negro"
(RIGHT):   Joe Garcia, Native American-Hispanic

:

```
8          Q     AND WHAT WAS THAT?

9          A     SHE LISTED HIM AS BLACK MALE.

10         Q     AND SHE DID ANSWER A QUESTION THAT'S FURTHER DOWN

11   ON THE PAGE AS HAVING HAD CONSENTING INTERCOURSE WITHIN 72

12   HOURS, BUT MY COPY SHOWS THAT BOTH YES AND NO ARE CHECKED.

13         A     THAT'S CORRECT.

14         Q     WOULD YOU EXPLAIN THAT, SIR?

15         A     CERTAINLY.

16               WHEN THE QUESTION WAS FIRST ASKED, HER MOTHER WAS

17   IN ATTENDANCE, AND AT THAT POINT, SHE SAID THAT SHE HAD NOT HAD

18   INTERCOURSE.

19               HOWEVER, WHEN WE BEGAN THE EXAMINATION, SHE

20   EXPLAINED THAT SHE, IN FACT, HAD HAD CONSENTUAL INTERCOURSE;

21   THAT SHE DID NOT WANT TO ANSWER THAT QUESTION IN THE AFFIRMATIVE

22   WHEN HER MOTHER WAS PRESENT.  SO SHE CHANGED AND WANTED US TO

23   KNOW THAT, IN FACT, SHE HAD HAD CONSENTUAL INTERCOURSE WITHIN 72

24   HOURS.
```

TRACEY DENISE ARCHER (STEARNS)
(SLO Police Report 89-285015; Transcript pages 0057-174, 1588,1603-22)

OCTOBER 12, 1989, at 3:30 PM in San Luis Obispo, Tracey Archer, 24, White, about 5'7" 125 pounds, with light shoulder length hair, said a man *without a mask* pushed his way into her home through the front door and *then* pulled a mask over his face. She described him as "Hispanic, in his late 20s, 5'10," 220 pounds, dark brown medium length hair, having no weapon, wearing a brown ski mask, tan short sleeve shirt, *no tattoos* on his forearms, and he drove a 1986-1988 gray Ford Mustang LX." A witness, **Kara Elizabeth Trapp**, saw the suspect, *without the mask*, talking to Archer at her door, and provided a description to **Officer Robert Espino**.

No composite was made in the Archer case as in the Brooks case, but police showed Archer some photos. At first, she said she *"wasn't sure,"* and picked someone, ***not Joe***, then, pointing to Joe's photo, said the man she saw was "chubby in the face *like* him, but ***not that old.***"

Once again, Joe's attorney overlooked a police report - one in which Archer's boyfriend described a *young, skinny Mexican guy"* who he had observed staring up at Archer's apartment for about half an hour while seeming to pretend to be looking at his car's engine with the hood up. Later, Archer testified that when she had *"picked Joe"* from a photo lineup, she was *"fairly sure"* it was Joe," which is not a "positive ID."

At the time of the incident, Joe had been driving to Santa Barbara to meet with a client, and produced a gas station receipt to prove it.

AND YET JOE WAS CHARGED WITH
BREAKING AND ENTERING AND ASSAULT WITH
INTENT TO RAPE TRACEY D. ARCHER (STEARNS)

31

CHERYL ANN PICCO
(Police Report #89-6020; Transcript pages 00196-00213,1777,1803,1828)

OCTOBER 16, 1969: at 10 PM in Morro Bay, Cheryl Picco, early 40s, about 5'7," 145 pounds, who Joe described as closer to "olive-skinned Italian" rather than White, with dark hair past her shoulders, brown eyes, and thick eyebrows, said she was attacked by a man who she described as Black, 38, 5'8" to 5'10," 220 pounds, with black curly hair, brown eyes, blotchy complexion, *no tattoos*, wearing tennis shoes and *having no weapon.*

As in the Dorgan case, Joe's attorney did not want Joe to admit he had ever met Picco. Again, his attorney's strategy failed. Despite testimony by Joe's alibi witnesses and despite that no weapon was found during a search of his car and home, police later claimed a "beebee gun" was found *outside* in the dirt next to the Garcia home, probably a neighbor child's toy, but it *was never entered into evidence.* This was at the time when LAPD "planted" evidence in the O.J. Simpson murder case. At the time of the Picco incident, Joe had been passing out Christian oriented tracts with a man named **Mario** who he was helping to locate a shelter and was walking to his car when he heard and observed a man and woman arguing in a car on the street in front of a hotel. The man had been fighting with an obviously inebriated woman who Joe later learned was the man's wife; the couple had just come from drinking at a restaurant bar. The man kicked her out of his car onto the street. Joe was right there, so extended his hand to help her up. But Picco began to flail her arms and pushed him away, screaming *"Help! He's tying to rape me! He's trying to kidnap me!"* Someone called police. A hotel manager witnessed all and corroborated Joe's story.

AND YET JOE WAS CHARGED WITH
ATTEMPTED KIDNAP OF CHERYL ANN PICCO WITH FIREARM.

CATHERINE TERESE PINARD (OWEN)
(SLO Police Report 89-291002; Transcript pages 00117-00136, 2011,-38,-58,--82,-84)

OCTOBER 17, 1989, at 9:30 PM in San Luis Obispo, Cathy Pinard, 25, White, about 5′5," 135 pounds, dark brown hair to middle of her back, thick brown eyebrows, while living with her boyfriend, **Dan Machbitz,** said a man entered her home through a small window over her kitchen sink. She and **Mickie J. Alleman,** who lived four blocks from Pinard, had also described a "Naked Man" in the vicinity as White, and weighing at least 300 pounds with a large belly, age 20s to 30s, 5′10" to 6 feet tall, whereas Alleman said he was 5′9," wearing a **red beanie cap,** tennis shoes, and had *no tattoos.*" Pinard said (in the police report) her attacker had a "**red ski cap on top of his head**" - later stated he had "**RED HAIR.**" Both women were "positive" about their descriptions. Pinard further stated that when he raised his red mask up to his forehead, *she saw is face,* and that he was brandishing a knife. She said he touched a lot of places in the apartment *without* gloves, spoke slowly with a Southern accent, and that she had seen his face on several occasions *in her home.* Several months later, when Joe's photo appeared in her local newspaper, Pinard phoned police alleging that Joe, "the man in the picture" was the man who broke into her home. Yet when detectives pointed to Joe's picture in a photo lineup, Pinard said *"No, that's not him"* and picked someone else.

Police dusted Pinard's apartment for fingerprints and not a single fingerprint was Joe's. Checking the window, an investigator found no pry marks on the screen or frame. And the Crime Report Information System

33

(CRS) Report, ID # 80204A54296, and DR# 89291002, states: *"I compared the lifts [fingerprints] from the scene against the inked fingerprints of the victim. A lift from a ceramic shoe contained insufficient ridge detail to make a positive identification. A lift from a glass mug was a print made by the Pinard's left thumb. The lift from the back door was made by fingers of Pinard's right hand."*

Joe's investigator interviewed **Maureen Nelly Denny**, 60, who lived next door to Pinard's apartment. Denny stated (per San Luis Obispo Police Report # 89290021) that she *"may have heard something over there, but it goes on all the time...Pinard's boyfriend beats the hell out of her all the time and curses her out calling her the foulest names. There are all kinds of people, drunks coming and going, all the time. The girl and her boyfriend smoke marijuana all the time,"* and Denny was *"sure they are selling narcotics out of their apartment... they always have a bunch of people passed out in the backyard and on the front porch."*

Denny showed the investigator the back yard where the kitchen window was located. The perpetrator would have had to climb over a wall to reach the window. The investigator found no marks on the wall indicating someone had climbed the wall. Denny added *"I don't know why he (the perpetrator) would have climbed through the window...All he would have had to do was walk right in through the front door like all those other people did."*

While Joe was in San Luis Obispo County jail awaiting trial, he met **James Medina,** an inmate in his early 20s, a friend of Pinard's boyfriend, **Dan Machbitz**, with whom he dealt drugs. Medina did not want to testify in Joe's behalf but Joe informed his attorney that he was positive Medina knew who attempted to rape Pinard and that they were all dealing drugs out of that house. Gudmunds shrugged it off, saying it was *"too late to look for Medina."* Pinard later said she again saw the perpetrator the next morning, wearing a red cap and riding a bike by her home at 7:00 AM -- the time that Joe was at work. No one checked Joe's alibi. But **Mickie Alleman's** claim of a "Naked Man" who had **NO tattoos** was *thrown out* when Gudmunds had Joe remove his shirt and the jury was shown that **Joe was *covered with tattoos*.** Prosecuting Attorney Estrada-Mullaney alleged that Alleman was probably focused on the Naked Man's *penis,* despite that Alleman said she "did not know if he was circumcised (when asked) because she was concentrating on his *face*."

AND YET JOE WAS CHARGED WITH BREAKING AND ENTERING WITH INTENT TO RAPE CATHERINE T. PINARD (OWENS)

DISSIMILARITIES of VICTIMS' IDENTIFICATIONS THAT DID NOT MATCH JOE in PEOPLE v. GARCIA, CA CR-15883 (1991)

DISSIMILAR VICTIMS' IDENTIFICATIONS
WITH ALIBIS and DNA RESULTS in PEOPLE v. GARCIA CR 15583 (1991)

	ARCHER	BROOKS	DEANE	DORGAN	PICCO	PINARD	WITTMEYER	SUSPECT GARCIA
	429/220	459/220	459	220	207	459/220	459/261/289	
	Burglary/ Assault/ Intent to Rape	Burglary/ Assault/ Intent to Rape	Burglary	Assault/ Intent to Rape	Burglary/ Kidnap/ Assault w/ Int to Rape	Burglary/ Assault w/ Intent to Rape	Burglary/Rape/ Sex Assault	
REPORT#	89-285015	89-5944	RT1921,-43-4	89-15980	89-6020	89-291002	89-2807	
DATE	10-12-89	10-11-89	7-14-89	9-9-89	10-16-89	10-17-89	9-17-89	
TIME	3:20 PM	4:00 PM	4:00 AM	2:30 PM	10:00 PM	9:30 PM	12:30 AM	
DAY	Thursday	Wednesday	Friday	Saturday	Monday	Tuesday	Sunday	
CITY	S.L.O	Morro Bay	SLO	Los Osos	Morro Bay	SLO	Atascadero	
RACE	HISPANIC	"NEGRO"	MEXICAN	Unknown	BLACK	WHITE	WHITE	NATIVE AMERICAN
SKIN	Not Noted	Light Brown	Not Noted	None Noted	Not Noted	Not Noted	Dark	
AGE	Late 20s	30-40	early 30s	None Noted	38	20-30	17-20	41
HEIGHT	5'7"	5'9"	5'10"-5'11"	Unknown	5'8"-5'10'	5'10"-6'	5'9"-5'-11'	6'1"
WEIGHT	180-220	180-200	185	Unknown	200	200-250	Heavy	220
BUILD	Unknown	Unknown	Unknown	Unknown	Unknown	Unknown	Wide	Muscular
HAIR	BROWN	Unknown	DARK	Unknown	BLACK curly	BROWN	Unknown	BLACK
EYES	Unknown	Unknown	Unknown	Unknown	Unknown	Unknown	Unknown	BROWN
Facial Hair	Unknown	Moustache	Stubble	Unknown	Unknown	Unknown	Unknown	
TATTOOS	NONE	NONE	NONE	Oriental	Unknown	NONE	Unknown	MANY TATTOOS
VOICE	Unknown	Hesitant	Not Noted	Unknown	Unknown	Unknown	Loud, Disguised	
ACCENT	None	Southern	Not Noted	Unknown	None	None	None	
ODOR	None	Bad Breath	Not Noted	Unknown	None	None	Marijuana	
WEAPON	None	Simulated Gun in Pocket	9mm Gray with Holster	None None	None	Kitchen Knife	6"Handgun Blue Steel	No Guns
DISGUISE	Brown Ski Mask	Not Noted JCPenney	None Noted	None	None	Red Ski Mask	Black Ski Mask Not Noted Ski Jacket	No Ski Caps WhiteBuick;
SHOES / CLOTHES	Not Noted; Tan shirt	bag LeathSlipprs BlueHoodie MauvePants	WhiteSneaker Red Shirt Bluejeans	Aqua Shirt RedFannyPak Bluejeans	Not Noted	White Tennis Shoes; Beige Windbreaker; LtShirtDkPant	GraySweatpants	Silver Ford Probe
CLOTHES				BluishGray				
VEHICLE	'86-88 Gray Mustang LX		None	VW Sirocco				
NAMED SUSPECT	No	No	No	"TERRY"	No	No	STEVE BOLT	
Boyfriend SexPrior		Don Burson Yes		Live-in BF		ScottMachbitz		
Admits Lie(s)		5pm at SLO Century 21		Lied to Sheriff				
Garcia Alibi	AM call		In jail	Witness	Witness		Salinas trip; Sbarro's Recpt & witness;	
Fingerprints	None	None	None	None	None	None	None	
DNA	None	No match	None	None	None	None	None DNA no match	DNA no match

San Luis Obispo Telegram-Tribune, Jan 23, 1991

Garcia trial could cost $500,000

By Leslie Morris
Special to the News

The six-month trial that led to a sentence of 72 years and six months to life for convicted rapist Joseph Belarde Garcia has so far cost more than $300,000 for defense attorney fees and Superior Court costs.

Garcia, 42, was convicted in June of 18 felonies and one misdemeanor and was sentenced last week by Judge William Fredman in San Luis Obispo Superior Court.

The $300,000 figure does not include costs for the District Attorney's office, the Probation Department, Superior Court staff, Municipal Court costs, facility costs and sheriff and transportation costs. With those items considered, the figure could soar as high as $500,000, according to Court Administrator Larry D. Reiner.

Unfortunately for Superior Court, there was no way to plan for such high expenditures in the budget. "Every once in awhile a case like this will come along and wipe out the budget," Reiner said. "You just can't anticipate those kinds of costs." When the budget is being prepared, Reiner explained, the criminal cases have not yet come through the court process. Therefore, cost assessment must be based on historical data.

But there was no previous indication that a case could cost so much because the Garcia trial was the longest and most expensive criminal case in San Luis Obispo Count history.

The trial resulted in Judge Fredman not handling the usual flow of criminal and civil cases for Superior Court; a program that brings in retired judges to try civil cases helped ease the caseload. "If we hadn't had the civil trials program, we would have had less than half the capacity to try long civil trial cases," said Presiding Judge Warren C. Conklin.

"It (the Garcia trial) significantly reduced our trial capacity for six months" Conklin said. "I did not have any idea it would go this long."

The court also incurred hard hitting financial strains. "The court knew it was going to take a big budget hit when the case went into its second or third month of trial," Reiner said, especially after the Kelly-Frye hearing that determined whether the District attorney could admit DNA evidence into the trial.

The largest single cost has been the defense attorney Jon Gudmunds' fee of more than $150,000. That figure reflects his hourly fee along with a variety of costs such as office supplies, car rentals and telephone bills.

The $150,000 figure may come under scrutiny by the public because the court possibly could have cut the cost in half, had it paid the defense attorney a flat fee. Local attorney Jeff Stein offered to defend Garcia for a flat fee of $75,000. But the county perceived that amount as being at the high end, so went with the hourly rate. "Gudmunds' attorney fees were not unreasonable," Reiner said, "though they added up to $133,000 for 1,565 hours."

Judge Donald G. Umhofer

As early as January 1990, media confirmed: *"Some of the women were <u>unable</u> <u>to positively identify</u> Joe as their attacker"*... and yet Judge Umhofer decided there was enough "evidence" to have Joe Garcia stand trial.

San Luis Obispo Telegram-Tribune, January 23, 1990

Defense musters evidence in rape case preliminary hearing

The prosecution closed its case Monday in the preliminary hearing of a man accused of attacking eight women.

Attorneys for Joseph Belarde Garcia will begin presenting evidence on behalf of their client on Wednesday.

Garcia faces 21 felony counts connected to the alleged attacks which occurred in 1988 and 1989. The Atascadero resident, who is being held in County Jail pending $325,000 bail, has pleaded not guilty to all charges.

Two sexual assault charges — the first two filed in the case — were dropped last month when the alleged victim refused to testify.

Municipal Court Judge Donald G. Umhofer will decide when the hearing concludes if there's enough evidence to have Garcia stand trial in Superior Court.

Most of Wednesday's testimony came from the prosecution's medical experts and law enforcement officials involved with the case.

The alleged victims were called to testify by Deputy District Attorney Teresa Estrada-Mullaney when the preliminary hearing began last month.

While describing the assaults, some of the women testified they were unable to positively identify Garcia as their attacker.

The preliminary hearing was postponed for a month under an agreement worked out between the attorneys and Umhofer. Defense attorneys said they needed additional time to compile their case.

37

MEMORANDUM OF PURPOSE

TO: Judge Fredman

FROM: S. Jon Gudmunds

DATE: May 7, 1991

RE: *People vs. Garcia*; Relevance of Law Enforcement Reports Regarding Other Reported Sex Crimes

The review of law enforcement reports ordered pursuant to the defendant's motion is for the following purposes:

1. To determine if a Ford Probe was described as the suspect vehicle;

2. To determine is the suspects wore a black ski mask (Wittmeyer) or a red ski cap (Pinard);

3. To determine if any of the suspects wore grey sweat pants (Wittmeyer);

4. To determine if any of the suspects wore a heavy ski jacket (Wittmeyer);

5. To determine if any of the suspects used the name "Jay" (Dorgan) or "T" (Pinard);

6. To determine if any of the suspects used a handgun similar to that used in the Wittmeyer, Pico, or Deane counts including the use of a holster (Deane);

7. To determine if any of the suspects modus operandi was similar to any of the instant offenses, i.e. pretended to be looking for someone else, relied upon notes and hand signals in communicating with their victims, directed the victim to wash herself after the offense and impersonated a detective investigating the offense;

8. To determine whether the physical descriptions provided by the victims were similar to the descriptions provided by our victims immediately following the offense:

Brooks: Black, 5'9", 180-200 lbs., 30-40 years of age, mustache.

Deane: Mexican, 5'9" 185 lbs., Mexican accent, thick brown hair in a square cut.

Pico: Black or possibly American Indian, 5'11", stocky, 38-40 years,

Joe's attorney sought police reports to show similarities of individual suspects in other sexual assault or rape cases at the time a "serial rapist" was speculated. Judge Fredman said the reports would "necessitate undue consumption of time, *OR* confuse issues, *OR* mislead the jury" and later, when Fredman had seen the list, said "none were relevant" **so the jury never knew if there were other sexual assaults and rapes at the same time that Joe was accused of being "the Central Coast Serial Rapist."**

SUPERIOR COURT OF THE STATE OF CALIFORNIA

FOR THE COUNTY OF SAN LUIS OBISPO

THE PEOPLE OF THE STATE OF CALIFORNIA,	)))
Plaintiff,	)) NO. 15883
vs.	)) RULING (OPEN) ON
JOSEPH BELARDE GARCIA, AKA JOSEPH PEACEMAKER,	) DEFENDANT'S MOTION FOR) PRODUCTION OF POLICE) REPORTS
Respondent.	))

The court, having personally received certain selected police reports in accordance with its order of May 1, 1991, and held an in camera hearing in the presence of counsel and their respective investigators, Mr. Conrad Feierabend and Mr. Thomas Talbert, finds and concludes that none of the referenced reports submitted for examination are relevant to the defense in this case within the exculpatory rules of People v. Hall (1986) 41 Cal.3d 826.

The court further finds that the information contained in the referenced reports should be excluded as its probative value is substantially outweighed by the probability that its admission will necessitate undue consumption of time, or will confuse the issues or mislead the jury.

The documents reviewed at the hearing, the minutes of the

- 1 -

39

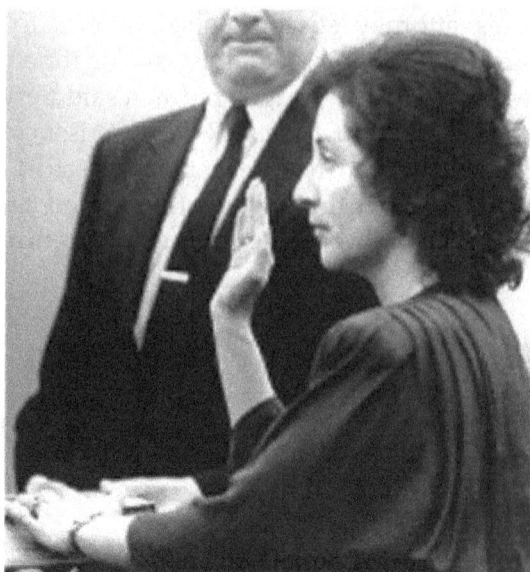

LEFT: Barry LaBarbera, District Attorney
RIGHT: Teresa Estrada-Mullaney, State's Prosecuting Attorney

S. (Steinthor) Jon Gudmunds, Joe's Public Defender

Chapter 3:
(1991) TRIAL of the CAREFULLY CRAFTED CENTRAL COAST RAPIST

Fifteen months had gone by before the Prosecutor and Defense lawyer were ready for jury selection in "People v. Garcia," in Superior Court of San Luis Obispo County, Case Number 15883. District Attorney Barry LaBarbera amended the Complaint three times, each time piling on a long list of unsolved cases to the indictment to create a Serial Rapist. Unable to post $325,000 bail, Joe was held in jail fifteen months while awaiting trial, at first on nine cases – eight cases after Gloria Johnson refused to testify.

On May 13, 1991, before trial began, Joe's Defense lawyer, **S. Jon Gudmunds**, complained to Judge Fredman *"This case has become so paper-intensive; I've got so much paper I sometimes lose things"* (Transcript pages 1281-1367). His requests for more time or more lawyers were Denied. His Objection to the inclusion of Joe's "prior crimes" was overruled. Attorney Gudmunds provided Joe with a copy of his "Motion for Change of Venue," promising it would be filed, but it was never filed. Despite that prospective jurors claimed they could be impartial, the Court concluded that the pre-trial publicity was so pervasive and prejudicial that the jurors could not possibly be impartial. Yet the Court rejected the notion of partiality of "any particular juror," so Joe's attorney said that was the reason he never filed the Motion for Change of Venue. The Memorandum with the Motion for Change of Venue would have informed the Court that, throughout the Fall of 1989, police agencies throughout San Luis Obispo County engaged in a manhunt for a Rape and Assault suspect. Despite that **Prosecuting Attorney Teresa Estrada-Mullaney** was admonished by Judge Fredman to *not leak any information to media,* beginning eight months *before* the trial, various details of the attacks and a police composite image of the suspect had been released to media. Thereafter, a photo of Joe Garcia was shown on television, prompting racial overtones. **Joe, being of a minority race, was depicted as raping *White* women, including a teenaged *White* girl, Tyra Wittmeyer,** despite that the sweet Mormon girl first said *"It wasn't Joe*, then *"It was Steve,"* and also that *she* **could not identify her assailant**.

Statements released to media by the District Attorney's office, about Joe having been "previously convicted of Rape and Sodomy," led to more complainants against Joe as citizens publicly expressed their concern that a "serial rapist" was in their midst.

Attorney Teresa Estrada-Mullaney's background by then was one of "second choices." According to news articles, she had originally wanted to become a teacher but the job market wasn't promising, so she became a lawyer out of sibling rivalry. Her brother, Nicolas Estrada, was a lawyer. Initially, she applied to be a Public Defender but wasn't offered the job, so she went to work for the Orange County District Attorney for the next eleven years. From then on, it was about *winning* – winning cases, winning awards, and winning notoriety. Joe's high profile case could provide all of that. [Jan Dean Howell, *"Teresa Estrada-Mullaney- Breaking the Mold & Making a Difference,"* SLO County Bar Bulletin, March 2020] Like a "perfect storm," Estrada-Mullaney, in behalf of San Luis Obispo County's District Attorney Barry LaBarbera, not only had a tidy bundle of nine cases in one trial, but also packaged and marketed Joe as **THE CENTRAL COAST RAPIST**, producing a windfall of media attention to bolster her bid for Judgeship.

Joe was already guilty according to media. All Estrada-Mullaney had to do was come up with *"theories"* to "prove" it... such as that the witness, Alleman, who said "The Naked Man" was Joe, simply didn't notice Joe was *covered with tattoos, including a huge gorilla on his back,* " was because she was *staring at his penis."* But when Alleman was asked if "The Naked Man" was *circumcised,*" she said she "didn't know" because she had been *"staring at his face."* In the Brooks case, Estrada-Mullaney alleged "Five of the seven license plate numbers were correct – *just in the wrong order!"* In the Wittmeyer case, police searched for suspect Steve Bolt, and when they could not find his car with the license plate number provided, they tried to find it *"by scrambling the plate numbers,"* and claimed to have eventually found Bolt, interviewed him, and even taken a blood sample that "didn't match," yet, at trial, there was no written police report nor mention of where Bolt was on the night when Wittmeyer was sexually assaulted, nor did Joe's defense Attorney Gudmunds think to inquire about it. To discredit Joe's good reputation for helping people in the community through his ministry, which his character witnesses confirmed, Estrada-Mullaney accused Joe of *"trying to use religion in his con game."* (Trial Transcript page 5571). And she justified her theories despite the mountain of *dissimilar* claims and *circumstantial* evidence, by calling her theories *"not too legally remote"* (Transcript pages 1281-1367). Additionally, Mullaney had to convince the jury that Joe was not just unlucky to have had previous contact with most of the women who were now victims of various crimes he was accused of, by also accusing him of crimes *that did not actually occur,* or *"could have* occurred," as in the case of Margarita Lucille Smith and Beverly Brian.

AND THAT IS HOW "UNREASONABLE DOUBTS" BECAME "REASONABLE" TO A JURY.

Santa Maria Times, April 14, 1991

Accused rapist finally to have trial

By Nancy Morse
Times Staff Writer

SAN LUIS OBISPO — The longest pending criminal case in San Luis Obispo County is finally under way in Superior Court.

Joseph Belarde Garcia, 42, of Atascadero, is charged with 19 counts including rape, assault with a deadly weapon, sexual battery and attempted kidnapping and burglary. The alleged crimes occurred in 1988 and 1989.

The case took one-and-a-half years to come to trial because of a hearing to determine whether DNA evidence — which determines genetic material — could be used in the trial.

Superior Court Judge William Fredman ruled that he would allow evidence using the defendant's genetic material into the trial. This is the first case in the county's history to use DNA evidence.

Samples from deoxyribonucleic acid, known as DNA, were taken from some of the crime scenes and compared to Garcia's blood. The semen samples were analyzed at the DNA laboratory run by the FBI in Washington, D.C.

Garcia was arrested by Atascadero police in October 1989. He has been in county jail with bail set at $400,000 since then.

Eight female victims, police officers and detectives have testified against Garcia so far.

Fredman ruled that a Ventura County woman Garcia was convicted of raping in 1979 can testify against him. The youngest victim Garcia is allegedly accused of raping cannot identify him because her attacker wore a ski mask and disguised his voice. She was 15 when the attack occurred in 1989.

Before trial began, Gudmunds, who was already overwhelmed by two of his other clients' cases at the time, filed a "Motion To Sever" the nine cases against Joe. The overwhelming volume of leads, witnesses, evidence, allegations and alibis needed to be properly and thoroughly investigated to insure an adequate Defense, let alone a *good* one. Joe had previously been assigned *two* attorneys for the Preliminary Hearing - **Joe T. Malone** and **Frank J. Pantangelo** - who similarly complained of needing more time and that there was no investigator for the Defense and no investigative interviews of Joe's alibi witnesses. But the Judge Denied all requests to increase the Defense team's staff and resources and for continuances.

A week before his trial, Joe learned that Gudmunds wasn't actually prepared to defend him. Four and a half hours before commencement of trial procedures, Joe filed a "Motion to Dismiss" his attorney... and to allow him to represent himself. Although he showed the Court that Gudmunds had not been adequately representing him, the Judge Denied his Motion for self-representation, stating *"In the middle of trial, you could at any time raise your hands and cause me to declare a mistrial and I can't have that."* Joe responded there was no legal basis offered for that presumption and that he knew the facts of his case better than his attorney. Also, there had been no actual evidence proving he was the perpetrator in *any* of the alleged crimes. He was still Denied.

On the opening day for jury selection, when the guards came for him, Joe was wearing a suit and tie provided by one of his new investigators. He was brought to the women's holding tank where he had to wait a few minutes in full view of the twenty or so women on the other side of the glass. A tall, slim blonde in an orange jailhouse jumpsuit called out *"If that guy's a rapist, he can rape me anytime!"* and the others laughed. One of the two guards, who then pushed Joe along the corridor to the courtroom, said to another guard, *"That gal is just as twisted as Garcia here."* Joe kept his composure and did not answer him back. Joe was convinced that there was not a single "serial rapist," but at least three or four perpetrators involved in the multiple crimes for which he had been charged... and he was even certain he knew one of them.

Finally, he was brought into the courtroom and immediately noticed the prosecutor, Teresa Estrada-Mullaney, and her investigator, **Bill Miller**, who were smiling at him every so often, as if to say *"Gotcha!"*

LEFT: Prosecution's Investigator, James William "Bill" Miller;
RIGHT: Defense's Lead Investigator, Conrad Feirabend

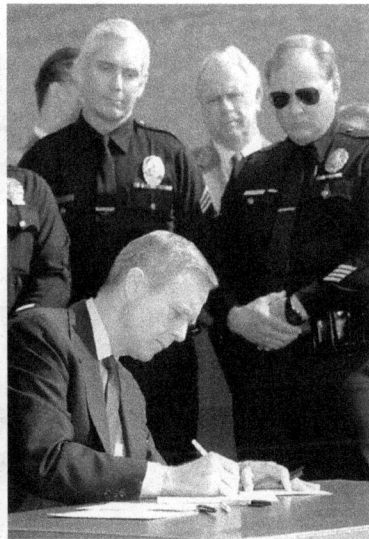

(LEFT): George Deukmejian, California's "Law and Order" Governor (R) 1983-1991
(RIGHT): Pete Wilson, California's "Tough On Crime" Governor (R) 1991-1994

Seated next to Joe, Gudmunds silently and methodically laid out his papers on their table. It all seemed surreal to Joe, as though he was watching actors on a movie set. And to a great extent, attorneys *are* actors trying to convince their audience - the judge, and twelve jurors - that their version of the story is the better one. **Bailiff Jack Heller** did not move from his post but occasionally placed his hand over his gun in its holster as if preparing to take down the dangerous criminal that Joe was alleged to be.

About one hundred prospective jurors, allegedly Joe's "peers," were led in, in a single line. Not one was Black or Native American. The pre-trial publicity, and having a defense attorney overwhelmed by now-eight cases in one trial, and a prosecuting attorney for whom eight solved crimes with "guilty" verdicts would be a huge stepping stone to a judgeship, and jury pool who Joe described as "White Republicans," raised doubts in his mind that he would get a fair trial, even before trial began. As the attorneys took turns questioning, accepting, and declining juror candidates, Joe slipped his handwritten comments to his lawyer. Eventually, twelve jurors - seven men and five women - who appeared to be between the ages of 38 and 55, were selected. Nothing really stood out, except that *all were White*.

Each juror was asked to fill out a questionnaire containing one hundred questions, including how often they watched TV, read the newspaper, or listened to news on the radio. Gudmunds had a copy of their answers, most of which Joe could glance on the table. Perhaps the most significant of the written questions put to the prospective jurors was whether or how they had already heard about the case and their perception of Joe's innocence or guilt. Most of them knew about the case from local media, and most of them said they believed Joe was guilty! Yet none admitted to what they wrote when verbally questioned in open court. Joe pointed this out to Gudmunds who dismissed many of the first 154 prospective jurors. The other questions asked about their formal education, whether or not they had relatives who had been sexually assaulted, and did they know whether Joe had been accused of Rape in the past, which almost certainly was intended to plant the idea in the jurors' minds that he must have such a history or else the question would not have been asked.

Finally, on January 14, 1991, Baliff Heller, having been signaled that the actual trial was to begin, announced *"Everyone please rise. The Honorable Judge William R. Fredman presiding. Take a seat please."*

Judge Fredman bid all a "Good Morning" as he introduced himself and apologized for the delay in getting started, explaining there were "*a lot of details in this case to take care of.*" He then instructed the jury that this was a criminal case and that the District Attorney had charged Joseph Belarde Garcia with two counts of Rape and the several other charges.... And that "*everyone is innocent until proven guilty **beyond a reasonable doubt.***"

The opening day of Joe's trial, was to be the first "DNA case" in San Luis Obispo County. Gudmunds would have to defend Joe against 19 felony charges in what started out as ten cases, reduced to eight separate cases and victims in one trial. He told the court that he "wasn't fully prepared" and asked for a Continuance but was Denied. Gudmunds appealed, repeatedly asserting he was "not yet prepared" to defend his client, but the Appellate Court insisted in maintaining the original trial schedule. In California, as in every state, the accused has "a right to a speedy trial" - and to counsel – but nothing in the law requires that counsel must be *competent*.

Investigations into the Prosecution witnesses' credibility revealed that some of Joe's young female accusers were known to be involved with illegal drugs, or that their boyfriends were associating with known drug dealers. But Gudmunds did not delve into the accusers' backgrounds as aggressively as Estrada-Mullaney attacked Joe's alibi witnesses and twisted their words to support her theories of the cases.

A young girl named **Lonnie** was supposed to be one of Joe's character witnesses as she had been attending Bible studies at Joe and Judy's home for over a year without any impropriety. But the DA's investigator, **Bill Miller,** had gone all the way to Tehachapi State Prison, allegedly to have Lonnie's incarcerated boyfriend phone her and persuade her *not* to testify in Joe's behalf, by alleging that Joe had been sleeping with her. Miller reportedly also tried to turn Joe's friend and character witness, **Tony Fasano**, against him, by alleging to Fasano that Joe had been sleeping with *his* wife. But Fasano knew better and told Miller to "go to hell" and reported it to Joe. Joe's own investigator, **Michael Raphael,** allegedly tried to get Joe's wife, Judy, to date him while Joe was in jail, by falsely claiming that Joe had been having an affair with Cyndi Wittmeyer before his arrest.

There seemed no limit as to how low some would stoop.

THE TROUBLESOME DNA

The Sexual Assault of Tyra Wittmeyer is one of two cases in which DNA evidence was collected from the victim's body and bedding and compared to Joe's DNA collected via his blood. Tyra described her assailant, within a very short time of the sexual assault, as "White, age 17 to 20, about 5'11, having an odor of marijuana and no tattoos" (in Police Reports documenting Tyra and Cyndi Wittmeyer's statements, that also even identified Tyra's attacker as *"Steve,"* in Trial Transcript Page 5427). Joe did not smoke marijuana. The arresting officer said Joe did not have a marijuana odor. At trial, Tyra still did not actually identify Joe as her assailant, only acknowledged that she was *told his DNA "matched" so it had to be him.*

For the first thirty days of the trial, the jurors looked alert enough, paying close enough attention to all that was being said. For sixty days, Gudmunds' focus was on deciphering the existing DNA technology by studying a 400-page DNA Manual and that was the portion of the trial where he shined. But during the more than sixty days of technical terminology by DNA experts on both sides, jurors' expressions changed to ones of confusion and exhaustion. And the experts on both sides had a problem with errors known to occur in RFLP proficiency DNA testing – most significantly, **that there were not yet uniform standards for forensic testing of DNA in criminal trials; nor did the FBI have a sufficient database for laboratories doing the testing.** (Trial Transcript page 5414).

Because the lab doing the testing was informed in advance that Joe, whose blood was being tested, was part "Native American," worthless DNA results were compared to only two American Indian tribes known as **"P-gabrielino"** and **"Gabrielino Band of Mission Indians,"** which was akin to taking only one or two characteristics of a fingerprint and "matching" it to a control sample. Joe's blood sample **could not identify him as the perpetrator,** only that he was one of the same class as the donors of "A," "B," or "O" alleles, and only if the samples compared sufficient characteristics, *which they could not,* but the Prosecution knew that without DNA they had no real evidence against Joe in any of the eight cases, so decided that Joe *"could not be excluded"* **which isn't the same as saying "it's a match."**

Their DNA expert told the jury that while 42% of the general population is Blood Type A, only 2.6% of the general population have a PGM sub-type of "1 minus 1 minus," as Joe was said to have, while the

Defense's DNA experts showed that the FBI inappropriately lumped all Indian tribes together in one database without necessary sub-structuring of mixed race samples (Joe was part Hispanic and part Native American). Reportedly, there are no "full blooded" Native Americans today. Some, but not many, may be three-fourths Native American.

Gudmunds further explained ..."They're trying to say that Mr. Garcia is one in 2,000, if he's an Indian, and there's less than 2,000 so therefore he must be the one. How about the guy standing next to him who happens to be 1/16th Indian?... That the Court instructions say there's evidence that the Defendant is within a statistical group of persons having certain blood characteristics is insufficient by itself to establish guilt."

For months, the experts belabored, ad nauseam, the differences and shortcomings of testing techniques employed by Cellmark, Gentech, and other labs, in comparison to the FBI testing, using terms such as "Restriction Fragment Length Polymorphism"(RFLP), "Polymerase Chain Reaction" (PCR), "allele dropout or degradation striping," "assumption of linkage equilibrium," "Ethidium Bromide Effect, " and other causes of "Band shift" – problems seen in the DNA samples in Joe's case. The jurors just wanted to go home. DNA Experts for both sides found several issues with testing of the DNA in Joe's case, as follows:

> **Bruce W. Kovacs:** "There's no national standard for DNA analysis" (page 288)"results are based on probability not certainty(p.277,L3-4)

> **Laurence D. Mueller**, was concerned that the small slice of the main database used had just 200 "Indians" in the database... seventeen or 18 different tribes... and some of these tribes were represented by maybe two persons, and some by three, up to six or seven... one of them had thirty-seven or thirty-five... Sioux Indians had about 81...and Mueller said that was not a representative sample... so if you had a database matched to only one tribe, you'd get one set of figures... and if you matched it to other tribes, you get a completely different set of figures. The database for Blacks isn't big enough; the database for Whites isn't big enough. The best way is to get *a large enough database* and *then* match the sample. *It simply wasn't done.*" (Trial Transcript pages 5425-5426).

> **Dwight Adams**: "DNA match or no match is subjective" (page 83); Joe's DNA "was computer matched digitally, which does not afford

the possibility of individualization of a body fluid stain; individuals can have the same DNA *pattern* yet are two entirely different individuals; there's no oversight, no proficiency testing of the labs (*not required to provide their error rates*)." (pages 422, 513);

Randell T. Libby (for the Defense): "The FBI used Ethidium Bromide dye, causing Band Shift without controls; there are extra Bands in some of Garcia's DNA (page 926); the FBI's attempt to validate that Ethidium Bromide has no affect on RFLP doesn't hold up scientifically at all (page 932, L1-3); FBI did not use substructure for Hispanic database" (page 859); Libby agreed with Adams: "Computer generated DNA analysis sometimes does not produce correct results" (984, L-16); "In Garcia's sample, FBI declared just 2 Bands...there were obviously more than 2... 6 in Lane 15, and Lane 20 is a failure, extensively degraded with multiple Bands observed and which should never have been interpreted, nonetheless it was scored as a 2-Band pattern." (page 1009); Errors were noted for multiple samples interpreted as American Indian by FBI that *actually failed*" (page 1011); "FBI analysis is unreliable or false regarding autorads analyzed in Garcia and other cases" (page 1029).

George Felix Levine, the FBI's DNA expert, *discredited* the FBI's own testing in Joe's case, partly because "the autorads in the control samples were [according to the report] *compromised and degraded.*" In addition to DNA testing of fluids, it was alleged that a hair found at one of the crime scenes "matched" Joe's hair. But Levine, stated "*We can't identify (match) a person by hair*"(pages 2464-2497). And in January 2021, Levine told me all 1980s-1990s DNA analysis was discredited for criminal cases because it could not be done, despite many self-proclaimed "experts" cashing in by claiming otherwise.

Simon Ford, PhD, and **Attorney Martin Shapeiro**, PhD, were also DNA experts for the Defense.

Judge Fredman stated: "The Court is *unable* to determine relevant scientific community acceptance of forensic DNA testing in criminal cases" (Trial Transcript page 532). In the end, the Court, believing there was already overwhelming *circumstantial* evidence to convict Joe, *never ruled on the DNA issue* but left it to the jury to decide what it all meant.

AND THAT IS HOW UNREASONABLE DOUBTS ABOUT A DNA ANALYSIS BECAME REASONABLE TO A JURY.

SURPRISE WITNESS

and the Alleged Rape of Margarita Bassin
(June 4, 1979, Simi Valley Police Report #79-11863;
and 1991 Trial Transcript pages 01009-01024 and 2932-2948)

That Joe was stunned would be putting it mildly, when prosecuting attorney Teresa Estrada-Mullaney called **Magarita Bassin** to the stand. Bassin had nothing to do with the 1989 cases, but Gudmunds caved and agreed to allow Bassin to testify about one of Joe's "past mistakes."

In 1979, Joe had confessed to raping Margarita Bassin after both had been drinking. In the 1970s, I did not report being violently raped because "date rape" was considered "as if consensual." In 1979, when Joe was accused of raping Margarita Bassin, California law did not actually define what constituted "Rape" and had been particularly silent on "spousal rape" until AB 546 Chapter 994 by California Assemblyman Floyd Mori made spousal rape a crime; yet California State Representative Bob Wilson sarcastically reacted by saying to a group of women "*If you can't rape your wife, who CAN you rape?*"

In 1979, as today, social psychologist Carol Tavris, best explained the *complexity* of distinguishing *actual* Rape from "*honest false testimony of Rape*" (Los Angeles Times, 10-4-15):

> "By far, the most well-traveled pathway from uncomfortable sexual negotiations to *honest false testimony* **is alcohol.** For some women, alcohol is the solution to the sex decision: If they are inebriated, they haven't said yes, and if they haven't explicitly said yes, no one can call them sluts. But for *both parties*, alcohol significantly impairs the cognitive interpretation of the other person's behavior. Men who are drunk are less likely to interpret non-consent messages accurately, and women who are drunk convey less emphatic signs of refusal. *And alcohol severely impairs both partners' memory of what actually happened.* When trying to reduce sexual assaults, labeling all forms of sexual misconduct, (including unwanted touches and sloppy kisses) as '*Rape*' is alarmist and unhelpful. *We need to draw distinctions between behavior that is criminal, behavior that is stupid and behavior that results from the dance of ambiguity.* "

(LEFT): Margarita Leticia "Maggie" Bassin,
aka "Megan" Bassin;
(RIGHT): Leticia Bassin (Margarita's mother)

According to Joe, while he was living with a male roommate on Haven Avenue in Simi Valley, he had dated **Leticia Bassin** a few times; she lived on Erringer Road, in Simi Valley, with her daughter, Margarita, and her son. In Leticia's statement, she said she had known Joe about 2 months. Leticia had been wanting Joe to move in with her and her family but Joe's friend, **Frank Tomlinson**, strongly advised Joe against doing so.

On Saturday, June 3, 1979, at about 2:00 PM, after Joe and a friend had been to a party with his friend **Anthony Gallina**, he went to Leticia's home. Joe's memory is hazy about that day, having had more than enough to drink at the party before he arrived at Leticia's, intending to sleep it off and to possibly have sex with Leticia. Whether that occurred or whether, because it was still early and they typically might have gone out to a local lounge for a drink or two before going to dinner, he can't recall. But he does remember that Leticia passed out asleep in her bedroom, nixing any hope of sex that night. So Joe let Leticia's big red dog out while trying to decide whether to pour himself "one final nightcap" or make coffee or a sandwich. On the way to the kitchen, he couldn't help but notice "Maggie," Leticia's 21-year old daughter, Margarita, through her partially open bedroom door, and stopped in his tracks as she slowly took off her panties and climbed into bed. Although Maggie had switched off her lamp when she saw Joe, she didn't shut her bedroom door. Maggie had been out drinking with **Harvey Simpson** that evening, and, like Joe, was feeling no inhibitions.

Previously, Joe had met Maggie when he and Leticia had lunch at La Fiesta Restaurant where Maggie was waitressing and caught Maggie eyeing him in a way that he was certain was a flirtatious invitation to get closer to the younger woman. And so, on that Saturday night, too drunk to consider potential consequences, he quietly slipped into Maggie's bedroom, and unzipped his jeans, letting them fall to the floor, as he watched the motionless young woman who was watching him close her bedroom door behind him, transforming the semi-darkness to pitch black. Neither did she move away as he slid between the sheets over to her warm body. *Absent any objection,* he slowly ran his hand over her curves. Finding the moistness as he teased her with his fingers, the young woman's spontaneous orgasm responded to the foreplay heightened by the total darkness. But too many drinks had a numbing affect on Joe, so his anticipation was all that was "growing." Even when she reached down trying to guide his penis to help him "even the score," he could not get an erection… and they soon fell asleep.

The next morning, a thin ray of light that pierced through a torn shade woke Joe who found himself in bed with his girlfriend's daughter peacefully asleep beside him, and unable to remember whether they had sex, nor whether she had wanted to. Either way, he knew he had better get out of there before Leticia finds out. Panicked, Joe scrambled to find his clothes as Maggie began to waken. She didn't say a word, which worried him even more. Feeling hung over, confused, and uncertain what he should do, he told her he was sorry and that he didn't want to get her in trouble with her mother, who he hoped was still asleep in the other bedroom.

Leticia, yawning as she stumbled into the kitchen for coffee, ran smack into Joe... who quickly exited without a word. Uncertain what kind of trouble he was in with Leticia, or Maggie, or both, he looked for a pay phone and called his friend, **Frank Tomlinson**. Whether Frank, a former LAPD Detective, believed that Joe was overreacting, or whether he was fed up with Joe getting himself into "situations," Frank decided to have police pick up Joe for his own protection to sort it out. Joe, feeling he had been a disappointment to Frank, told police he wanted to "turn himself in," although he didn't know for what, but then changed his mind and denied that he had done anything wrong.

What is known is that Leticia was interviewed by police, on Sunday morning, June 4, 1979, stating she was too tired to remember details but that she had known Joe about 2 months and that they had sex the day before, then she asked Joe to drive Maggie to work. Maggie was interviewed by police, several hours after Leticia's interview, which would have given Maggie plenty of time to convince Leticia that she didn't *choose* to have sex with her mother's boyfriend but was *raped* by him. ... She then told police she had never known Joe before that event, despite that Leticia acknowledged she had been dating him for 2 months, during which time Joe had been to their home multiple times.

The women claimed that Joe "broke into their home" in the middle of the night via a glass slider at the side of the house, entered Maggie's bedroom with a knife and "threatened to kill her if she screamed." Oddly, no one removed any possible "evidence" from Maggie's bed or bedroom and the alleged knife, found in the kitchen, did not have Joe's fingerprints on it.

Knowing that she had consensual sex with her boyfriend, **Harvey Simpson**, just hours before the alleged rape, and knowing she had to submit to a "rape kit" analysis, Maggie knew what the exam would reveal,

54

so told the officer that she had been repeatedly raped both vaginally and anally for about two hours until just before dawn. Maggie's "rape kit," done by Sharon Tarborch, RN, determined that Maggie had perianal bruising and rectal bleeding. By then, police told the women that Joe was in custody.

In a follow-up police investigator's report, Maggie told the officer she had sex with Harvey Simpson at his home just hours before the alleged rape. When the officer asked Maggie why she hadn't volunteered that information before, she said she didn't want her mother to think she was having consensual *anal sex* with Harvey Simpson.

The women said they "couldn't believe Joe could do such a thing."

On Monday, June 5, 1979, at Joe's Preliminary Hearing, after Frank Tomlinson had been talking with the Superior Court judge in judge's chambers for about 30 minutes, Joe pled "Guilty" and "No Contest," as his Public Defender advised, in order to receive a lighter sentence. When Maggie and Leticia both showed up at Joe's sentencing hearing, as did Frank and his partner, the Judge granted Joe's request to address the two women and he apologized to them. Both women began to weep. Frank tried to convince the judge to sentence Joe to a rehabilitative clinic instead of prison, but that was Denied because there had been a psychiatric evaluation that determined Joe was *not* a "Mentally Disordered Sex Offender" that would qualify him for the clinic. Joe says he pled guilty partly because he "*felt* guilty" for being drunk and stupid, and not to lose his friendship with Frank. **THAT IS HOW UNREASONABLE DOUBT IN A CLAIM OF RAPE BECAME A REASONABLE OUTCOME**.

> Joe was convicted of False Imprisonment, Forcible Rape, Sodomy and Burglary and was sentenced to 13 years in prison. He paroled after 8 years, in 1987. Upon his release, Joe's photo was posted as a sex offender on a "Megan's Law" Community Notification website.

Those who knew Joe in 1979 considered it a wrongful conviction. Joe admits attempting to have sex with Maggie, but denies *sodomizing* her – something he was sure he *couldn't* have done as he had seen and heard enough rapes at juvie and San Quentin to know the viciousness of forced rape-sodomy and knew he could never enjoy doing that to anyone.

PASTOR FRANK TOMLINSON,
former LAPD Homicide Detective

JOE GARCIA
during 8 year imprisonment for 1979 conviction
based on claim by Margarita Bassin

After Joe's 1991 conviction, **Governor Pete Wilson** was calling for passage of bills that would put first-time rapists and child molesters in prison "for Life without possibility of parole," expand the Death Penalty, make it easier to try juveniles "as adults," and further limit use of "credits" to reduce sentences. Joe was convicted and sentenced "with enhancements" (added time) for his "past acts," in 1991 – this was *before* President Bill Clinton introduced a "Three Strikes" crime initiative and even before Pete Wilson officially enacted "Three Strikes Law" in California in 1994, a law that contributed to the problem of over-populated prisons.

Since Joe's trial, Margarita, now calling herself "Megan" Bassin, created a Facebook page, joined an online dating service, and was shown, in an online news article with her photo, selling items at a charity social event. On November 10, 2008, as "Megan Bassin," she filed for "Dissolution of Marriage Without Children" against Vladimir Parhomchuk. But a year later, on December 12, 2009, the matter was Dismissed for Failure to file Proof of Service. The status of their relationship, and Vladimir's whereabouts, is unknown.

Neither Joe's 1979 trial, nor his 1991 trial, would be the last time Margarita Bassin would come back to haunt Joe.

Lacking hard evidence that Joe had committed any of the crimes, nor even that actual crimes occurred in most of the eight cases, Prosecuting Attorney Teresa Estrada-Mullaney could only speculate *theories*. So she compared the fact that Margarita Bassin's mother was asleep in the next bedroom, *and* her brother was asleep across the hall, while Joe allegedly raped Margarita, with the fact that Karla Gearhart was asleep in the next bedroom when Joe allegedly raped Tyra Wittmeyer. Mullaney theorized that the perpetrator risked entering the Wittmeyers' home knowing that Karla, and possibly Travis, would be there, because "*the thrill* for him was having other people in the house while forcing the frightened victim to be quiet." (Trial Transcript page 5555).

That theory is contradicted by the behaviors of known serial rapists and killers such as Ted Bundy, and Rex Allan Krebs, who had "*nothing to lose*," whereas Joe had *everything* to lose, having worked hard to gain the respect of his community, a loving wife, about to have a child, and his work at Homes and Land was about to pay off big time. Why would he throw that away? And where was the *evidence* that placed him at the scene at the time of *any* of the crimes for which he was charged?

When Margarita Bassin took the stand in 1991, before a word was said, she theatrically wept for the jury as Estrada-Mullaney handed her a tissue in case any juror could not see the artificial tears. Most of the jurors' expressions then changed from blank to cold.

Gudmunds then asked Maggie point blank whether she had sex a few hours before the alleged attack. Maggie answered, *"I don't recall."*

The jury never saw the 1979 follow-up report in which Bassin *admitted* having had consensual sex with her boyfriend, Harvey Simpson, just hours before the alleged rape. The report also said the reason she had not previously disclosed this was to "avoid embarrassing her mother."

The jury also never heard that when police asked her if she could identify her attacker, she stated the room was dark and *"I don't know that I would recognize him if I saw him again."*

Neither Estrada-Mullaney nor Gudmunds produced Transcripts from the 1979 case, so Gudmunds couldn't impeach the woman when she **added things that *never* happened, and that were never in her 1979 testimony.** But where was the 1979 police report?

As Estrada Mullaney questioned her, Maggie wept three more times, over-playing her theatrics in front of the jury as she was about to discredit herself:

Estrada Mullaney: *"Did he sodomize you?"*
Bassin: *"I'm not sure what you mean by that."*

How could any woman who claimed to have been raped and sodomized, as she claimed Joe had done to her, not know the meaning of *"sodomized?"*

Estrada Mullaney: *"Did he penetrate your rectal area with his penis?"*
Bassin: *"Yes."*
Estrada-Mullaney: *"More than once?"*
Bassin: *"I believe so."*
Estrada-Mullaney: *"How long did this go on?"*
Bassin: *"Over and hour."*
Estrada-Mullaney: *"Was it painful?"*
Bassin: *"Yes."*

And she added that she suffered pain *"for several weeks and months,"* yet neither her mother nor her brother were awakened by her crying out from such pain, and she had to be reminded that she had been allegedly sodomized? The jury never heard that although Joe admitted he had been in bed with Maggie, he was so intoxicated that he could not penetrate her and, despite that he pled guilty on a plea bargain to lighten his sentence, he maintains that he did *not sodomize* her.

In her original 1979 statement, Maggie Bassin said she *"reached down several times and tried to insert Joe's penis into her vagina so he could finish and leave."* When asked *"Did he tell you to do this?"* She answered *"No."*

Joe's 1991 trial would not be the last time Margarita "Megan" Bassin would return to haunt Joe.

At the time of Joe's trial, California's then newly elected Governor **Pete Wilson** had run on a "tough on crime" campaign with the slogan *"Lock 'em up and throw away the key,"* setting the stage for an ambitious Estrada-Mullaney to win points with Joe's high profile case. Gudmunds was particularly astounded, with regard to the confused reversal of testimony by Tyra Wittmeyer when he told the jury:

> *"Yesterday you were told that Tyra said **she didn't know who her attacker was** and then points to Mr. Garcia and she knows 'he's the one who raped me **because of the DNA.**' **Who put that idea in her head?"*** (Trial Transcript pages 5411-542)

But Gudmunds did not provide the jury with an *answer* to that question and the jury never heard that Tyra had initially identified Steve Bolt as her rapist. In Gudmunds' closing argument, after *each* recital of the allegations and facts in each of the eight cases, he told the jury: **"It doesn't add up. It doesn't make sense."** And he cautioned the jury against using one charged offense to "bootstrap" another, adding: *"Otherwise, you have a domino effect without ever having proof **beyond a reasonable doubt."***

AND YET, UNREASONABLE DOUBT BECAME REASONABLE IN THE MINDS OF THE VICTIMS AND THE JURY.

And so, the all-White jury came back a *second time* saying they were "deadlocked," unable to reach a unanimous verdict. And each time, Judge Fredman ordered them to *"Go back and do your job,"* instructing them to return with a verdict, as there was no way he was going to have a hung jury and retrial. It had already cost taxpayers a six-month trial, and an estimated $500,000, and by God, they were going to "get justice."

And so, the jury came back a *third time.*

They had to consider each charge individually – 2 Counts of Rape; 4 Counts of Assault with Intent to Commit Rape (including in the Brian and Deane cases where had been determined "no crime was committed"); 3 Counts of Sexual Penetration by a Foreign Object (Finger); 6 Counts of First Degree Burglary (although nothing was actually taken nor claimed to have been taken); 1 Count of Assault with a Deadly Weapon despite no gun or knife was found when Joe's car and home were searched, other than a beebee gun of dubious origin, and none was entered into evidence; 1 Count of Attempted Dissuasion of a Witness for having written to Travis Wittmeyer his concern for Tyra and how her changed testimony would weigh on the conscience of the devout Mormon girl.

The jury deliberated *eleven days…* eleven days in which loud voices arguing about case details were heard by all who were in earshot, and Joe's lawyer commented to him "*Someone in there is on your side."*

On June 14, 1991, despite the glaring inconsistencies, victims who could not identify their attackers, as well as victims who named their attackers and said "*It wasn't Joe,"* and despite no actual DNA match, and no hard evidence, the twelve men and women found Joe to be "**GUILTY on all Counts." All Counts**!

On July 19, 1991, in his pre-sentencing statement to Judge Fredman, Joe maintained his innocence (Transcript page 5769). Estrada-Mullaney piled on "Enhancements" to the sentence she proposed to Judge Fredman - including for use of a gun never in evidence, and his "past bad acts," including the 1979 Rape of Margarita Bassin for which he had already served his sentence and about which he was very likely wrongfully convicted - by adding 5 years to each of the 1989 cases for which convicted; she also added an enhancement, making **her unreasonable doubt reasonable** by citing he was convicted of **Rape of Margarita Lucille Smith,** *who was never raped, never testified, and for which Joe was never charged* and which the Court never questioned (Transcript page 5806). Where was the evidence of this non-event?

Times Press-Recorder, Arroyo Grande, California, June 14, 1991

Jury finds Garcia guilty on all 19 counts

SAN LUIS OBISPO — Joseph Belarde Garcia was convicted Thursday of raping two young women and attacking six others, ending the longest trial in county history.

A jury of six men and six women deliberated seven days before pronouncing Garcia, 42, of Atascadero, guilty on 18 felony counts and one misdemeanor count. The entire trial lasted 67 days.

Garcia was accused of attacking eight county women in 1988 and 1989. He pleaded not guilty to all the charges.

He was convicted of two counts of rape, six counts of first degree burglary, four counts of assault with intent to commit rape, three counts of sexual penetration with a foreign object — a finger — one count of sexual battery, one count of assault with a deadly weapon or force likely to produce great bodily injury, and one count of attempted kidnapping.

In addition, the jury found from one to three special circumstances in seven of the counts.

Superior Court Judge William Fredman set sentencing for July 10.

As the verdicts were read by the clerk of the court to a packed courtroom, Garcia gazed impassively at the wall with occasional glances at the jury. He occasionally conversed with defense attorney S. Jon Gudmonds and wrote frequently on a yellow legal tablet.

Garcia's trial was the first in county history to use genetic evidence.

61

SENTENCING HEARING
July 19, 1991

(TOP):   Judge William Fredman;
(LEFT): Prosecuting Attorney Teresa Estrada-Mullaney;
(RIGHT): Joe Garcia and his Court Appointed Attorney Jon Gudmunds

One of the factors that had to be influencing Judge Fredman's sentencing decision in Joe's case was the fact that, in 1987, just two years before the alleged crimes for which Joe was tried, Fredman had been criticized for sentencing serial rapist-killer, **Rex Allan Krebs,** to a State Hospital for "Mentally Disordered Sex Offenders" when Krebs pled "No Contest" to Rape, Forced Sodomy with Use of a Knife, and Burglary with Intent to Commit Rape and Sodomy. Fredman said he had hoped Krebs could be rehabilitated.

But when Krebs paroled in 1999, after serving just ten years of his twenty-year sentence, Krebs committed the Rape-Torture Murders of local colleges students, Rachel Newhouse and Anishka Crawford. Krebs was then sentenced to "Death by Lethal Injection," to be carried out at San Quentin Prison. In January 2020, the California Supreme Court upheld his Death Sentence. However, months prior, on March 13, 2019, Governor Gavin Newsom issued his Executive Order N-09-19 instituting a moratorium on executions in California, providing Krebs, now 54, with a reprieve. At this writing, Krebs, Prisoner Number D69844, remains alive and well at San Quentin Prison. Fredman was not about to make another political misstep so late in his career when Joe appeared for sentencing.

And so Fredman did not question or object to Estrada-Mullaney's wish list of additional *Enhancements,* when he maximized Joe's sentence to **72.5 Years to Life, then justified his decision to media, stating Joe was a "career criminal who** *cannot be rehabilitated."*

AN UNREASONABLE DOUBT MADE REASONABLE TO DEPRIVE A MAN OF THE REST OF HIS LIFE.

On January 28, only six months after Joe's wrongful conviction and sentencing, Judge Fredman died.

Governor Pete Wilson, aware of Joe's high profile case and conviction, rewarded Teresa Estrada-Mullaney by appointing her as the first woman judge in San Luis Obispo County to fill the vacancy left by Fredman.

Wilson also appointed the D.A. in Joe's case, Barry LaBarbera, to the bench in 1998.

Teresa Estrada-Mullaney continued to make headlines as being "tough on criminals" – including in 1996, by sentencing a repeat sex offender to 84 years, and, in 2010, when she tried **Ollie Rayshawn Tinoco**, age 15, "as an adult" for Rape. That she was "out for blood" was most evident in 2006 when she sentenced 14-year old **Robert Holguin**, who, at age 13, had beat and killed 87-year old Gerald O'Malley with a skateboard. Estrada-Mullaney rejected the Defense's recommendation that the boy, who has a low IQ, brain damage, mental problems, and learning disabilities, be sent to a group home with psychiatric supervision for extensive mental treatment and potential rehabilitative programs before he is returned to society. She instead decided the boy had to be *punished*, and sent him to California Youth Authority where racial and gang violence was prominent, to serve his sentence until he was 25 in 2017. Estrada-Mullaney also thought the public had a *"right to know the 14-year old boy's name and see his face,"* despite that names and photos of minors are not normally disclosed. As result of Estrada-Mullaney's decisions to throw him away in the system, the boy requested counseling *more than 100 times and was put on suicide watch 3 times.* Cruel and unusual? Perhaps. **Unreasonable?** Absolutely.

Months after Joe's trial was over, verdict read, and sentence decided, Joe became privy to a June 20, 1991 six page report by his investigator, **Michael Raphael** about **Arthur Charles "Archie" Kuentzel**, who had been a juror at Joe's trial. Kuentzel revealed that his own granddaughter had been raped and that her assailant had never been caught. Kuentzel evidently did not admit this in his responses to the juror questionnaire that asked whether anyone in a prospective juror's family had been raped. Kuentzel also admitted that he *"felt the legal system is not just,"* and that *"some of us just went along with the majority."* He said he *"previously served on a jury, also a rape case, and that case was heard and decided in just one week,"* that he had *"been on tranquilizers during the last two months of the trial,"* and that Judge Fredman *"did not provide clarifications repeatedly requested by jurors but instead told them to 'go back and read their workbooks.'"* Additionally, Kuentzel's son, a Chaplain at the jail where Joe was held, pre-trial, kept telling Joe *"My Dad asked me to inquire of you about this Wittmeyer case because he is having great difficulty deciding whether you are guilty of the charge."* Joe replied he was not permitted to talk about his case to anyone, as his attorney had instructed him. The Chaplain grimaced and said *"My Dad will have a hard time finding you not guilty when I tell him you were evasive and not forthcoming with any information proving your innocence."*

ANOTHER UNREASONALE DOUBT MADE REASONABLE.

The Charges Against Joe Garcia
in the 1991 Trial of Combined Cases

Penal or other code section or sections:

	(A)	(B)
Count I	Assualt w/ intent to commit rape	§220 California Penal Code
Count II	Forcible penetration w/ foreign object	§289(a) California Penal Code
Count III	Burglary, 1st Degree w/ intent to commit rape w/ firearm use	§§ 459, 460.1, and 12022.5(a) California Penal Code
Count IV	Burglary 1st Degree w/ intent to commit rape	§§ 459 and 460.1 California Penal Code
Count V -	Assualt w/ intent to commit rape	§220 California Penal Code
Count VI	Burglary, 1st Degree w/ intent to commit rape w/ firearm use	§§ 459, 460.1 and 12022.5(a) California Penal Code
Count VII	Forcible rape w/ Great Bodily injury and use of Deadly weapon	§§ 261(2), 12022.8, and 12022.3 California Penal Code
Count VIII	Forcible penetration w/ foreign object w/ Great Bodily Injury and use of deadly weapon	§§ 289(a), 12022.8 and 12022.3 California Penal Code
Count IX	Sexual Battery w/ firearm use	§§ 243.4(c0 and 12022.5(a) California Penal Code
Count X	Burglary, 1st Degree w/ intent to commit rape	§§ 459 and 460.1 California Penal Code
Count XI	Forcible rape	§ 261(2) California Penal Code
Count XII	Forcible penetration w/ foreign object	§ 289(a) California penal Code
Count XIII	Burglary, 1st Degree w/ intent to commit rape	§§ 459 and 460.1 California Penal Code
Count XIV	Assault w/ intent to commit rape	§ 220 California Penal Code
Count XV	Attempted Kidnapping w/ firearm use	§§ 207, 664, and 12022.5(a) California Penal Code
Count XVI	Burglary, 1st Degree w/ intent to commit rape	§§ 459 and 460.1 California Penal Code
Count XVII	Assualt w/ intent to commit rape w/ use of deadly weapon	§§ 220 and 12022(d) California Penal Code
Count XVIII	Assualt w/ a Deadly Weapon	§ 245(a)(1) California Penal Code

/// ///

65

Santa Maria Times, July 19, 1991, by Leslie Morris

Judge comments on longest trial in county's history

Not only was the Joseph Garcia trial the longest and most expensive in San Luis Obispo County history, it also was one of the most difficult for Superior Court Judge William Fredman.

"The mass of the case, with all of its ramifications, puts the pressure on," Fredman said. "There are so many decisions to be made and each one depends on the others."

Fredman described the case as "somewhat worrying" at times because of the technical and scientific elements involved.

For the first time in SLO County history, DNA evidence was used to link the defendant to the crime scenes.

Fredman had to determine the scientific community's confidence in DNA identification and whether to admit the evidence. The DNA evidence was obtained from semen samples from the crime scenes and compared to Garcia's blood.

The appeal Garcia already has filed is likely to focus on the reliability of that evidence.

"A good portion of the pre-jury testimony was like going to class every day," Fredman said.

"It was a scientific learning process. the tests at the end will be the decision that will go to the Court of Appeals — that will hopefully be upheld."

The Garcia trial gave Fredman headaches beyond the nature of the evidence.

"Garcia didn't have good relations at the jail. He kept bringing up those problems on a daily basis — not before the jury, but before me. That didn't make things too easy."

In remarks before his sentencing, Garcia referred to his poor relations with jail staff, saying he refused to let them treat him with disrespect and filed complaints against dozens of staff members.

The number of charges — 18 counts ranging from rape to attempted kidnapping to attempting to dissuade a witness from testifying — added to the complexity of the case.

Garcia frequently addressed Estrada-Mullaney in his remarks, calling her "Terry" and accusing her of using his case to further her career.

"Terry doesn't care if I'm guilty or not. She started something. She was under pressure. You and I both know you have used this to showboat your career," he said.

He also spoke of the Rodney King beating by Los Angeles police.

"The criminal element does not only exist in people locked up, but in people who wear uniforms, people who wear three-piece suits, women who wear suits," he said.

"I am leaving this court as a winner, and my definition of a winner is a person who's able to love in spite of all the hardship."

> The appeal most likely will focus on the admissability of DNA evidence used to link Garcia to the crime scenes.

Fredman praised the jury — 12 regular jurors and four alternates who served for 40 days.

"It's difficult for them, under the pressure and stress, to be away from home and to keep their spirits up," he said.

"We were fortunate not to lose any of them. None missed more than a day."

During the trial there were allegations some jurors were overheard discussing the case.

Fredman addressed the allegations with investigations and a hearing, but no misconduct was found.

Despite those allegations, the jurors seemed in good spirits, Fredman said.

Despite the complexities, Fredman said he found the trial challenging and interesting.

"But if it were my choice," he said, "I'd rather have a more compact case with (fewer) elements to it. And it would be over in a shorter period of time." — By Leslie Morris

Convicted rapist gets 72½ years

By Scott Swanson
Staff Writer

SAN LUIS OBISPO — An Atascadero man was sentenced Thursday to 72½ years to life in prison for the rapes of two young women and assaults on six others.

Superior Court Judge William R. Fredman pronounced the sentence, saying he had little hope that Joseph Belarde Garcia would ever be rehabilitated. Garcia will be eligible for parole in about 36 years.

Garcia appeared relaxed and happy through the hourlong proceeding. He occasionally smiled and winked at audience members in the crowded courtroom and he appeared to be singing to himself at times.

About 50 people attended the sentencing, which was under heavy security with nine bailiffs present.

Fredman said later that the trial was one of the most difficult he had ever presided over.

(See related story in this issue.)

Prosecutor Teresa Estrada-Mullaney, a Grover City resident who just completed a term on the city planning commission, said that society will be safer with Garcia behind bars.

"Mr. Garcia won't be eligible for parole until he's a very old man," she said. "With this long sentence, he won't have the opportunity — we

> "This county has never seen a sexual assault case like this one or a defendent like Joseph Belarde Garcia and we hope we never will again."
> — Teresa Estrada-Mullaney

hope — to victimize any more women. I think the 72-years-and-six-months-to-life is exactly what the consequences should be."

Defense attorney Jon Gudmunds was unavailable for comment following the sentencing. Gudmunds has declined to comment to the news media throughout the trial.

Garcia, 42, was convicted June 13 on 19 counts after a 67-day trial, the longest in county history.

He was arrested on Oct. 19, 1989.

The trial cost the county $303,582 — excluding costs to the District Attorney's Office — up until the sentencing hearings conducted this week, according to Superior Court

(Continued on back page)

67

Investigator's report on juror Arthur Kuentzel, who disclosed, after trial, that his granddaughter was raped, that he had been on tranquilizers during the last 2 months of Joe's trial, that the judge did not clarify things concerning to the jurors, and he felt "the legal system is *not just*":

INVESTIGATIVE REPORT
Pages 1 thru 6
June 20, 1991

Foz: S. Jon Gudmunds, Attorney at Law
         426 E. Barcellus, Suite 303
         Santa Maria, CA 93454

By: Michael Raphael, 330 E. Enos Dr., #20
         Santa Maria, CA 93454   / Defense's Investig

Case: People vs. Joseph Belirde Garcia
         aka Joseph Peacemaker

Jury report #3

Report of an interview with a juror who made decisions in the case of P. vs Joseph Garcia.

Juror: Arthur Charles "Archie" Kuentzel
         501 Grand Avenue
         Arroyo Grande

         Tel: 481-6560

I contacted Archie Kuentzel after the jury had been excused by San Luis Obispo County Superior Court Judge William Fredman shortly after the jury returned its verdicts in which the jury determined that Joseph Garcia was guilty of all charges lodged against him. I caught Kuentzel in front of the courthouse. We talked while sitting on a bench in front of the courthouse. I asked for permission to tape record our conversation. Kuentzel granted me permission to do so. A portion of our conversation was recorded. I discovered this when I later reviewed the tape for purposes of writing this report. I was using a new recorder that day and apparently pushed the play button, rather than the record button, for the first phase of the interview. I wrote notes on my recollections of what he said. Thus some of the following report is based on those notes and recollections.

Although Kuentzel granted me permission to record his comments and answers, he asked me on four occasions to turn the recorder off so he could tell me things he did not want on the record. One of these things is that his granddaughter was raped. He did not identify her or indicate whether he has more than one grandchild, but said her assailant has not been identified or caught.

(1) of (6)

Kuentzel said he had to make an effort to keep his
grandaughter's rape out of his mind while deciding
Garcia's fate. Kuentzel said he was able to do
that, keep his granddaughter's rape out of his mind
and separate from the task of deciding on the
charges against Garcia.

Kuentzel told me he would never serve on another
jury again, even if forced to do so at gunpoint.
"I'd rather be shot," he said. He said the legal
system is "not just," and was not just in this
case. He said he had previously served on a jury,
also a rape case, and that in that trial, the case
was justly heard and decided. That trial lasted a
week, he said.

Kuentzel was obviously distraught, and visibly
emotional, as he talked to me. He was friendly
enough. At the very end, he wished us good luck.
At one point, when a woman lingered nearby, he
asked if I knew who she was. When I said no, he
asked if we could move to another bench. We did
and continued our conversation at a distance from
the woman.

Kuentzel said he had been using tranquilizers for
the last two months of the trial. He was critical
of Superior Court Judge William Fredman, the
prosecutor, Teresa Estrada-Mulaney, and the defense
attorney, Jon Gudmunds, for not making things more
clear for the jury. He was particularly critical
of Judge Fredman, saying the judge did not
understand some of the questions the jury asked and
that Judge Fredman did not provide clear
explanations for some questions asked by jurors.
He said the judge would refer jurors to their
workbooks rather than provide clarification that
jurors needed.

Kuentzel was quite direct in some answers and
avoided giving clear answers in others. When I
asked him if he ever talked about the trial with
anyone, he said he only did so with his wife of 40
years. He said he talked to her about the case
because he relies on her judgement and input. He
said that she would simply tell him to "sleep on
it" or "think about it."

"I talked to my wife about it. My wife is a good
counselor to me," he said. He said he did not talk
to her about details of the case, just general
aspects of the trial.

69

Attorney Richard Power was assigned Joe's direct Appeal.

It was Denied.

Joe was sent to California State Prison at Corcoran. He had requested a hardship transfer to be closer to Judy and Jordan but was Denied. However the Captain got word from another guard that an attempt was planned on Joe's life. Corcoran housed gangs and high profile killers including Charles Manson. Joe once shared a cell with Manson family member, **Charles "Tex" Watson**, through whom Joe gained a phone interview with **CNN reporter Ted Rowlands,** who did a story on Watson but Rowlands wasn't interested in Joe's wrongful conviction. The combined enemy threat and hardship on family qualified as "special needs," so Joe was promptly escorted out of Corcoran and into Mule Creek State Prison at Ione, in Northern California, as Prisoner Number H01695.

It took four or five years for Joe to get his anger under control over being wrongfully convicted, and to "move on," mentally, with the belief that a person who cannot forgive is truly trapped.

At Mule Creek, Joe shared an eight foot by ten foot "cage" with a six inch window, that was to be his permanent home. There were two tiers to his housing unit. Joe's cell was on the first tier with a cold, bare, unpainted cement floor, cement walls, crowded by metal lockers and a lidless stainless steel toilet. That space was brightened only by his orange prison jumpsuit, white t-shirts, blue pants, white socks, brown boots, white tennis shoes, blue jacket and beanie cap with "CDC PRISONER" in large yellow letters stamped on all his clothing.

In place of bars, his cell had a six foot by six foot metal door with a small glass window. A small steel desk was welded to the back wall. A thin pillow and Army blanket covered each of the two metal bunks. His was the lower bunk. When he or his cell-mate needed privacy to use the toilet, a sheet that hung on a string was pulled across the cell. On the ceiling, a large white fluorescent lightbulb was framed in a white metal box. Joe had a small TV which helped him keep him current on events in the outside world, and a typewriter that he used to type his appeals and letters. The noise level depended on time of day.

Each of the five housing units at Mule Creek held about two hundred inmates. Meals were laced with Salt Peter to curb sexual urges. Breakfast consisted of pancakes, a small carton of milk or cup of strong coffee, hot or cold cereal, a piece of fruit, or occasionally dried scrambled eggs – served military style in the chow halls. Dinner was at 6:00 pm and usually consisted of soybean based products in place of meats. Chicken was served once a week but eaten at the inmate's risk of food poisoning from it, which frequently occurred. "Special diet" meals were available with a doctor's card. Inmates could walk, exercise, pitch horseshoes, or even "kiss and make out" with other inmates. The Day Room was open from 10:00 am until 9 pm "lights out" although inmates could leave their own lights on. A cacophony of loud voices, TVs, clanking of metal and general noise resonated throughout.

Joe's psych records understandably indicated a diagnosis of "Episodal Depression" and because prison psychiatrists saw him as the "Central Coast Rapist," records also note "anti-social personality traits."

Joe participated in "Lifers Support Group Therapy," passed a twelve week "Anger Management" program, and was commended for his participation and commitment toward self improvement. But prior to his job at Mike Raike's real estate office, the only jobs he held in between incarcerations involved dishwashing, janitorial chores and manual labor. Back in prison, he was assigned to work in the main kitchen and in Office Services where he learned about computers and the printing trade. His letters reflected excellent comprehension, composition and writing skills. Over time, Joe demonstrated marketable skills in graphic art, small business, typography and typing. But the only prison job at Mule Creek that paid $38 per month was as EOP Aide assisting other inmates.

He was an avid reader and applied his creative skills to making and selling a large variety of different cell furnishings, from a shelf offered for $2.00 to a TV stand with large drawers for $20 – each item constructed from cardboard but sturdy as wood. Thus he became known as "Brother Joe the Cardboard King."

Not long after arriving at Mule Creek, one of the "good" guards informed him there was a plan to falsify a report that Joe was "overly familiar" with three female staffers who Joe was merely communicating with about the treatment of mentally and emotionally challenged inmates. To avoid trouble, and in order to retain the bit of "freedom" he had at Mule Creek, he gave up the $38 a month job that would have put him in harm's way.

Joe, 2012

(TOP LEFT): Peter Neufeld, Barry Scheck, Co-Founders, The Innocence Project;
(TOP RIGHT): Lori Carangelo, Founder, Americans For Open Records (AmFOR)
(BOTTOM LEFT & RIGHT): "People v. Garcia" – 6,000 pages of Trial Transcripts

Chapter 4:
(2014-2013) INNOCENCE PROJECTS,
MISSING DNA and GOVERNOR JERRY BROWN

On October 30, 2004, the **Innocence Protection Act** (aka "Innocence Act") became the first federal Death Penalty reform. More than 100 people were released from Death Rows across the United States because of procedural errors or newly discovered evidence of their innocence. The Act was a first federal attempt at ensuring that innocent people are not put to death. Thirty-six states also enacted legislation, including California (Penal Code Section 1404-1405). Of the thirty-six, Texas had executed 24 inmates during 2009; there were 52 executions out of 3,173 serving Death sentences nationwide. Advances in science, and in particular DNA testing, became a method for the wrongfully convicted to be exonerated.

In 2005, Joe was granted a court appointed attorney to file a "Motion for Post-Conviction DNA Testing under the Innocence Act." On November 3, 2005, **Attorney Raymond H. Allen** notified Joe of his appointment by **Judge Michael Duffy**, asking Joe to provide an "**evidence list**"... and stated his impression that DNA testing "was already done" [in 1991] and that Joe *"had been positively identified as the perpetrator of the crime and convicted based on numerous witnesses who had prior knowledge of him."* Joe wrote back that the undertone of Allen's letter implied that Allen had a predisposed mindset that Joe was guilty. On June 30, 1995, Judge Duffy, himself, took a plea bargain to avoid a charge of Driving Under the Influence (DUI), thus proving justice is not the same for all.

Judge Michael Duffy

EVIDENCE LIST

EXTANT BIOLOGICAL MATERIAL FROM VICTIMS
In re People v. Garcia, Case No. 15883
and in District Attorney's Chain of Custody
according to Clerk's Transcript on Appeal, January 2, 1990, Vol. 1, p. 0232-0285

Sex Evidence Kit from San Luis Obispo General Hospital SART Exam
By Jane Ann Kulick, RN,
Re victim TYRA WITTMEYER:

Blanket and Clothing from Residence of Tyra Wittmeyer

Sex Offense Evidence Kit from San Luis Obispo General Hospital
SART Exam by Christine Clickard, RN,
Re victim JACQUELINE BROOKS:

Comforter, Bath Mat and Other Items from Residence of
Victim Jacqueline Brooks

And Other Biological Material

BIOLOGICAL MATERIAL TAKEN FOR DNA TESTING
From JOSEPH BELARDE GARCIA
(per same January 2, 1990 Transcript pages 0232-0295)

Head and Pubic Hair, Blood and Saliva Samples

Seized from DEFENDANT GARCIA'S Home:
(according to Atascadero police report, October 10, 1989, Report No. 89-2807:

Pinks Tank Top
Grey Sweatpants
Black Heavy Ski-Type Jacket with "Victory In Jesus" on Back
Two Towels, One Pair Men's Underwear (from Vehicle)

Also:
Video Tape (Exhibit WWW; CT 1376: RT 5169-5170)
of 3-1/2 Hour Interview of Joseph Garcia
And by phone on October 19, 1989 (RT 5222-5235)

It was not until 1996 that Joe learned his prosecutor, Estrada-Mullaney, had his car confiscated indefinitely "in case" it could be *"evidence"* in future cases – just as she had asked that **the DNA evidence** be kept indefinitely, yet it disappeared without "Notice of Intent to Destroy Evidence."

**POLICE SERVICES
CITY OF ATASCADERO**

December 10, 1996

Mr. Joseph B. Garcia #H-01695
CSP - Sacramento, A-6-204
P.O. Box 290066
Represa, CA 95671-0066

RE: 89-2807

Dear Mr. Garcia,

We received your letter concerning the location of your vehicle (Ca Lic#2NAT419) which was seized by our department in 1989.

As you know, the car was initially seized as evidence and later held at the request of the District Attorney's Office pending all appeals in the case. The Atascadero Police Department was responsible for the storage of the car for nearly two years. During that time numerous persons inquired about the release of the vehicle, including Ford Motor Company, the legal owner.

At the time the car was ready for release Ford Motor Company was notified about the excess storage fees due. They made arrangements to pay the storage fees to the City of Atascadero and pick up the car. The transaction took place in 1991.

Should you have any questions concerning the whereabouts of the vehicle, I suggest you contact Ford Motor Company.

Sincerely,

WILLIAM E. WATTON
ACTING CHIEF OF POLICE

BY;

JOHN S. BARLOW, LIEUTENANT
FIELD SERVICES DIVISION

JSB:jb
cc: File

R.H. "BUD" McHALE
Chief of Police

5505 EL CAMINO REAL • POST OFFICE BOX 911 • ATASCADERO, CA 93423

On February 16, 2006, Attorney Allen sent note to Judge Duffy and Joe stating Mr. [Gary] Simms received *no reply* from the department's Santa Barbara office, that there was *no reply* from Detective Bergantzel, and that **"Mr. Dutra,"** Atascadero Police Department Property Technician, found *"no evidence listing"* so *"**theorized** the file was purged."*

Alton & Allen, LLP

974 Walnut Street
San Luis Obispo, California 93401
Office (805) 541-1920
Facsimile: (805) 541-5657

February 16, 2006

HAND DELIVERED

Honorable Judge Michael Duffy
San Luis Obispo Courthouse
San Luis Obispo, California 93401

> Re: **Appointment of Counsel Pursuant to**
> **Penal Code Section 1405(b)(1)**
> **People v. Garcia**
> **Case No: F000147281**
> **File No: 05.034-01C**

Your Honor:

This correspondence serves to provide an update on the aforementioned matter. I have made contact with Gary Simms at the Department of Justice, Property Technician Dutra at the Atascadero Police Department, and Detective Bergantzel at the Morro Bay Police Department regarding extant biological samples. Mr. Simms indicated that he has sent a request for any samplings to the department's office in Santa Barbara, but has not received a response. Mr. Dutra indicated that there is no evidence listing for Mr. Garcia's matter, and theorized the file was purged. Detective Bergantzel has not responded as of the writing of this letter.

Should I discover any extant biological samplings, I will proceed with a PC §1405 motion. In the meantime, should you have any additional questions, comments, or concerns regarding any of the aforementioned information, please do not hesitate to contact the undersigned.

Very Truly Yours,

ALTON & ALLEN, LLP

Raymond H. Allen

Alton & Allen, LLP

974 Walnut Street
San Luis Obispo, California 93401
Office (805) 541-1920
Facsimile: (805) 541-5657

March 27, 2006

HAND DELIVERED

Honorable Judge Michael Duffy
San Luis Obispo Courthouse
San Luis Obispo, California 93401

> Re: **Appointment of Counsel Pursuant to**
> **Penal Code Section 1405(b)(1)**
> **People v. Garcia**
> Case No: F000147281
> File No: 05.034-01C

Your Honor,

This correspondence serves to provide an update on the aforementioned matter. I have maintained contact with Gary Simms at the Department of Justice. Unfortunately, as of this date, he has been unable to indicate whether or not the Department of Justice has any extant biological samples. Although he assures me that he has made repeated attempts to get this information, I am no further along than I was last month with regards to the Department of Justice.

Moreover, Detective Bergantzel of the Morro Bay Police Department Evidence Room has responded and indicated that his agency is not in possession of any evidence, biological or otherwise, as it pertains to this matter.

Due to the age of the case, seventeen years have elapsed since some of the crimes were committed, there might be no DNA to test. The motion for re-testing, therefore, is likely not proper.

I have calendared myself to call Mr. Simms on April 12, 2006. At that time, he should be able to state definitively whether the Department of Justice has any extant biological samples. In the interim, should you have any questions, comments, or concerns regarding any of the aforementioned information, please do not hesitate to contact the undersigned at your earliest convenience.

Very Truly Yours,

ALTON & ALLEN, LLP

Raymond H. Allen

Alton & Allen, LLP

974 Walnut Street
San Luis Obispo, California 93401
Office (805) 541-1920
Facsimile (805) 541-5657

April 11, 2006

VIA REGULAR US MAIL

Joseph Garcia, H-01695
Mule Creek State Prison
Post Office Box 409020
C-13-149
Ione, California 95640

> Re: **Appointment of Counsel Pursuant to**
> **Penal Code Section 1405(b)(1)**
> **People v. Garcia**
> **Case No: F000147281**
> **File No: 05.034-01C**

Dear Mr. Garcia:

I have received your correspondence dated March 31, 2006 wherein you inquire about the status of the aforementioned matter.

As of today, I still have not established that there is any extant DNA samples available to test. As you know, the prosecution brought forward the DNA evidence. The remaining samples, if any, would be with them or their agents. To that end, I had the court issue an order directing the San Luis Obispo County District Attorney to turn over their file for review. However, the district attorney's office had previously purged its file.

Moreover, I made contact with the law enforcement agencies involved in this matter. I have personally spoken with their evidence technicians. They have indicated that they do not have any evidence, biological or otherwise, in their possession.

I have also been in contact with the agency that tested the DNA. The DNA was tested by the Federal Bureau of Investigation, Department of Justice. I have made repeated attempts to confirm whether extant samplings are at the regional office in Goleta, California. To access this information, one must go through Mr. Gary Simms at the DNA laboratory. To date, I have not received confirmation.

In addition, I have spoken with the defense expert, Randell T. Libby, PhD. He indicated that he did not do the testing, but only reviewed the testing that was done. He, of course, did not have any extant samplings. He has been of assistance in trying to find extant samplings and would be the logical person to re-test the samples if any are discovered.

Finally, I am pursuing the possibility that extant samplings remain in the FBI laboratory in Washington, D.C. To this end, I am seeking the assistance of Richard Nediermeyer of the FBI DNA laboratory.

Obviously, I have been trying to find extant biological samples. There is no reason to file a motion to test DNA pursuant to PC §1405(b)(1) unless there is in fact DNA to test. However, once the samples, if any, are located, then testing would be appropriate. As you state, the science has dramatically changed over the last decade and this change could inure to your benefit.

Should you have any additional questions, comments or concerns regarding the aforementioned please do not hesitate to contact the undersigned at your earliest convenience.

Very Truly Yours,

ALTON & ALLEN, LLP

Raymond H. Allen

78

Alton & Allen, LLP

974 Walnut Street
San Luis Obispo, California 93401
Office (805) 541-1920
Facsimile (805) 541-5657

April 17, 2006

VIA REGULAR US MAIL

J. Richard Nedimyer
Paralegal Specialist
935 Pennsylvania Avenue, N.W.
Room 7879
Washington, D.C. 20035

> Re: **Appointment of Counsel Pursuant to**
> **Penal Code Section 1405(b)(1)**
> **People v. Garcia**
> **Case No: F000147281**
> **DOJ Nos: SBC 035-91 and 144-89**
> **File No: 05.034-01C**

Dear Mr. Nedimyer:

I received your name and mailing address from Dr. Randell T. Libby of Genequest Diagnostics, Ltd. I am a criminal defense attorney that was appointed to represent Mr. Joseph Garcia. Mr. Garcia was convicted of several rapes in 1991. DNA evidence was collected and tested by the FBI. He now seeks to have his DNA samples re-tested pursuant to an applicable California statute. However, I am having difficulty finding extant samplings.

I have learned that the FBI identification numbers for his cases are SBC 035-91 and SBC 144-89. According to Mr. Gary Simms of the local Department of Justice office, on or about February 15, 1994, the DNA samplings were sent back to the San Luis Obispo County District Attorney's Office. The evidence technician, Cindy Scoles, for the district attorney's office assures me that any such evidence from that period has been purged.

Thus, in my pursuit I have been led to the FBI office in Washington, D.C. It is my understanding the Department of Justice and FBI testing was conducted in Washington, D.C. back in the early nineties. Does the FBI in Washington, D.C. have any of the extant samplings or DNA data remaining from this case, or, in the alternative, do you know of any way to track down extant biological samples regarding this case?

Please contact the undersigned with whatever information you can provide. I look forward to your response.

Very Truly Yours,

ALTON & ALLEN, LLP

Raymond H. Allen

No one inquired who last had signed in as required for access to the stored evidence. Allen just took Detective Gary Simms' verbal assurance there was "no DNA to test" by Detective Gary Simms -- the same Gary Simms who arrested Joe and who would not want a 16-year old cold case re-opened- and never filed the required Motion for DNA testing. **UNREASONABLE DOUBT AGAIN BECAME REASONABLE**.

On June 26, 2006, Joe, dissatisfied with Allen, filed a "Motion for Substitution of Counsel with Statement of Facts, Declaration and Points and Authorities." On July 7, 2006, **Judge Duffy** Denied the Motion noting:

"The Court will take no further action regarding his request which was untimely from the outset. Any further requests should be submitted elsewhere."

In 2008, almost eight years after Joe's conviction, nine boxes of his elusive Trial Transcripts, police reports, and other records that had been withheld from Joe during the time he needed them to reference in support his Appeals, were suddenly and unceremoniously dropped into his cell. He was not permitted to retain more than a single boxful and was forced to quickly sort through it all, under pressure of a guard standing watch. Material that appeared to be duplicated was discarded. After pulling out what he thought he should hang onto, he then mailed all the rest to a friend for safekeeping in case an attorney should agree to help him pro bono.

In 2008, **Michael Brennan** of University of Southern California's Gould School of Law, and Innocence Projects in New York and California, to whom I sent requests in Joe's behalf for representation and DNA testing, declined to take up Joe's complex case. And **Governor Arnold Schwarzenegger** Declined Joe's *"Application for Pardon,"* stating Joe hadn't "exhausted all legal means."

Governor Arnold Schwarzenegger

Thereafter, a note appeared in my post office box indicating there were packages for me to pick up over the counter – seven large Priority Mail boxes containing Joe's voluminous Trial Transcripts and documents. Reading the testimony as I sorted the heavy volumes of Transcript pages, that I spent a month scanning to a flash drive, confirmed that "everything was wrong" in his case. Hundreds of long letters from Joe on lined yellow legal pad paper followed, as he went over the details of each accusation, incident and testimony. For 12 years, his letters never failed to include a note of hope no less fervent than his earliest letter:

> *"Dear Lori... Thank you for taking the time to write... For us, HOPE has never died and daily we live with great expectation of a 'door' to open for us. I have chosen long ago not to live with regrets or bitterness, but instead to live in a positive manner and help out others here who might not be doing too well or are mentally and emotionally challenged. Someone once stated that a 'bad attitude' is like a flat tire; you don't go anywhere in life 'til you change it, whether you're in the White House or the Poor House. I concur..."*

On April 29, 2009, **Appellate Attorney Richard Power,** who had unsuccessfully handled Joe's Appeal, replied to my request for further assistance in Joe's behalf, saying he remembered Joe's Appeal fifteen years prior, and that "the statistical method used in the DNA portion of Joe's trial was *questionable.*" But he didn't know whether the DNA samples from Joe's cases still existed, and said *"Unless Joe's friends want to put up the money,"* he wasn't going to try to locate Joe's DNA evidence.

Attorney Richard Power

On May 28, 2009, as aka Americans for Open Records (AmFOR), I submitted Joe's case to **Linda Starr,** Director of California's Innocence Project at Santa Clara, for review. She declined.

On July 11, 2009, AmFOR submitted Joe's case to **Professor Justin Brooks** of "the other" California Innocence Project at California Western School of Law in San Diego. Brooks' Denial was swift, but was due to a young intern's error in basing it solely on a previous Denial. After my phone call to the IP's Case Manager, **Trevor Luxor,** Joe's updated submission was reinstated. But, after reviewing Joe's revised submission for an entire year, the San Diego Innocence Project Declined without explanation. We assumed they simply had too many Death Row cases and could not spare any time to search for Joe's DNA evidence.

In June 2013, I phoned Joe's former defense attorney, Jon Gudmunds for help or referral. He informed me he'd had a stroke, was no longer practicing law, so could not help Joe. When I inquired as to what I needed to do to compel a search for the allegedly "missing" DNA evidence, Gudmunds seemed unaware of the 2004 Innocence Protection Act and whether compelling a search for the DNA evidence via a Discovery Motion was possible. But also, he unexpectedly stated *"That was the longest case – He raped nine women. These guys want to end up back to jail."*

While such a false statement could be chalked up to his having had a stroke, or poor memory after 24 years, his comments left me wondering whether he had a long-held bias against Joe as he did not sound as though he had believed Joe was innocent while being paid $150,000 to defend him

After Barry LaBarbera was no longer District Attorney and Teresa Estrada-Mullaney had retired from the bench, I continued to compose Joe's Motions, including a renewed *"Motion for Post-Conviction DNA Testing Under the Innocence Act and for a Court Appointed Counsel,"* citing Trial Transcript page 5747 where Estrada-Mullaney had required that the DNA evidence was to be *retained indefinitely, "in case of further Rape claims or trials."* It was Denied. We then filed a *"Request for Reconsideration,"* directing the Court to specific points covered in the denied Motion but adding that *"the Court may now be in violation of the Innocence Protection Act."*

Joe's renewed Affidavit of Innocence, 2013,
that accompanied his renewed Motion for Post-Conviction DNA Testing

----

PEOPLE OF THE STATE OF CALIFORNIA)
)   CRIMINAL CASE NO: 15883

v.   )

JOSEPH BELARDE GARCIA   )

AFFIDAVIT OF INNOCENCE
PURSUANT TO THE INNOCENCE PROTECTION ACT
AND CALIFORNIA PENAL CODE SECTION PC 1405 (a-n)

    I, Joseph Belarde Garcia, hereby affirm that I am actually and factually innocent of the nine (9) crimes for which I was convicted that are the subject of Case No. 15883 and the attached Motion, regarding Beverly Joan Brian. Tracey D. Archer Stearns, Jacqueline D. Brooks, Cheryl A. Picco, Stacia Michelle Deane, Carrie S. Dorgan, Cheryl A. Picco, Catherine T. Pinard, Tyra Dawn Wittmeyer.

    I declare, under penalty of perjury under the laws of the State of California and the United States, 28 U.S.C.A Sec. 1746, that the foregoing is true and correct.

Executed on this _21_ day of _Nov._ , 2013

Joseph Belarde Garcia

    Within about 30 days after filing the "Request for Reconsideration" regarding his 2013 Motion for Post-Conviction DNA Testing that was Denied, Joe received a letter from the San Luis Obispo County Superior Court Clerk stating that **Judge Dodie A. Harman** had reviewed the matter and it was again Denied, claiming, as Joe's previous attorney had claimed, that DNA testing had *"already been done in 2005,"* and so, the case had been closed and *"no further motion or appointments will be considered"* nor any attempt to locate Joe's DNA evidence that would exonerate him.

Judge Dodie Ann Harman

October 9, 2013

Joseph Garcia
ID # H-01695 A2-23-34
Valley State Prison
PO Box 92
Chowchilla, CA 93610-0092

RE: CR15883

Mr. Garcia,

Your Notice of Motion and Motion for Post-Conviction DNA Testing Under the Innocence Protection Ace has been received and reviewed by this court. Per **Judge Dodie Harman**, as Previously advised on August 28, 2013, a request was made by you pursuant to Penal Code 1404-1405 in 2005 at which time as attorney was appointed. The matter was closed after an investigation by the attorney and no further motion or appointments will be considered pursuant to Penal Code section 1404 or 1405.

Sincerely,

SUSAN MATHERLY
COURT EXECUTIVE OFFICER

His black hair now white, taking Elanapril for high blood pressure, wearing a back brace and walking with aid of a cane, and sharing a cramped 8-foot by 10-foot cell with a cell-mate, Joe was beginning to feel even older than his 60 years. In the past, he had been allowed to relieve stress in prison by working out with a punching bag as he did in his youth. To maintain a healthy body despite his confinement, he exercised at every opportunity. But two hernia surgeries and a surgery for a lower back disk from over-exercise with weights, now limited his exercise routine.

Like actors Robert Downey Jr. and Charlie Sheen, Joe had found redemption through sobriety. Downey and Sheen overcame being judged by their "past mistakes" and "bad boy" image. Downey's movies, and Sheens sitcoms *Two and a Half Men* and *Anger Management,*" financially support the actors in style. But Joe is still paying for his "past mistakes" and other men's crimes, while hanging onto his faith and spirit for dear life.

Judy became Vice Principal at a Christian school. While she did not press Joe for a divorce, neither did she think she could handle his possibly being on parole as a "registered sex offender" with an ankle bracelet. It took more than two decades for Judy to lift herself from the depths of depression. While the biggest challenge had been the financial debt incurred from Joe's trial and providing for their son, including putting him through school, Joe's arrest and conviction caused Judy, like Joe, to endure every emotion -- from denial, sorrow and depression to anger and resentment -- until she reached a point of acceptance to some degree. She prayed for herself but forgave everyone who had lied and hurt them and changed their lives. Still, when asked to talk about it today, she describes her pain in terms of the present, not just the past. And, according to Joe, her letters over the years have ranged from distant, to chastising, to professing renewed love for him.

When Jordan was three, Judy found a job at a day care center; when he was five, she started his schooling. They remained in California until Jordan graduated eighth grade as valedictorian, then they moved to New Jersey, with many day trips, including to see lighthouses, Disneyland, the White House. In 2019, Jordan, then an adult, got a job in China; Judy followed him there and they sent Joe their photo at The Great Wall." Jordan then hadn't seen his father since he was eleven, and was an adult, when he eventually went to visit him in prison, taking his fiancé along to meet Joe.

California Governor Jerry Brown
Served 1st & 2nd terms in office, 1975-1983 and 3rd & 4th terms 2011-2019

When I spoke with Jordan, he very much wanted to be supportive of his father and explained:

> " When I was a kid, from age three until seven, my father seemed 'always there' because he was. It seemed normal. My Mom drove us to the prison at least every Sunday. Most often we stayed for the whole weekend since there was housing on the prison grounds where visiting family members could stay. And then suddenly one day he was gone from my life. Sure, there were male role models as I grew up, but they weren't my Dad. I tried to compensate for that loss with alcohol and friends."

In 2013, when Joe was transferred to Valley State Prison in Chowchilla, California, California, **Governor Jerry Brown** was resisting complying with the federal District Court's Order to reduce California's prisoner population by 10,000 inmates. Brown claimed that the Court had overstepped its authority in blocking his plan to send thousands of inmates to out-of-state prisons instead of sending them back into local communities and he asked the U.S. Supreme Court to intervene. It was no secret that Brown wanted to build more prisons to make more prison jobs and get more funding. From 2009 to 2017, GEO, the second largest private prison company in the U.S., gave $12.7-million and Core Civil gave $7.9-million to Brown who also received $122,100 from private prison groups.

In 2013 to 2014, when Joe Garcia submitted his 2014 *"Application for Clemency and Commutation of Sentence"* to Brown's Legal Affairs Office, Brown received $91,000 from corrections companies, and a $54,000 donation from GEO to double the number of prison beds, increasing GEO's 4-year revenue from $38,132,640 to $66,394. Meanwhile, Corrections Corporation of America (CCA), the largest private prison operator, contributed hundreds of thousands of dollars to California lawmakers and received a contract worth *$700-million* to have California prisoners sent to out-of-state CCA facilities

Because PC 1405 prohibits Appeal of a Denial for Post-Conviction DNA Testing, I composed a *"Writ of Mandate"* asking California's Second Appellate Court, Ventura Division 6 (which covers San Luis Obispo County cases) to compel the lower Court to review the matter. Governor Brown was still challenging the federal Court Order forcing him to cut California's overcrowded 120,000 inmates in 33 prisons by nearly 10,000 inmates that should have occurred by the end of January 2013. October 15, 2013, the U.S. Supreme Court rejected Brown's challenge that claimed the

Court lacked jurisdiction.

California's financial statement was "in the red" and Brown had to come up with a balanced budget. More prisons and even more prisoners would mean more jobs for prison staffers and *more funding*. The deadline for prisoner releases was again delayed until end of January 2014. January passed with another delay Granted until June 2014. The question remained as to whether Joe would be among those released, if ever. But, to Joe, there was no "if" about it. In his mind's eye, he could see himself a free man.

On April 17, 2014, an AP news story by Jennifer Pelts, *"Fund Raised Thousands for Exonerated NYC Man,"* revealed the circumstances of Jonathan Fleming, a Black man whose 1989 wrongful conviction by an all-White jury was similar to some of the circumstances in Joe's case. Fleming was able to get funding through a crowd funding website, Indiegogo.

That's when I started a *"Petition to Free Wrongfully Convicted Joseph Belarde Garcia"* at Causes.com. Joe's son, Jordan, added his post in support of his father's release, and, within a day or so of Jordan's post, there were 106 signers, then 215, whose names and comments I attached as one of the Exhibits to Joe's *"Application for Clemency and Commutation of Sentence,"* which was acknowledged as received by Brown's Office of Legal Affairs … but was never acted on.

Chapter 5:
(2015) A BITTERLY BIASED
PAROLE HEARING

*"…Okay, one, two, even three cases, maybe they're incorrect.
But we're taking a whole lot of people."*
-Commissioner Nga Lam (9-16-15 Parole Hearing Transcript, page 118)

In 2015, Joe became eligible for parole. Since 2011, California had been under U.S. Supreme Court Order to reduce the prison population to a 137.5% benchmark due to overcrowding, so it was hoped Joe would be paroled. But the reduction was accomplished by moving inmates as follows: 8,000 were transferred to prisons in Arizona, Mississippi and Oklahoma; 2,077 were relocated to a private prison in California City, California; 2,035 who had been convicted of low level felony crimes had them changed to misdemeanors such as drug offenses and property crimes; 975 were released after seeking re-sentencing, if the inmate's "third strike" was not considered **serious or violent**; 115 were released through an **"elderly parole"** program for elderly inmates not considered a threat to society.

California inmates "age 60 and older, who served at least 25 years of their sentence" have since been eligible for early release, unless they were sentenced to Death or were serving Life Without Parole. Additionally, inmates who have medical conditions that require skilled nursing care are eligible for admission to health care facilities; however, those who recover are sent back to prison. Governor Jerry Brown's administration estimated that 85 inmates would meet criteria for the expanded "elderly parole" and 100 inmates would be eligible for the expanded "medical parole."

On September 16, 2015, a Parole Consideration Hearing was held in the matter of Joseph Belarde Garcia, who was then 67, had served 27 years, had various medical issues and walked with a cane.   Representing Joe was **Attorney Dejon R. Lewis**. The Parole Panel included: Brian Roberts, Presiding Commissioner; Nga Lam, Deputy Commissioner; Linda Dunn, San Luis Obispo County Deputy District Attorney; John Barrick, Ventura County D.A.'s office; Richard Jallins (Parole Board Commissioner and

Joe and his wife and son at time of his 2015 parole hearing.

ATTORNEY DEJON RAMON LEWIS,
Joe's court appointed attorney for Joe's 2015 parole hearing

Observer); Margarita Bassin (identified as "Victim"); Helen Chang (San Luis Obispo County Victim's Support); James Miller (Victims' Support Advocate); William "Bill" Miller (retired Private Investigator who worked for San Luis Obispo County's District Attorney at Joe's 1991 trial).

At the beginning of the hearing, and repeatedly during the hearing, Commissioner Roberts emphasized *"We're not here to retry those cases today. We are here to try to understand it, but not to retry it."*

And yet, whenever Joe attempted to clarify a point for their *"understanding,"* the Commissioner would cut him off. Neither had any of those present, except for "Bill" Miller, been at Joe's trial and none had seen Transcripts of his trial. Joe was, in fact, *retried* each time he was asked to detail the Bassin case and the cases of each of the eight women whose conflicting identifications resulted in his Life conviction.

According to the Parole Hearing Transcript (pages 109-110), Joe was starting to clarify that his wife not only provided verbal alibi testimony but also provided receipts that supported his alibi on the day they were out of town when one of the incidents occurred, adding *"But I know we are not here to retry the whole thing,"* which gave Commissioner Roberts an opening to say *"No, we're not going to retry it...* **You're GUILTY and that's that."**

From the outset, so that there was to be no mistake as to what D.A. Dunn's decision was going to be, Dunn responded to Joe's mention of having been recruited by his friend, former Los Angeles Police Department (LAPD) Homicide Detective, Frank Tomlinson, as a Confidential Informant (CI), Dunn fired back: *"He wants to tell us, oh, I helped solve cases with the Mexican Mafia and I was chairman of this...* **He's a narcissistic grandiose liar."** (Parole Hearing Transcript page 110).

Actually, Tomlinson's August 30, 2015 (on the next page), and older letters in his Central File, confirmed Joe's life saving assistance as a Confidential Informant who testified at risk of his own life, and it was also reported in *"The Wonderland Murders 1981"* in *"The Cops"* chapter:
> "The late seventies found **Frank [Tomlinson]** involved in the Garcia witness case. Garcia was a lifelong criminal, but Tomlinson and his partner **Richard Szabo** had Joe released to police custody since Joe agreed to turn state's witness in order to try to bring down Mexican Mafia captain Arthur Blajos, known as 'Conejo' ('The Rabbit')."

Neither Joe's psyche evaluator, Jana R. Larmer, nor the Parole Panel looked for the support letters urging Joe's release and offering transition help - letters from Frank Tomlinson, Pastor Roger Willis, Anita Conner, Susan Allen, Linda Stephens, Johnny Willis Transition Team, myself, and others.

HOPE COMING

Biblical Counseling & Consulting

4545 Industrial Street #5L
Simi Valley, CA 93063

805-558-2226

August 30, 2015

CDCR Parole Board

In Re Joseph Belarde Garcia H-01695

Dear Sir/Madam,

I first met Joseph in 1979 in Visalia where he was incarcerated. Having been around many prisoners and ex-cons, I was struck at the vulnerability of Joseph. He expressed a burning desire to know God better, and we began a discussion that lasted for many months. During that time, Joseph did not ask me for any favors, only to meet with him.

He assisted law enforcement with some intelligence information, and testified in Superior Court to his knowledge of certain prison gang members. Again, Joseph did this because he felt compelled to do the right thing, not because he wanted any favors.

I have recently visited Joseph at C.I.M. and he assured me (I trust him to keep his word) that if he is released, he would begin a counseling regimen with me. He does this completely aware that if I discover that he is not following all of the requirements of the law and his release, that I will report it to the proper authority.

I trust that you see I believe it is time for Joseph to be released from his incarceration. I am a retired homicide detective (supervisor) for the Los Angeles Police Department, currently a licensed pastor who has founded a biblical counseling center.

Respectfully submitted,

Frank Tomlinson
President

92

Joe's "past mistake" with Margarita Bassin, still a single woman at 57 when she returned to "bear witness against him" at his parole hearing, continued to be a curse he can never escape. Joe's attorney, Dejon Lewis, immediately Objected to her presence and to Ventura County DA's Attorney John Barrick's presence or participation in this parole hearing:

> "Ms. Bassin was not a victim in his crimes – the Life crimes. She was a victim from 1979, which has nothing to do with these proceedings"... And with regard to Barrick: "None of these cases for which he's serving his Life sentence came out of Ventura County."

Deputy D.A. Dunn responded, addressing the Commissioner:

> "Well, actually, Commissioner, that's somewhat incorrect in that Ms. Bassin testified in the San Luis Obispo Court trial and was allowed to testify by the trial judge. And so it was her testimony that was relevant to this case and therefore we request that she be allowed to speak."

Lewis countered:

> "She gave testimony which basically assisted the D.A. with regard to him being found guilty, but she is not a victim in this particular issue... of the crimes that he's been convicted of in this term, so therefore..."

Roberts:

> "She's a victim of a crime he's been convicted of.... I think...?

Lewis:

> "But not the Life crime."

Roberts:

> "Okay. I believe she qualifies. All right?"

Lewis:

> "Still noted."

Roberts:

> "All right. Your objection is noted. Overruled. Okay? All right..."

And Barrick was allowed to "observe."

Whenever there is an upcoming parole hearing, the D.A. solicits any victims from the original trial in order to prevent a parole... especially a parole of a prisoner claiming wrongful conviction that could risk overturning a case. Bassin waited hours from the start of the hearing until she was allowed to speak at the very end. According to Parole Hearing Transcript page 146, her brief, disjointed comment was as follows:

"*I am Margarita Bassin. I live with the pain that Joseph Garcia – of him putting a knife point and raping me at 21. I am here today to stand tall on behalf of all the victims who have shared the horrendous crimes of a mentally deranged human who I strongly feel he should remain here forever. I have conquered many things in my life. And I will continue to have a beautiful and peaceful life. But I live in fear now. I believe strongly for all of us. I continue to live with God on my side. No weapons form against me shall prosper. And I say this in the name of Jesus Christ. Amen. I know my presence shows more than any words could ever say. I did not choose this to happen to me, but I want to thank you, the Parole Board, and everyone that's here. Thank you kindly – and graciously.*"

Such a short paragraph with so many contradictions. Joe's debt to society, and to Bassin, was not only paid in full for their one drunken night together in 1979 – by his imprisonment until 1987 – but also his debt was "overpaid" when Bassin interjected herself into his 1991 trial, twelve years later, hoping to assure that he would spend the rest of this life in prison. Still not having exacted sufficient revenge, nor taking any responsibility for their drunken mistake, here she is again, center stage, self-appointed to represent "*all*" victims, declaring that Joe is "*mentally deranged*," contradicting his psyche reports, and stating she'll "*continue to have a beautiful and peaceful life*"…or, no, she "*lives in fear*" although "*God is on her side.*" What happened to God's edict "*Vengeance is mine sayeth the Lord*" and His Commandment "*Thou shalt not bear false witness*"?

The Parole Panel never heard that, in a follow-up police report, Bassin told the officer she "had sex with Harvey Simpson at his home" just hours before the alleged rape, and when the Officer asked why she hadn't volunteered that information previously, she said she "*didn't want her mother to be embarrassed.*" Or was it that she didn't want her mother to know that she also had sex with her mother's lover, Joe Garcia, so made up the rape story? The Parole Panel never heard that Joe's fingerprints were not on any of her kitchen knives, and that Bassin did acknowledge Joe had been so drunk he could not perform (so no Rape occurred).

Not only was Joe "re-tried" at his parole hearing for his "past mistakes" from childhood, and his entire non-violent criminal history examined in detail, but also the Ventura County D.A. who was supposed to just be "observing" alleged that Joe committed crimes for which Joe was never charged, and which never occurred, but which were added as "Enhancements" during sentencing to assure a Life sentence.

The Ventura County D.A. simply said whatever sounded good, such as *"There was DNA"*... but not that the DNA was inconclusive and mysteriously went *"missing"* when Joe sought a post-conviction DNA test under the 2004 law and new science, that would have exonerated him. And D.A. Dunn alleged: *"And then there was another woman that was a DNA match. And that was not just Tyra, but also the one who was 18."* (Transcript page 47), referring to Jacqueline Brooks, who identified her attacker as "Negro" per the composite of the suspect that she instructed the police artist Darrell R. Klasey to draw, and, no, there was no "DNA match" nor was the DNA ever ruled on in any of the eight cases.

Dunn decided: *"He is still in a state of complete **denial** about his culpability and his responsibility, so he's just too **dangerous.**"*

Actually, Joe took responsibility for drunken sex with Margarita Bassin by pleading guilty, apologizing to her and her mother in Court, and serving the resulting prison sentence. For 32 years since his 1989 arrest, he consistently has denied guilt in the eight 1989 cases.

"Bill" Miller then offered to "read statements" by the "survivors" and their families, but began by alleging (Transcript page 134):

"I have spoken to Tyra, Jackie, Cathy's mother Peg, and Stacie. They told me they remain afraid of what they know this inmate is capable of doing. I see sitting here an inmate who in 25 years has never admitted these crimes, has never shown any remorse for his actions."

He then read a lengthy statement alleged to be from "**Peg Pinard**," in behalf of her daughter, Cathy Pinard, about the publicity resulting from Cathy Pinard's demeanor in court (Transcript page 135-139):
"...a demeaning and fictional account describing the account of my daughter's reactions to his vicious attack appeared on the internet... His modus operandi was the same each time."

"Peg" Pinard

95

Cathy Pinard was observed "laughing and giggling" one hour after the October 17, 1989 event (Transcript page 5172), and in Court. Also, the "modus operandi" was actually different in each case. So much for "not retrying" Joe's case, let alone retrying it with "alternate reality."

> Bill Miller read a statement he said was from Jacqueline Brooks:
> "...He was found guilty on all Counts, not only because of my testimony, but because of the DNA that was found at the crime scene... Prior to the string of attacks in San Luis Obispo, he was in prison for molesting a child."

It was odd that a "victim impact statement" made no reference to what *she* alleged Joe did to *her*, just a recital of patently false claims that he was convicted "based on the DNA" and that the "prior" case for which he was imprisoned involved a "child"– referring to Bassin at age 21, who admitted to having sex with two men that day -- her boyfriend, Harvey Simpson, and Joe. No mention that the Brooks' composite and description of her assailant, nor that the DNA did not "match" Joe.

> Miller then read a statement alleged to be from Tyra Wittmeyer (Transcript page 142-143):
> "I was sleeping on my favorite unicorn sheets after watching a unicorn movie and was very proud of being a virgin... He had a ski mask on... He had been in jail before, for the rape of a young girl..."

The statement omits any mention of Tyra having **identified** her attacker as being **Steve Bolt**, a teenager bearing no resemblance to Joe who was 42 at the time, nor that she had been adamant that *"It wasn't Joe"* who she had known for months, nor that she didn't actually accuse him at trial, only parroted that she was told "his DNA matched," and, again there's the false statement that Joe had previously "raped a young girl," when referring to Bassin who was 21 at the time she had consenting drunken sex with two men that day. So, no, they were not *"re-trying the case"*; they were inventing a totally different reality.

THE DECISION (beginning on Parole Hearing transcript page 147): Commissioner Roberts recapped the charges for which Joe was convicted, naming the victims, including Margarita Bassin, who was not a victim in this case and about whom he was not charged in this case. Roberts acknowledged (on Transcript page 151):

*"The record does reflect some circumstances tending to show **suitability for parole**. Namely, we found that his age of 67 and the fact that there were elements of **elderly parole consideration** that we and the clinician (Jana R. Larmer) discussed and both considered independently, that we felt those things, your age and those things, tend to **indicate a reduced probability of recidivism**. We believe you've made realistic plans... However those positives are far outweighed by other circumstances tending to show unreliability and suggest, if released, Mr. Garcia would pose a threat to public safety... The mere number of victims are staggering in our mind... And that victim was here, a previous sexual attack on her... **We also considered your claim of innocence, and today we found that implausible.**"*

According to Commissioner Nga Lam (Transcript page 158):
"I'm just going to be really frank. You scare me... Your claim of an overzealous D.A. who's now a judge, I mean, it's ludicrous, sir. It's so ludicrous... I mean, forget the DNA. And they have DNA on you... When you look at all these crimes they look very similar... It's just not plausible, it's ludicrous when you sit here and tell everybody in this room that you're the – you know... I mean, come on. You're so far from where you need to be – I had a serial rapist here – and I believe that's what you are sir – just a couple of months ago. He gets it, you know. He's working toward it. He tells us about, you know, the fact that he lives a double life."

Joe was then informed he could not request parole again *for another ten years.* He will then be 77 years old.

After the hearing, I phoned Joe's attorney, Dejon Lewis, requesting the hearing transcript and to verify that he will appeal the Denial of parole. And soon thereafter I received Joe's reaction to the parole hearing:
"Glad to hear you got the parole hearing transcripts. That entire hearing was a setup. But my attitude is good as I see light at the end of the tunnel... just another bump in the road. I'm not discouraged at all. If the Feds really step in and take control of the prison system as rumored, I would automatically be released. Laws are changing daily which can affect all Lifers."

The California Court of Appeals Denied Joe's Habeas appeal of his 2015 parole Denial, which cited the Parole Panel's illegal, unethical basis mostly being his consistent claim of *factual innocence.*

"...Your claim of innocence we find to be,
   you know, implausible and not believable."
--Commissioner Brian Roberts to Joe Garcia,
September 16, 2015 Parole Hearing Transcript page 160

The following year, on December 14, 2017, a California Court vacated a Denial of Fred Swanigan's parole due to the same Parole Board basing their Denial of Swanigan's claim of innocence. Joe appealed in 2015, prior to the Swanigan ruling, and also since, and was again Denied.

California Court of Appeals Vacates Parole Denial for Claiming Innocence

Loaded on DEC. 14, 2017 by Matthew Clarke (/news/author/matthew-clarke/)

Filed under: Appeals (/search/?selected_facets=tags:Appeals), Parole (/search/?selected_facets=tags:Parole), Habeas Corpus (/searc /?selected_facets=tags:Habeas%20Corpus). Location: California (/search/?selected_facets=locations:1476).

by Matt Clarke

On September 1, 2015, a California court of appeal vacated the decision of the Board of Parole Hearings to deny parole to a prisoner who had been convicted of first-degree murder and sentenced to life in prison because the decision was impermissibly based upon the prisoner's claim of innocenc

Fred Swanigan was convicted of fatally shooting a man during an argument over money the man owed him for damaging his car. The conviction was based upon the imperfect eyewitness testimony (three witnesses--two children and an adult. A jury sentenced him to life in prison for the 1980 murder. He consistently denied committing the crime and had an alibi witness.

Swanigan's first parole hearing was in 1996. He denied committing the crime, and the board denied parole. That was the pattern for 18 years. Then, in 2009, without admitting guilt, Swanigan "accepte responsibility" for the murder. Not satisfied, the board denied parole.

In a 2012 hearing, the "Board told Swanigan at least 10 times that his denial of parole centered on th denial of the life crime." In a 2014 hearing, Swanigan briefly admitted the offense, but immediately recanted when his lawyer told him to tell the truth. Parole was denied for failure to admit the crime and lying to the board when he confessed.

Swanigan filed a petition for a writ of habeas corpus in Los Angeles County Superior Court, challenging the 2014 parole denial as unsupported by "some evidence" of future dangerousness. The court denied the petition.

Swanigan filed an original petition for a writ of habeas corpus in the court of appeals. The court appointed attorney Rich Pfeiffer to represent him. It then issued a decision agreeing with Swanigan.

DeJon R. Lewis

Law Office of DeJon R. Lewis
674 County Square Drive, Suite 204
Ventura, CA 93003

DeJon R. Lewis, Esq

Tel. (805) 658-1225
Fax (805) 658-1608
dalaw@prodigy.net

September 18, 2015

Chief Counsel
Howard Moseley
Board of Parole Hearings

     RE: Request for Decision Review of Joseph Garcia H-01695

Dear Mr. Moseley:

On September 16, 2015, I represented Joseph Garcia (H01695) at his initial parole consideration hearing at CIM. I was not appointed by the Board in this matter but was hired privately by Mr. Garcia. The Commissioners presiding over the hearing on behalf of the Board were Commissioner Brian Roberts and Deputy Commissioner Lau. Please accept this letter as my request for review of the Board's decision in this matter wherein Mr. Garcia received a 10-year denial.

From the beginning my client has asserted his innocence and claims that he did not commit any of the crimes for which he received his life sentence. At the hearing there were representatives for some of the victims of the life crimes, which are unequivocally acceptable under Marcy's law.

The first issue that my client and I have is the fact that the victim assaulted in Mr. Garcia's fourth prison term (CDCR No. C16145), Ms. Marjorie Bassin, **(a prison commitment that took place years before the life crimes)** was allowed to sit in the hearing room and make a victims impact statement despite my numerous objections that were subsequently overruled by Commissioner Roberts.

During his recital of the Board's decision in this matter, Commissioner Roberts stated that Ms. Bassin's statement was "helpful" in rendering the Board's 10-year denial decision. Mr. Garcia was sentenced to 13 years 8 months for that crime and paid his debt owed to Ms. Bassin and society years before the life crimes. We believe to allow Ms Bassin to make a victim's impact statement when she **WAS NOT** a victim of any of the crimes that make up the life crimes related to those proceedings, was in violation of Marcy's Law, my clients due process rights, and was a blatant abuse of Commissioner Robert's Administrative discretion.

After a thorough reading of Marcy's Law under *California Penal Code* § 3043(3)(b)(1), I interpret that section to allow a victim of the instant matter for which he or she has been affected to give an victim's impact statement for the crime(s) that the inmate committed against that or those victims, for crimes that the inmate has served a determinate sentence for which he has been paroled and other crimes, but it does not provide for a victim of past crimes for which that victim was affected wherein the inmate has served his time and paroled to give a victim's impact statement at a parole consideration hearing for crimes unrelated to that victim.

The second issue my client and I have is the fact that despite my client taking years self help related courses addressing his drug and alcohol issues, by attending Criminal and Gang Members Anonymous (CGA), and a four (4) year course called "Intervention for Sexual Behavior," the Board members openly made statements and opinions to discredit and/or minimize his participation. Most of my client's crimes that make up the life crimes were drug and alcohol induced sexual assaults and he has addressed those issues despite proclaiming his innocence.

Thirdly, my client received a nonviolent CDC 115 for "over familiarity with staff" dated 10/6/14. Prior to receiving the latest 115, my client was disciplinary free for over 14 years because the few 115's received during that 14 year time span were either dismissed or reduced to CDC 128's. In some of Commissioner Robert's questions of my client he asked Mr. Garcia "why did he fight the 115's" and appeared to be upset with my client that he had done so successfully.

My client and I knew that the 2014 115 would be a problem and we were of the belief that if he was to be denied parole that it would be either a 3 or 5-year denial given that this was his initial hearing, his latest 115 coupled with his positive programming and nonviolent record. Never in my wildest dreams did I believe that my client would receive a 10-year denial.

Therefore, we respectfully request that you commence a decision review of this ruling for the reasons outlined above and review the transcript of this hearing. We believe that clear and convincing evidence (under Marcy's Law) was not shown or presented during the hearing that would warrant or justify such a lengthy denial period. Thank you

Sincerely,

DeJon R. Lewis. Esq.

/drl

Law Office of DeJon R. Lewis
1655 Mesa Verde Avenue, Suite 120
Ventura, CA 93003

DeJon R. Lewis, Esq.

Tel. (805) 658-1225
Fax (805) 658-1608
dalaw@prodigy.net

April 30, 2019

Joseph Belarde Garcia, H01695
California Institution for Men
P.O. Box 368
Chino, CA 91708

   RE: Response to Your Appeal

Hello Mr. Garcia.

I know that you wrote me some months ago. I have been really busy doing my work with the Board of Parole Hearings. My work with the Board formally ends on May 28, 2019.

Any Board work that I do now, will be on a solely private attorney basis. As for any response from the Board regarding your appeal, there is no written response. I came to find out that Mr. Mosely was on his way out and their new legal counsel was on the way in exactly at the time we were waiting for a response.

When I called in, after several months of waiting, I was informed by the Board's Legal office that your appeal was summarily denied because past victims from other crimes not connected to the life crime are allowed under Marcy's Law. When I asked why I had not received a written response, I was told that it was because of the "changing of the guard," and all of the confusion that goes with that.

If you would like to have an earlier hearing, all you have to do is fill out a Petition to Advance, BPH form No. 1045. You can receive this from your counselor. So long as there has been a change in circumstances, e.g. (finishing a new self-help course, obtaining an advanced degree, acquiring a new trade or skill, good behavior etc.) you should be approved and placed on the next available calendar within 8 months or so.

Good luck with your quest for freedom. I would be willing to represent you so long as I can have minimal contact with your girlfriend.

Enclosed, please find my brochure that I am distributing out throughout the CDCR system.
I invite you to pass it around to all of those inmates interested in quality legal counsel at their hearing at a fair reasonable price.

Congratulations on your kid and their living abroad. It must be great for them.

Sincerely,

DeJon R. Lewis
/drl

101

A **1994** psychological evaluation by **Gerald Hollingsworth, MD,** had noted *"Most all of the commitment offenses were denied and the DNA figured prominently,"* but he found that Joe had no mental illness. Joe's **2015** psychological assessment by **Jana R. Larmer,** suggested Joe has PTSD and bouts of Depression and anger, and alleges Joe's claim of innocence is "denial," which influenced the parole panel. Perhaps it hadn't occurred to Larmer that a *wrongfully convicted* individual has reason to sometimes feel depressed and angry. Larmer's report had many factual errors about Joe and his case, including that he was convicted based on DNA, which the Parole Panel, media, and the parole panel parroted, because she had never read the trial transcripts. So Joe wrote Larmer requesting corrections of errors in her report, or re-assessment of him. *Larmer never responded*

Lighthouse Bible Church

Roger D. Willis
Pastor

August 27, 2015

Ref: Mr. Joseph Belarde Garcia
    #H-01695

To Whom It May Concern,

I have added my support in favor of the release of Mr. Joseph Belarde Garcia from incarnation to a transitional living arrangement, and eventually back into "normal" life.

I have not met Mr. Garcia, however I know the character of the individuals who are willing to establish a team to facilitate his transition back to "civilian" life. I have great confidence in the discernment and dedication of the ones who are on his "team."

As the pastor of Lighthouse Bible Church, Simi Valley, I will be able to provide additional encouragement, and accountability to Mr. Garcia's reintroduction to "normal" life.

Sincerely,

Roger D. Willis, Pastor
Lighthouse Bible Church
4910 Cochran Street
Simi Valley, CA 93063
805-584-8222

CC: Counselor Prill,
Mr. Joseph Belarde Garcia

The SLO District Attorney acknowledged one of many support letters sent by Anita Conner over the years, before and since his parole hearing, advocating for his release based on his innocence.

OFFICE OF THE DISTRICT ATTORNEY

COUNTY OF SAN LUIS OBISPO, STATE OF CALIFORNIA

DAN DOW
District Attorney

ERIC J. DOBROTH
Assistant District Attorney

JERRET C. GRAN
Chief Deputy District Attorney

SHERYL M. WOLCOTT
Chief Deputy District Attorney

January 9, 2019

TERRY O'FARRELL
Chief, Bureau of Investigation

VIA U.S. MAIL & ELECTRONIC MAIL
(Joy4thejourney@outlook.com)

Ms. Anita Connor
6422 Indio Avenue #B
Yucca Valley, California 92284

CIM APPEALS

AUG 28 2019

Re: *The People v. Joseph Belarde Garcia*
San Luis Obispo County Superior Court Case No. CR016036
DA Case No.: 07-219546

Ms. Connor –

I have received your letter dated November 27, 2018, requesting reconsideration and the resentencing of Mr. Joseph Belgrade Garcia. After review of our records we respectfully decline your invitation to petition the Court for a modification of the sentence Mr. Garcia is presently serving. The crimes for which Mr. Garcia was convicted of in 1991 are extremely serious. It is the nature of these crimes, coupled with his prior criminal history, which resulted in what is functionally a life sentence for Mr. Garcia.

Although mindful of your broader concern that Mr. Garcia remains incarcerated at the age of 70, the legal opinions expressed in your letter of November 27th are incorrect. The law is complex in this regard. If you wish further review, I encourage you to seek legal counsel.

Very truly yours,
Dan Dow
District Attorney

CIM APPEALS

NOV 21 2019

By: Eric Dobroth
     Assistant District Attorney
Enclosure: Copy of November 27, 2018 Letter

*"Your claim of an overzealous DA who's now a judge,
I mean, it's so ludicrous sir. It's so ludicrous."*
--Commissioner Nga Lam to Joe Garcia (September 16, 2015 Parole
Hearing Transcript page 158)

Ironically, while Joe's high profile case was making headlines, on October 20, 1989, in a movie titled *"False Witness,"* actress Phylicia Rashad portrayed "an Assistant District Attorney who realized she could be promoted if she can convict a suspect in a controversial rape case"... Art imitating life?

Nipomo Adobe Press May 10, 1991

Deputy DA receives award from governor

SAN LUIS OBISPO — Deputy District Attorney Teresa Estrada-Mullaney recently received a public safety award from Gov. Pete Wilson.

The award was presented to Estrada-Mullaney, a Grover City resident, on April 15 by Attorney General Dan Lungren on behalf of the governor at the Governor's Conference on Victim Services and Public Safety.

Estrada-Mullaney has been a prosecutor for 12 years. She was a deputy district attorney with the Orange County District Attorney's Office for two years. She has been with the San Luis Obispo County District Attorney's Office since May 1981.

Her current assignment is the prosecution of career criminal cases, which is the basis for the governor's award. In this assignment, she has a 100 percent conviction rate in the prosecution of career criminals.

These cases involve the prosecution of serious felony crimes, including repeat or multiple residential burglary and robbery cases.

She is currently prosecuting Joseph Garcia, who is charged with 19 felonies, mostly sexual assault crimes, involving nine victims.

Estrada-Mullaney has taught other prosecutors statewide in the areas of sexual assault and mentally disordered offenders. She has also authored or co-authored articles regarding child witnesses. She has participated in Law Week through the County Bar Association.

Margarita Bassin being called to testify against Joe, not only in his 1991 trial, but also at his 2015 parole hearing, was the capstone of the pyramid of carefully crafted strategies to keep Joe in prison. Lacking hard evidence, the D.A. continued to use Bassin to support a circumstantial case and to forever deny him parole.

On November 19, 2015, when I received the electronically transmitted 165-page parole hearing transcript, I phoned Joe's parole hearing attorney, Dejon Lewis, and asked where we can go from here. Lewis commented that the parole hearing *"was entirely unfair"* but he also said *"sex offenders should go through a program while in prison..."* when I cut him off, asking *"Do you believe he's innocent?"* Lewis replied,

> *"When so many women are coming forward,*
> *like in the Bill Cosby case, with all those women accusing him,*
> *it's pretty convincing."*

Dejon Lewis, whose practice includes personal injury, criminal appeals including sex crimes, knew little about Joe or the case, but apparently believed his client "must be guilty." Lewis did not even bother to respond to Joe's repeated requests for the Parole Board's written Decision on his Appeal. It was not until April 3, 2019 – 4 years after his 2015 parole hearing – that Lewis informed Joe "there is no *written* response" to the appeal, but Joe *did* receive the Parole Board's *written response* to his *own* Appeal, which was "summarily Denied" stating past victims of crimes *not* connected to the Life crime (Margarita Bassin) *ARE* allowed under Marcy's Law"– which is what had been contested.

One ray of hope was Lewis' referral to a Ventura County attorney, **Wendy Lascher**, known as a *"Super Lawyer."* I wrote to her immediately.

Attorney Wendy Cole Lascher, "Super Lawyer"

Cathy Singer, Producer
NBC Dateline

"The media's the most powerful entity on earth.
They have the power to make the innocent guilty
And the guilty innocent
And that's the power."
Because they control the minds of the masses."
-Malcolm X

Chapter 6:
(2016-2019) INNOCENCE: A "TOUGH SELL": LOYOLA and LARRY HOBSON

My chat with Joe's parole attorney, Dejon Lewis, refueled my hope for possible legal assistance when he referred me to Ventura County's "Super Lawyer," **Wendy Cole Lascher**, to whom I immediately wrote in Joe's behalf. We didn't have long to wait for Attorney Lascher's reply but it told us what we had already surmised – that there are more who are wrongfully convicted than there are lawyers willing or able to lend pro bono assistance to exonerate them.

The first "Conviction Integrity Unit (CIU)" that was established in Santa Clara County, California, in 2002, was, by 2016, one of twenty-four such units nationwide – not a huge number, considering there were more than 2,300 prosecutors' offices across the country, but the presence of CIUs coincided with the recent record-high numbers of exonerations – By 2015, almost 150 had been cleared for crimes they never committed, more than any previous year, according to the National Register of Exonerations. However, critics of CIUs say the close relationship that CIUs have with county Prosecutors is a conflict of interest and little more than "public relations ploys," especially when the unit has no external oversight, nor any relationships with other key stakeholders such as local Defense attorneys or groups advocating correcting wrongful convictions.

So I refocused efforts on trying to interest media in Joe's story. Media had "tried and convicted" him in 1991. Would they help exonerate him in 2016 if I was as good a writer as Attorney Lascher had commented in her letter?

In February 2016, I subscribed to LinkedIn.com, a website for professionals to showcase their expertise, because it provided a way to communicate with TV and movie producers to request their email in order to submit Joe's story. One of the TV producers I tapped had produced NBC Dateline's *"In the Shadow of Justice"* series that featured wrongfully convicted cases.

FERGUSON CASE ORR PATERSON LLP

ATTORNEYS AT LAW

1050 SOUTH KIMBALL ROAD, VENTURA, CALIFORNIA 93004

PHONE: (805) 659-6800 FACSIMILE: (805) 659-8818

www.fcoplaw.com

MICHAEL W. CASE
JOHN C. ORR
THEODORE J. ENGLAND
JOSEPH L. STROHMAN, JR.
DAVID W. TREDWAY
WENDY C. LASCHER

DAVID L. SPAIN
SCOTT P. SAMSKY
WILLIAM E. SMITH
CHRISTOPHER R. ALTADARI
GARY D. P. SHEA

JAMES Q. McDERMOTT
MARA F. BARNEY
MICHAEL A. VELTHOEN
DOUGLAS K. GOLDWATER
JESSE F. CAHILL

LESLIE A. McADAM
BRET G. ANDERSON
JOHN H. ANDERSON
NEAL F. MAGUIRE
JOHN A. HRIBAR

JOSHUA S. HOPSTONE
KYMBERLEY E. PECK
LAUREN E. SIMS
LAUREN S. BAO
LANE J. LOPEZ

THOMAS H. FERGUSON
1926-80
WILLIAM E. PATERSON
RETIRED
Of Counsel
ROBERT B. ENGLAND

Writer's Email:
wlascher@fcoplaw.com

November 23, 2015

<u>By U.S. Mail</u>

Lori Carangelo

Palm Desert, California 92211-2733

    Re: *Joseph Garcia*

Dear Ms. Carangelo:

    I hate injustice, and I applaud your hard work on behalf of Joseph Garcia. Unfortunately, however, I am not in a position to take on any pro bono exoneration, even in the hope of winning eventual literary rights. (In fact, I already have the rights to a share of another inmate's future book.)

    You are a good writer and it's an interesting story. I hope you can find an attorney to assist, but this time it can't be me.

    Best of luck.

                    Very truly yours,

                    Wendy C. Lascher

WCL/ad
cc: DeJon Lewis, Esq.

108

On March 28, 2016, I submitted Joe's story to **Cathy Singer,** one of **NBC Dateline's** producers. She informed me of her initial interest in his case and asked for Joe's trial transcripts which I immediately provided on a flash drive by mail. She also said she would be traveling while covering another story but would get back to us in about a month. Two months later, I received the following email from Singer:

> *"I'm sorry to just be getting back to you. I have been thrown onto a bunch of different stories since we last communicated, which have sent me on the road on numerous trips. I will try to look at the material you sent me this week, but I cannot promise that Dateline will produce a story on that case. Thank you, Cathy."*

On May 31, 2016, two months after submitting Joe's story to Cathy Singer for Dateline, it was 8:00 pm California time, which was 10:00 pm in Chicago where Cathy Singer was at home when she decided to send me a one-line text message to my cell phone stating she decided not to pursue Joe's story. So I emailed her asking her to share the reason she lost interest. She replied that she felt his case is a *"tough sell"* because of his *"criminal background"* and because it's *"not just one but many cases."*

Tough sell, indeed.

In May 2018, Investigation Discovery (ID) TV aired a story about serial killer Rex Allan Krebs, in which retired San Luis Obispo County criminal case investigator, **Larry Hobson**, commented. I asked Joe whether he had encountered Hobson and whether he thought it might be beneficial to contact him. Joe recalled that Hobson "sat in" at Joe's trial but at first didn't recall having any direct contact with Hobson whose Facebook page reveals he is a family man with two children, so I emailed him as follows:

> *"Saw you on ID regarding Krebs – Congratulations. ID aired one of my murder stories, loosely based on my non-fiction book, "Blood Relatives," but the re-enactment falsely depicted a wrongfully convicted Georgia man entering the crime scene according to the Prosecution's theory of the crime, and edited out part of my narration that explained why he gave a false confession and that he has claimed innocence ever since. Thought you might like to read a PDF of my book about another high profile San Luis Obispo case from 1989 (1991 trial). I'd love to know what a seasoned investigator as yourself might be able to do or suggest.*

Larry Hobson, former Investigator
for the D.A. at time of Joe's 1989 arrest.

Joe's son, Jordan, grown up knowing his father
only during prison visits.

Larry Hobson replied: *"Thanks Lori – Can you email the PDF – I'd like to read it.* I emailed Hobson a PDF of *"The Case of the Carefully Crafted Central Coast Rapist"* and waited for his reaction. And waited and waited.

August 9, 2018 - Almost two months had gone by, so I sent Hobson a follow-up inquiry to his direct email that he had provided:

"As it's been some time since you requested a PDF of 'The Case of the Carefully Crafted Central Coast Rapist,' I've been wondering whether you've since had a chance to read it, and, as Joe has been waiting in prison 30 years, I would like to give Joe, and his wife and son, some indication, either way, as to whether you agree that he was wrongfully convicted...

August 10, 2018 – Reply from Larry Hobson: *"Hi, Lori. Yes, I read the PDF copy you sent me about "The Case of the Carefully Crafted Central Coast Rapist." After reading the first few pages I remembered this investigation and my official law enforcement contact with Joe Garcia. At the time of the Garcia rape investigations I was a Senior District Attorney Investigator at the San Luis Obispo County District Attorney's Office. I was not the primary investigator assigned to the Garcia investigation, **but I remember conducting several interviews / interrogations with Joe Garcia.** During this lengthy investigation I came to know Joe Garcia very well – based on both his past and current criminal activities. I'm sorry to tell you I cannot help you by telling you I believe Joe Garcia was wrongfully convicted and I will not provide investigative assistance for you with the Innocence Project. Lori, based on the statements from the various victims and witnesses, along with the case facts and evidence gathered during this extensive investigation, there is absolutely no doubt in my mind that Joe Garcia is responsible for all the crimes for which he has been charged and convicted...*

I'm not sorry for Joe Garcia, but I am sorry I cannot help you with this follow-up investigation for which you obviously have very strong thoughts, feelings and opinions that Joe Garcia has been wrongfully convicted.
Good luck to you Lori.
Larry Hobson"

On August 22, 2018, I wrote to Larry Hobson: *" As a non-fiction writer, I feel I am owed at least some specific example of what you believe is 'untrue' in the book, just as you would expect something more specific from someone who alleges your polygraph results or past interrogation report was in some way false to gain a conviction. We are just seeking the truth, even if it upsets someone.* **Would you at least provide a record of your interrogation of Joe Garcia?** *Thank you, Lori."*

On Aug 22, 2018, Larry Hobson replied: *"Lori, I'm sorry I didn't reply to your request, but at this point I feel an ethical responsibility to stay out of your investigation and any follow up since I was a part of the original investigation that lead to the arrest and conviction of Joe Garcia."*

On Aug 22, 2018, I responded to Larry Hobson: *"Since you referred to an "**ethical**" responsibility, given you are no longer employed by the D.A., but your polygraph business may rely on a good relationship with that office, I would understand if you feel a "conflict of interest"...but isn't a human being, who you say your investigation "helped to convict," while others say he's innocent, a greater "**ethical**" concern? If he is wrongfully convicted, as I believe, wouldn't it be better to know you've also helped free, not just convict, an innocent man? From that perspective, I'm still hoping for some guidance from you and have enclosed my phone number in case you would like to talk with me "**off the record**."* ~Lori

There was no further email response from Larry Hobson, no "off the record" phone call, no specific "evidence" that he had alluded to, and I found no written record of Hobson ever having interrogated Joe Garcia as he had claimed.   Historically. Some investigators never made a written report, just gave the D.A. a biased verbal opinion, which seems unlikely in a multi-victim case such as Joe's. Joe also states that upon his arrest he requested a polygraph but was denied and that his long interrogation was videotaped – a videotape the Court refused to allow the jury to see.

If I ever had any qualms as to Joe Garcia's innocence, Larry Hobson's evasive emails, like President Trump's "denial tweets" intended to confuse rather than to inform, removed any doubt.

In 2019, Joe learned that his 2002 Habeas appeal by a jailhouse lawyer, titled "Successive Writ of Habeas Corpus Based on Newly Discovered Evidence in Case No. S-056219 [Innocence/Miscarriage of Justice Exception to Timeliness] had never been filed.

Effective January 1, 2019, in California, AB 1812 and AB 2942 on re-sentencing and early release were passed into law. The new laws require that a prisoner has to have been incarcerated at least 10 years and had no serious "115s" (violations that are written up on a "Form 115" report) in the past 5 years, in order to be considered for early release. Joe Garcia qualifies. He also contested Jana Larmer's evaluation that contains misinformation.

112

Under the new laws, murderers and other violent criminals have already been released, yet Joe, who never killed anyone, was still on a "Recall Waiting List."

Freeing Joe Garcia may be perceived as presenting risks – not to the public but to those who lied in order to prosecute and convict an innocent man. But retribution is not on Joe Garcia's mind. Enjoying the freedom to be with his family and to see, touch and inhale the great outdoors at national parks are on Joe's "bucket list."

While the new laws may be small consolation to a person who has spent over 30 years in prison on a wrongful conviction, at least it seemed an end to Joe Garcia's nightmare, in the form of Release, may be in sight, even if it does not include exoneration. But since Joe was convicted for Rape, a violent crime, it seemed futile to hope he would be among the supposedly "non-violent" inmates to be released.

And yet the first 26 who were released had convictions for Murder and Joe hadn't killed anyone.

But Joe was about to be in the middle of a "perfect storm," caught between a deadly pandemic, an economic crisis, old enemies, and an unjust legal system.

On August 7, 2019, I submitted Joe's completed "Questionnaire" (application) to Loyola Project for the Innocent. It was reviewed by Loyola's **Attorney Cassandra Olsen** and filed, together with emailed documents and six paperback copies of an earlier version of this book as one of the Exhibits. It then became part of their computer file on Joe. And on September 9, 2019, Attorney Olsen stated in a phone call that her review of Joe's submission and supporting documents was completed and that her volunteer, **Paige McGrail**, would be working on his case.

(L) ATTORNEY CASSANDRA OLSEN, and
(R) ATTORNEY NIKKI HERST-COOK,
Loyola Project for the Innocent

In December 2018 Congress passed the bi-partisan "FIRST STEP ACT" (which stands for "Former Incarcerated Re-enter Society Transformed Safely Transitioning Every Person"). President Donald Trump signed it into law, taking credit as if he had inspired the Act that was actually the "next Step" after fifteen years of successful reforms to the *federal* criminal justice system, including 1980s drug crime sentencing reforms, the Clemency Project, and the Fair Sentencing Act (FSA) signed into law by **President Barack Obama** on August 3, 2010.

Trump's son-in-law, **Jared Kushner,** became a prime mover for sentencing reform, mainly because Kushner's father was convicted of illegal campaign contributions, tax evasion, and witness tampering and served 14 months in *federal* prison.

Months passed without further word from Loyola attorney, Cassandra Olsen. And then, finally, Olsen emailed an apology for not notifying me sooner that she was no longer working at Loyola Project for the Innocent and referred me to **Nikki Herst-Cook** at Loyola, who would "answer any questions."

Herst-Cook's introductory email did not indicate whether she was an attorney, just invited me to direct "any questions" to her. So my reply email asked her whether she was an attorney, whether she had an opportunity to review Joe's case, whether his file at Loyola had been assigned a Case Number or File Number, and the status. She only replied asking if I would be available for a phone call on a certain day, and of course I would be. But that day came and went with no call. Nikki then suggested a day and time, but weeks passed and she did not call. Eventually, she emailed back that she still needed more time to review Joe's matter.

On March 13, 2019, Governor Newsom signed an Order putting a moratorium on executions in California, granting a reprieve to California's 737 Death Row inmates, for as long as he is governor. It does not change convictions or sentences, nor enable releases. But on the day that Newsom signed that Order, President Donald Trump, evidently preferring to *keep* Capital Punishment, tweeted *"…Friends and families of the always forgotten victims are not thrilled and neither am I."*

ENDING CALIFORNIA EXECUTIONS

California Governor Gavin Christopher Newsom

"There are three kinds of lies:
Lies, damned lies, and statistics."
-Mark Twain

Chapter 7:
(2020) GOVERNOR GAVIN NEWSOM.
WARDENS, MURDERS, and COVID-19

In February 2020, America began to hear about the novel coronavirus, "COVID-19," which began in China in late 2019. And in February, President Donald Trump confided (on tape) to Washington Post reporter, Bob Woodward, famed for breaking the story on the Watergate scandal, that he was aware the airborne coronavirus virus was more deadly than the flu, but that Trump was "downplaying" it to the American people, alleging he was doing so to "prevent a panic," despite that he was hindering *prevention*, even alleging that the alarmingly increasing number of cases and deaths nationwide reported by Centers for Disease Control and Prevention (CDC) and by CNN and mainstream media, was "a hoax by Democrats. "

It was then that California's new governor, **Gavin Newsom,** began making headlines by stating his intention to **release** a significant number of non-violent prisoners from California's overcrowded prisons, starting with 3500 inmates, as the prisons were a "petri dish" for rapid spread of the coronavirus. Because the coronavirus pandemic prompted the state to release some inmates early, and to put a hold on accepting new ones, California's prison population was reduced to just over 106,000 – a drop of nearly 6,000. It still brought the system to 127% of capacity. Opponents to early releases said it's a terrible idea to reduce all services available to inmates coming out of prison while also accelerating the release of inmates.

On April 14, 2020, I mailed Joe's new *"Application for Clemency and Commutation of Sentence,"* with USPS Tracking, to **Governor Newsom's** Legal Affairs office, citing Innocence, Proposition 57, and that, given that his age was now 71, he also fit the "elderly release" criteria and was at high risk for COVID-19. A week after USPS Tracking showed the material had reached Sacramento, I emailed and phoned the Office of Legal Affairs, requesting acknowledgement of it having been received and the status, but was informed they couldn't tell me the status "because it had not yet been scanned to their system." My follow-up inquiries did not elicit a response.

3 More Inmates from California Institution for Men in Chino Die from Coronavirus Complications –
by Richard De Atley, The Press Enterprise, May 24, 2020

"A caravan protest passing outside Chino Prison's man entrance after the 9th inmate death on May 23rd from coronavirus."

The Supreme Court and courts across the country will see an increasing number of pandemic-related disputes in the coming weeks concerning prison conditions and whether prisons are violating the constitutional rights of inmates by failing to adequately protect them against the coronavirus.

Inmates are raising concerns about what they call the deliberate indifference of prison officials during a serious public health crisis and asking for home confinement or appropriate resources to improve hygiene and block the spread of Covid-19. For their part, state and federal officials are pushing back hard arguing that they are trying to respond to evolving risks while battling an unprecedented global pandemic.

Justice Sonia Sotomayor sent up a flare up this month after inmates argued that their prison conditions amounted to cruel and unusual punishment.

> "It has long been said that a society's worth can be judged by taking stock of its prisons," Sotomavor wrote.
> "That is all the truer in this pandemic, where inmates everywhere have been rendered vulnerable and often powerless to protect themselves from harm."

The issue is further complicated by the fact that federal law that governs prison conditions requires an inmate to exhaust a grievance process set up by correctional officials before turning to litigation.

On May 11, 2020, Alene Tchedmedyian and Richard Winton, LA Times, reported that Los Angeles County Jail inmates *were trying to infect themselves with coronavirus* by sharing a cup of water as a way to gain early release. The next day, nine inmates fell ill and were removed from the dorm. Eventually 21 inmates tested Positive for the virus.

On May 28, 2020, a Los Angeles Times headline reported:
"700 CHINO INMATES TO BE TRANSFERRED AS CORONAVIRUS SWEEPS PRISON"

and Alexei Koseff, San Francisco Chronicle, reported
"GAVIN NEWSOM WANTS TO CLOSE PRISONS AS CORONAVIRUS SHREDS CALIFORNIA'S BUDGET."

As the coronavirus was spreading at California Institution for Men at Chino, known simply as "Chino," where Joe was then incarcerated, Joe and other Chino inmates were permitted free phone calls. For the first time in 11 years, Joe was calling me several times a week for two weeks, while he anxiously awaited transfer out of Chino. So far, Joe had tested Negative for COVID-19 but it seemed inevitable that the pandemic would easily spread through Chino's close-quarter dormitories. Although Joe was assuring me, as he always had, that he would be fine, I feared that this wrongfully convicted man was now facing a possible Death sentence from COVID-19.

Newsom proposed closing down 2 California state prisons within the next 3 years, to ultimately save about $400-million annually. California was facing a projected $54-billion deficit and tens of billions more to come. Newsom was looking everywhere for a solution, including allowing thousands of inmates to earn quicker releases while facing off with politically influential labor unions spreading fear that releasing inmates would lead to a spike in crime, and also resistance from prison guards whose jobs are on the line in the community for whom the prison may be an economic lifeline. Newsom's intention was to spend less on incarceration and more on education and rehabilitation.

In the first week of June 2020, Joe was propelled out of the frying pan at Chino, and into the fire at California State Prison for Men at Corcoran, known simply as "Corcoran."

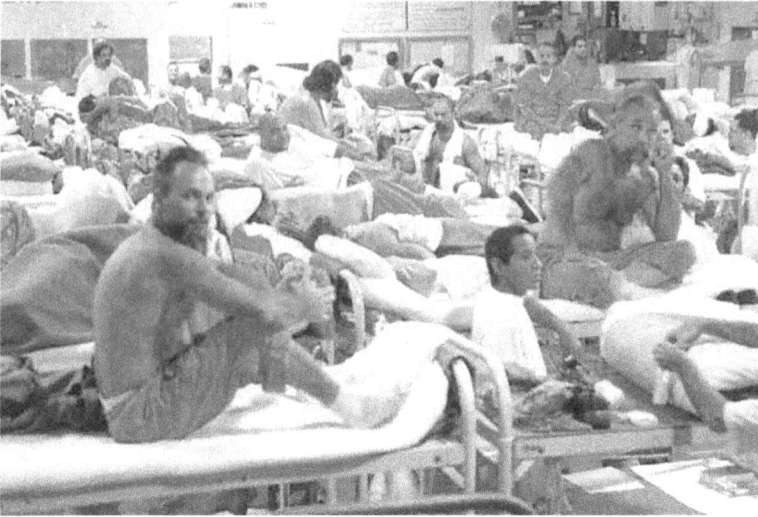

"12th INMATE AT CHINO DIES
AFTER TESTING POSITIVE FOR COVID-19"

by Richard Winton, Los Angeles Times, June 3, 2020:

"A 12th inmates from the California Institution for Men in Chino has died after testing positive for the coronavirus as corrections officials contend with major outbreaks at three state prisons. The death of the unidentified inmate came after the California Department of Corrections and Rehabilitation transferred nearly 700 inmates considered vulnerable to the coronavirus because of their age or medical condition from the Dan Bernardino County facility to a dozen other prisons around the state, officials said. The latest death occurred at a hospital near the prison, officials said…. About 672 inmates at the prison have tested positive for the coronavirus, with 447 of those still in custody."

Whether intentionally or by accident, Joe's Protective Custody or "Sensitive Needs" status was overlooked and he was placed in general or mixed population, meaning his former enemies,' the Mexican Mafia, were within reach. Joe's and my combined efforts to correct his situation fell on deaf ears.

On June 11, 2020, Matt Ormseth, at he Los Angeles Times, reported the June 10, 2020 murder at Corcoran in

> **"DANNY ROMAN, MEXICAN MAFIA MEMBER, A SOUTH L.A. GANG CHIEFTAN, IS STABBED TO DEATH AT CORCORAN"**- just days after Joe arrived at Corcoran. **Danny Roman**, 64, who controlled swaths of Los Angeles from various prison cells throughout California through extortion and drug trafficking, was stabbed to death at Corcoran. Two inmates, Raul Alvarado, 47, and Edward Cisneros, 31, both serving Life sentences for Murder, began stabbing Roman in his body and face

On June 12, 2020, as Corcoran's Warden was inundated with phone calls from inmates' concerned family members and friends, Corcoran's phone number resulted in a recording suggesting leaving a message for a call back "in 5 days." So I contacted **Xina Bolden,** Ombudsman for Corcoran prisoners, asking her to help me communicate to the Warden the gravity of Joe's situation. Her June 12, 2020 email told me Joe was on his own, as she believed safety concerns were addressed upon his transfer (although that was clearly not the case), that it was up to Joe to raise the issue, and that she had no authority to affect or recommend a transfer.

The Danny Roman killing was not the only murder at Corcoran in the same time frame. On June 6, 2020, the death of Antonio Vasquez, 27, was investigated as a Homicide. Adrian Madrigal, Vasquez' cell mate, was later sentenced for Vasquez' death to 33 years for Voluntary Manslaughter.

> In **"CDCR INVESTIGATING INMATE DEATH AT CORCORN AS HOMICIDE,"** KGET.com, June 12, 2020," Joseph Luis, KGET.com, reported the murder of inmate Anthony Roberson-Anderson, 30, allegedly killed by inmate Brandon Caine, 38.

> In **"INMATES COLLUDE IN KNIFE ATTACK ON GUARD AT CORCORAN PRISON,"** Lewis Griswold, The Fresno Bee, January 7, 2019, reported: *"Inmate Jubenal Mendoza, 27, distracted staff while inmate Edwin Perez, 31, retrieved an inmate-manufactured weapon and stabbed the [unnamed] Officer in the face several time."*

Danny Roman, Mexican Mafia Chieftan; Raul Alvarado; Edward Cisneros

Antonio Vasquez, Adrian Madrigal; Anthony Roberson-Anderson

Mexican Mafia, prison gang at Corcoran

Ken Clark, Warden,
California State Prison-Corcoran

Gray haired Joe, before COVID-19

June 15, 2020 - via USPS First Class Mail, Tracking # 9114 9014 9645 0960 2354 51

KEN CLARK, WARDEN
CORCORAN STATE PRISON
4001 King Ave / PO Box 8800
Corcoran, CA 93212-8309

Ref: JOSEPH BELARDE GARCIA, #H-01695, B-303, 135-L
Re: ONGOING EFFORTS TO SAFEGUARD, RELEASE OR RELOCATE HIM

Dear Warden Clark,

On June 5, relying on websites that had not been updated for quite some time, I addressed an urgent letter to "Warden Michael Sexton" in error (copy **enclosed**). My concern was, and still is, that while Joseph Belarde Garcia was thankfully transferred out of Chino while still Negative for COVID-19, he is now in need of "witness protection" from the Mexican Mafia gang members at Corcoran. His Application for Commutation has been pending at Legal Affairs since April.

On June 11, my fear was amplified by news of the June 10 murder at Corcoran of Mexican Mafia leader, Danny Roman, as Joe Garcia had been a voluntary key witness enabling successful prosecution of Mexican Mafia boss, Art Blajos, aka "Conejo" (The Rabbit) and assorted gangs. Blajos is now deceased, but the SAME MM gang members from the 1980s who made Death threats against Joe Garcia in retaliation for his assistance in prosecuting their members, are still incarcerated at Corcoran and are apparently newly agitated. Media speculates whether there will be retaliation against other inmates, such as Garcia..

Joe Garcia, a Native American and former street kid with a record for thefts for drugs, never hurt anyone, and has survived over 30 years of his wrongful imprisonment to date. I would think those who could "influence" protecting and releasing Mr. Garcia would do so, rather than place responsibility for Mr. Garcia's safety on Mr. Garcia alone, as Prisoner Ombudsman, Xina Bolden's, email (**enclosed**) seems to suggest. Among Garcia's supporters who know he was wrongfully convicted of 8 unsolved 1989 crimes in one trial in San Luis Obispo in 1991, and who has been urging Release of Mr. Garcia, is former LAPD Homicide Detective, Frank Tomlinson. One of Tomlinson's letters to the Parole Board (**enclosed**) verifies Garcia's part in prosecuting the aforementioned gang. Also **enclosed** is the book explaining how and why Joe Garcia was wrongfully convicted, which will be updated as to current events. While I understand that you cannot *unilaterally* decide to transfer Mr. Garcia to a safer facility, if one exists that does not pose severe risk of exposure to COVID-19, nor Mexican Mafia, nor can you *unilaterally* release him to Pastor Tomlinson, **please inform us of your plan for keeping Joe Garcia alive.**

Sincerely,

LORI CARANGELO - ███████████
aka AMERICANS FOR OPEN RECORDS (AmFOR)
███████████████████ Palm Desert, CA 92211-1952

cc: Joseph Garcia; Nikki Herst-Cook (Loyola Innocence Project); Frank Tomlinson;
Richard Winton, Matt Ormseth (LA Times); Gov. Newsom's Legal Affairs staff, et al.
enclosures: (5)

124

DIVISION OF ADULT INSTITUTIONS
CALIFORNIA STATE PRISON - CORCORAN
P. O. Box 8800
Corcoran, California 93212

June 30, 2020

Mrs. Lori Carangelo

Palm Desert, CA 92211-1952

RE: Joseph Garcia CDCR# H01695

Dear Mrs. Carangelo,

This letter is in response to your correspondence sent to the Warden, Ken Clark dated, June 12, 2020. I have reviewed your letter in its entirety and understand your concerns. The issues you have raised have been forwarded to the appropriate supervisory staff for review, to ensure compliance with California Department of Corrections and Rehabilitation policies and procedures.

Your letter indicates that Inmate Garcia is in need of witness protection and that Inmate Garcia has survived over 30 years of his wrongful imprisonment to date. You stated that you feel Mr. Garcia should be transferred to a safer facility. Additionally, you have listed COVID-19 is of concern and gave a brief synopsis of Mr. Garcia's alleged wrongful conviction.

Mrs. Carangelo, please know the Department of Corrections and Rehabilitation (CDCR) in conjunction with California Correctional Health Care Services (CCHCS) have our facilities health as well as the health of all those incarcerated at the forefront during this time of the unknown. CDCR has taken numerous steps in order to decrease populations in housing units by transferring inmates to vacant facilities throughout the state, as well as many other additional protocols to allow you and others to continue to program as normal as possible. Housing Units have been provided additional cleaning supplies, all inmates and staff have been given and required to wear facial coverings and social distancing is now required in order to reduce the risk of exposure. In addition, all staff members require screening prior to entering all areas of the institution. Many measures are in place to help all those incarcerated stay safe and healthy.

On June 22, 2020, Mr. Garcia's case was seen by the Unit Classification Committee for Transfer Review where case factors and housing placement status were reviewed to ensure proper placement/endorsement.

On June 24, 2020, Mr. Garcia was endorsed again to California State Prison-Corcoran. (Originally he was transferred from CIM because he was deemed an "at-risk" inmate for possible COVID exposure)

At this time, your request for Mr. Garcia to be safeguarded, released or relocated has been reviewed but unfortunately does not meet any type of criteria for an early release or relocation, and is appropriately housed at Corcoran State Prison based on his particular case factors.

Please keep in mind, CDCR offers various programs that could potentially assist Mr. Garcia in reducing his sentence shall he meet the criteria.

A copy of your letter will be placed into the Electronic Records Management System of Mr. Garcia. Should circumstances necessitate an early release in the future; Inmate Garcia's requests will be taken into consideration by the Classification Services Representative. Should there be any further concerns or questions, Mr. Garcia is able to contact Correctional Counselor A. Muhammad during open line hours or through the GA-22 Interview request form.

Sincerely,

KEN CLARK
Warden
California State Prison-Corcoran

125

Subsequent to Warden Clark's June 30th letter stating *"the issues you have raised have been forwarded to the appropriate [unidentified] supervisory staff for review,"* Joe was contacted by a staff member who asked him to explain his problem, as if unaware of his situation. The only solution he was offered for his safety was to be placed in "the Hole" (Administrative Segregation or "Ad Seg') - solitary confinement. Joe declined, because being placed in "solitary" would conflict with the time frame required to process him out of Corcoran, if those in charge eventually decide to transfer him to another facility.

But also, the sensory deprivation in "solitary" has been termed "cruel and unusual punishment." George Christie Jr., former Hell's Angels Leader who spent a year in "solitary," explained: *"I've had people shoot at me, take contracts out on me, but nothing compares to solitary confinement."*

At the same time that I had been pressuring Warden Ken Clark to address Joe's precarious housing situation, Frank Tomlinson, retired LAPD Homicide Detective who Joe called his friend, but who never replied to my 2018, 2019 and June 2020 letters asking if he could use whatever influence to convince Warden Clark to help Joe, emailed me to inform me Art Blajos was *not* deceased but very much alive. Tomlinson did not offer to intercede with Warden Clark or anyone on Joe's behalf, until after our further exchanges, when he wrote that he "had contacts inside" who he was "waiting to hear from" but would not be more specific.

Whatever "contacts" were made, Joe was not moved to a safer location and remained vulnerable to past and present factions of the Mexican Mafia at Corcoran, as well as any new elements that that Joe's years as a "Sensitive Needs" inmate had not prepared him to handle.

Name: GAR IA, JOSEPH

CDC #: H01695   PID #: 11078974

ICCS007B

Classification Review

CC Request Date: 11/16/2017

Request Time: 15:21:54

Institution: California Institution for Men
Facility: CIM-Facility A
Correctional Counselor: Cortez, Guillermo
Committee Type: Institution Cls. Committee (UCC)
Review Type: Annual
Scheduled Hearing Date: 11/29/2017

Scheduled Hearing Time: 09:00:00

Critical Case Factors

Factor	Current Value	New Value
Security Level		Placement Score: 19 Level: II-Level 2
Custody Designation	Medium (A)	Medium (A)
Custody Suffix - 1st	R	R-Committed a Sex Crime
Custody Suffix - 2nd		
Custody Suffix - 3rd		
Custody Suffix - 4th		
Housin Placement - 1st	SNY	SNY-Sensitive Needs Yard
Housing lacement - 2nd	SNY	SNY-Sensitive Needs Yard
Housing Configuration	CD	CD-Dorm
Institution (Primary)	CIM	
Institution (Alternate)		
Transfer Override	ZZZ	ZZZ-None
Exceptional Placement	Z	Z-None
Custody Upon Transfer	Medium (A)	Medium (A)
Detention Procession Unit	0	0-N/A
Work Change Clearance	No	No
Back Dock Clearance	No	No
Gate Pass Clearance	No	No
Access to Computer Clearance	No	No
ORWD Clearance	No	No
SVP Status Considered		No
MDO Status Considered		No
Annual IHR Conducted		No

127

August 8, 2008 · via USPS First Class Mail, Tracking #9114 9014 9645 0960 2354 75

KEN CLARK, Warden
California State Prison - Corcoran
PO Box 8800
Corcoran, CA 93212

Ref: Your 6-30-20 Reply (copy enclosed)
Re: JOSEPH BELARDE GARCIA - <u>Witness</u> Safety Housing Designation Ignored

Dear Warden Clark,

Thank you for your Reply to my June 12, 2020 concerns re Joseph Belarde Garcia's housing, which was NOT just due to COVID-19 but **ALSO his overlooked "witness protection status,"** in which **you stated:** "*...unfortunately [Mr. Garcia] does NOT meet ANY type of criteria for an early release or RELOCATION and is APPROPRIATELY HOUSED at Corcoran State Prison based on his particular case factors.*' No, sir, you are seriously mistaken. And the mistake could cost Mr. Garcia his life.

The Committee's denial of his request for Transfer out of Corcoran's "general population" is thought to be due to Mr. Garcia's records in Central File, over the past 30 years as well as pre-1991 records, having **different CDCR prisoner numbers** (including **H-01695** post-1991, **B-41970** in 1973 and **C-16145** in 1981) And so, the enclosed letters **authorizing his "permanent protective status"** were not available to me when I write you previously, nor to the Committee, so not considered. Because Mr. Garcia, long ago a gang dropout, assisted in prosecution and conviction of key Mexican Mafia members, which CDC determined (**in their letters, <u>enclosed</u>**) presented a **continuing** death threat to Mr. Garcia who is on MM's "hit list," and, indeed, the **Mexican Mafia** is *still* rampant at Corcoran where they accomplished **3 murders just since Mr. Garcia's May-June 2020 transfer** from Chino due to COVID, to Corcoran's 'general population' without "appropriate" P.H.U. Protective Housing Unit, classification or relocation to a safer prison, and Mr. Garcia's, and my, and even Retired Homicide Detective Frank Tomlinson's communications endeavoring to correct the situation **have been ignored**, if not corrected upn receipt of this information, and if anything happens to Mr. Garcia, I assure you that you will be held personally responsible.

Currently, Attorney Nikki Herst-Cook, of Loyola's Project for the Innocent, is endeavoring to persuade Governor Newsom to release Mr. Garcia, based on his April 14, 2020 "*Application for Clemency and Commutation of Sentence (Based on Innocence and other Qualifiers).*" In the meantime, I trust that you will want to "do the right thing" to keep Mr. Garcia alive long enough for others to secure his release as he also happens to be an innocent man (per the book I sent you <u>about his case</u>).

Respectfully,

LORI CARANGELO
aka Americans For Open Records (AmFOR)

128

LOS ANGELES POLICE DEPARTMENT

DARYL F. GATES
Chief of Police

TOM BRADLEY
Mayor

P. O. Box 30158
Los Angeles, Calif. 90030
Telephone:
(213). 485-2531
Ref: 8.2.4

October 29, 1981

Mrs. Mari Olsen
Probation Officer
Ventura County Probation Department
3190 Cochran
Simi Valley, California 93065

Dear Mrs. Olsen:

This letter is in regard to Joseph Belarde Garcia, AKA Joseph Peacemaker, and his pending appearance in Ventura County Superior Court.

Mr. Garcia came to the attention of this Department during the investigation of the murder of Nicholas Villa, which occurred in Van Nuys on November 25, 1978. Villa was executed at his residence, with his wife and children present. Because of Villa's associates and the circumstances of the murder, it was investigated as a Mexican Mafia "hit" and was assigned to Detectives Frank Tomlinson and Richard Szabo of the Robbery-Homicide Division.

It was early in 1979 that Mr. Garcia initiated contact with Tomlinson and Szabo indicating that he had information regarding the Villa homicide. His information proved accurate and relevant in preparing a case against Mexican Mafia "soldier" Arthur Blajos and his accomplice and "trainee," Michael Moreno. Mr. Garcia subsequently testified for five days at the preliminary hearing of Blajos and Moreno and his testimony is anticipated at the trial which is still pending. Mr. Garcia's cooperation regarding this case has enabled us not only to clear the Villa homicide, but to remove an extremely dangerous criminal from society. Blajos, who is 31 years old, has spent virtually his entire adult life in State prison during which time he has engaged in numerous attacks on guards and inmates. He has been allegedly involved in several inmate murders and has also engaged in riots and escape attempts.

129

Mr. Garcia's cooperation with law enforcement has also included
his ongoing supply of information to the prison gang task
force and has included information relative to the improvement
of security in one of our police facilities.

Obviously, Mr. Garcia has placed his life in jeopardy through
his cooperation and we hereby submit these facts for the courts
consideration. We also emphasize that as long as Mr. Garcia
remains incarcerated, special consideration regarding his housing
should be considered critical. He currently is and will remain
on the Mexican Mafia "hit list."

Very truly yours,

DARYL F. GATES
Chief of Police

WILLIAM H. COBB, Captain
Commanding Officer
Robbery-Homicide Division

**LAPD Police Chief Daryl Francis Gates
served from 1978 to 1992**

Memorandum

To: O. A. Loggins
Associate Superintendent
CTF-Central

Date: 10/30/73

<del>CONFIDENTIAL</del>

File No: GARCIA, J. B.
B-41870
RUIZ, G.
B-39901
DIRECTOR'S INTEREST CASE
"NUESTRA FAMILIA"

This document meets the validation requirements established in CCR Title 15 Section 3378

From: **Correctional Training Facility, Soledad 93960**

Declassified by originator of document on 12/9/74 ▨▨▨

This report will speak to two (2) of the Director's Interest Cases designees
(Nuestra Familia), their attitudes, desires and some staff assumptions.

On September 17, 1973, a letter addressed to me was received and signed by the
two subject inmates along with two other Director's Interest Cases. From this
letter and other information, Lieutenant I. T. Gutierrez submitted to me a
confidential report which was placed into the Central File of each man on the
letter. This report is dated September 18, 1973, and may be found on the right
hand side of the Central File.

Since that time, a great deal of dialogue observing behavior and information
gathering has transpired regarding the two subject inmates. They still verbally
maintain that they have withdrawn their alliances from the Nuestra Familia
and by staff observation in this controlled situation, have withdrawn their
affiliation.

Both of the subject inmates have been extremely cooperative in information
regarding the Nuestra Familia as to the leadership of the faction and especially
what they plan. For example, inmate Garcia gave us information regarding
possible "contracts" directed at staff personnel in various institutions in
the state. All of the concerned staff were alerted so that safeguards could
be taken. One staff member, W. Estelle, Program Administrator at CMC, began an
investigation based on this information and did come forth with strong indications
that he was, in fact, in physical danger. I have not received a written report
from Mr. Estelle, but the point is that the information was for the most part,
very beneficial.

We, the staff of Unit III, as well as the two subject inmates recognize the fact
that they are in danger by withdrawing from this faction, as are their families.
Whether they will ever be able, due to their affiliations, to be returned to
general population is a sensitive classification action and decision. However, I
am recommending that you approve my action in the form of recommending to the
Director that the Director's Interest Case, Nuestra Familia leader designation,
be removed. This would allow the Superintendent's Main Classification Committee
to decide what action to take from this point. Furthermore, in my opinion, it
would demonstrate to the two subject inmates our interest in the apparent "break-up"
of the Nuestra Familia.

R. M. Depue, Captain
Unit III

cc: Central File (S. inmates)
Mr. Ben William, ACCER
N.F. File, Unit III

September 15, 2020 - by USPS First Class Mail. Tracking # 9114 9014 9645 0960 2354 82

KEN CLARK, WARDEN
CA STATE PRISON -CORCORAN
PO Box 8800
Corcoran, CA 93212-8309

REF: JOSEPH BELARDE GARCIA, #H-01695, B-303, 135-L
       and my previous letters advising about his safety issues from enemies
       and requiring protective housing

RE: UPDATE - JOE GARCIA'S WORSENING CIRCUMSTANCES,
       ART BLAJOS ERROR, HIT LIST, and FORMER LAPD FRANK TOMLINSON

Dear Warden Clark,

In one of my previous letters to you with enclosures from officials advising you of Joseph Garcia's permanent protective housing status, in error I stated Art Blajos (Mexican Mafia "hit man)," as dead – He is very much alive and Mr. Garcia remains on your Mexican Mafia inmates' "hit list." At this writing, Mr. Garcia remains in mixed population and is now informed that :
(1) he may have been exposed to someone with COVID-19 and
(2) Mr. Garcia is to be "quarantined at Building 3 or 4" which he states is will have "Level 4 inmates" who are waiting to be transferred and where EOP inmates are located, and that those inmates are let out "6 at a time for showers" which greatly increases the risk to Mr. Garcia. He has told the Nurse that he is a Protected Custody inmate, not now appropriately housed. You need to step in.

Frank Tomlinson, former LAPD Detective, emailed me that he will be contacting you about housing Mr. Garcia in a Protective Housing Unit (PHU), or transferring him out to a safer security situation. He has all the documentation proving Mr. Garcia is supposed to be in protected housing. And I'm copying this to Mr. Tomlinson to update him about Mr. Garcia's current situation.

As you've been repeatedly advised of both the Penal Code and proof of Mr. Garcia's protective status, if this matter continues to be ignored, there will be a full investigation.

Lori Carangelo
LORI CARANGELO

132

By early August 2020, Warden Clark had the documents I sent him, verifying Joe was to remain in Protective Custody, as he had been protected at other California prisons for the past 30 years, and was to be protected "for as long as he is incarcerated." Yet Joe was formally Denied protective housing, broadly and vaguely citing that the department's needs and population pressure "override" Joe's documented classification. The Denial did not specifically claim there was no room for him in Protective Housing.

On July 2, 2020, I received a "form letter" type email from **Governor Newsom's Office of Legal Affairs**, which merely repeated former Governor Brown's staff's 2014 *"Don't call us, we'll call you, but don't hold your breath"* type response.

On August 1, 2020, **Sandee Ogilvie,** who had known Joe before his arrest and had attended his trial, emailed me:

> *"It really disturbs me how everything was handled. I still do not believe he was guilty. I do find it so sad that the life he deserved to have with Judy and Jordan was stolen from him."*

Ogilvie was also was particularly alarmed for Joe's safety. She informed me that she had contacted a good friend of hers, Joe Bush, a warden in Northern California, who she believed had some influence with Governor Newsom. For two weeks, Sandee reported that Bush was still trying to contact Newsom about Joe. Then Sandee simply stopped responding to my requests for an update. Evidently there was nothing more she or Bush could do for Joe, and so I did not hear from her again.

Sandee Ogilvie

Ed and Marietta Ostini, who had also attended Joe's trial, firmly believed he is innocent and stayed in touch with Joe by mail, sharing photos and well wishes.

Marietta Ostini, with husband Ed Ostini (now deceased)

On July 20, 2020, Governor Gavin Newsom's Commutations Unit responded by email to my request to know the status of Joe's April 14, 2020 *"Application for Clemency and Commutation of Sentence*, stating they were receiving a "high volume of correspondence" and "We are working hard to track and move forward commutation applications as quickly as possible."

===

RE: URGENT- PENDING COMMUTATION, & REQUIRE RELEASE, DUE IN PART TO DEADLY TRANSFER OF JOSEPH BELARDE GARCIA
1 message

Thu, Jul 2, 2020 at 9:01 AM
Office of Governor Newsom – Commutation Unit Commutations@gov.ca.gov
To: Lori Carangelo ,accesspress@gmail.com>

Thank you for contacting the Governor's Parole & Clemency Teams. At this time, we are receiving a very high volume of correspondence and are not able to respond to each one. If you are Writing to check on the status of a commutation file, we will send notification when our office takes action on the case or requires additional information. Unfortunately, we cannot provide a timeframe for this process. We understand that this is a very worrisome time, and we are working hard to track and move forward commutation applications as quickly as possible.

On August 25, 2020, Johnny W. Lewis, Community Health Worker, provided Joe with a letter of support, offering the services of Transition Clinic Network, which provides health care as well re-entry support, as part of Joe's parole… if Joe is ever granted parole.

TRANSITIONS CLINIC

08/25/2020

To whom it may concern,

I am writing a letter of support for Joseph Garcia based on the goals and mission of Transition Clinic Network. Transitions Clinic Network supports healthy reintegration back into the community by:

- Re-Entry Support
- Primary Care
- Care Coordination
- Mental Health Services
- Substance abuse treatment
- Podiatry
- Nutrition
- Optometry

Our clinic is a specialty clinic that serves men and women returning from incarceration. We promote quality healthcare reintegration into the community for chronically-ill recently released individuals. We are community based, patient centered intervention that provides transitional care and a primary care medical home for recently released people and their families. Although we are a primary care service, we also provide social service navigation and patient centered case management services from specially-trained formerly incarcerated community health workers (CHW's).

Mr. Garcia has reached out to our clinic on his own asking for us to be a part of his parole plans. I commend him for adding a medical home for his health care and case management as a part of his parole plans. I am attaching our flyer which outlines our organization's services. Please feel free to call me with any questions about our clinics and services.

JOHNNY W. LEWIS
Community Health Worker
Chapcare Pasadena, L.A.COUNTY
626-460-9008
jlewis@chapcare.org

135

On August 28, 2018, before COVID,
Alex Koseff, Sacramento Bee, reported:

> ## "CALIFORNIA LAWMAKERS MOVE TO CAP PRISON TIME FOR FELONS
>
> "Decades of "tough on crime" mentality devastated communities of color in California. Senate Bill 1279 introduced by Senator Steven Bradford (Dem.) refines the complex approach to sentencing by providing a greater balance between felonies and enhancements."

On July 10, 2020, after the virus had swept thorough California's prisons, Bill Chappell, NPR News, wrote:

> ## "CALIFORNIA WILL RELEASE UP TO 8,000 PRISONERS DUE TO CORONAVIRUS
>
> "California's prison system reported 5,837 coronavirus cases, a rise of 860 in 2 weeks. Release of roughly 4,800 people were eligible for release, including those with fewer than 180 days left on their sentence."

On July 13, 2020, **Loyola Attorney, Nikki Herst-Cook,** phoned me, confirming that she is an attorney, although on a first name basis, that she had reviewed Joe's case, and that her student volunteer, **Analleley Martin Gonzalez,** a UC-Berkeley student who was also on that conference call, would be helping with Joe's matter. Nikki asked me several questions while Annallely spoke not a word beyond introductions. I asked whether we were starting from scratch because of Attorney Olsen's departure - which she confirmed. Nikki said that due to COVID-19, she and other Loyola staff were working *from home*, and would not be able to pursue cases *in court*, but that they could try to get Joe released *via Governor Newsom.*

Weeks passed. My follow-up emails to Nikki, requesting an update, were never answered. Not even when I asked *"Has Loyola again abandoned Joe Garcia?"* Yet, in September 2020, Loyola Project for the Innocent freed another wrongfully convicted prisoner, Emmon Barnes... It was then that Joe wrote he was ill and tested Positive for COVID-19. My phone calls to the prison to check on his condition reached a recording instructing callers to leave a message but the earliest response time would be 5 days, if at all. In the meantime, I received an email from Frank Tomlinson saying Joe's Positive COVID test was "an administrative error."

Joe then he informed me he'd had a cold for weeks, but that it had been a False Positive for COVID. He was fine, even if his living conditions weren't actually habitable…

Despite that California had committed in 2019 to $260-million (over the next four years) to repair leaking roofs, clear out dangerous mold, and even maggots, mice and feces from pigeons at more than two dozen deteriorating prisons, the cost of overdue maintenance was pegged at more than $1-billion. Roofs at only eight of California's thirty-four prisons were replaced, but another twenty, including at Corcoran, still need to be done. Governor Newsom wanted to save repair costs by *closing* some prisons. In the meantime, winter 2020 found Joe's cell cold from swamp coolers used to keep air circulating in an effort to mitigate spread of COVID, and one wall in his cell was wet. Not one to give up after 32 years of wrongful imprisonment, Joe continued to have his jailhouse lawyer file appeals.

Around the first of October 2020, when Joe was out of quarantine at Corcoran and again tested Negative for COVID-19, he was moved back to his previous location at Corcoran, instead of to the Protective Housing Unit (PHU). There being no response from Loyola's Attorney Nikki Herst-Cook, nor Paula Mitchell, Loyola's Innocence Project Legal Director, nor Adam Grant, their Program Director, it was apparent that Joe was no longer of interest to Loyola's Project for the Innocent.

On October 2, 2020, the New York Times reported **President Donald Trump** tested Positive for COVID-19 and was hospitalized after spending months "downplaying" (lying) to the American people about the severity of the outbreak when it had killed more than 207,000 in the United States and devastated the economy. Trump continued to "the end of the pandemic was in sight.

On October 5, 2020, even while still sick with Covid-19, President Donald Trump removed his face mask, which he sees as a symbol of weakness, while standing on a White House balcony before entering the White House to resume his activities, without a mask and without regard to those who must work in close proximity to him. **By early December, more than a dozen people in Trump's personal orbit tested Positive for COVID-19,** while he resumed his re-election campaign rallies and events attended by maskless crowds without social distancing, which became "Super Spreader" events.

President Donald Trump, ill from COVID-19,
defiantly removing his mask.

In November, 2020, San Quentin Prison was under Court Order to reduce it's inmate population down to 50%. Instead of being released, San Quentin prisoners were *merely moved around to other prisons, including to Corcoran,* where Joe was then housed, so that it would appear that the Court Order was being complied with, but thus increasing Corcoran's population and the risk of COVID-19 exposure to Corcoran inmates.

In the meantime, Corcoran's Warden Clark had not only resisted honoring Joe's "Protected" status, but had also dispatched his staff to *intimidate* Joe and this writer. According to Joe, **Captain Nathan Scaife** had paid him a visit. Joe asked him *why* there was such resistance to placing him in the Protective Housing Unit (PHU) at Corcoran when, clearly, he was classified as requiring "Sensitive Needs Housing"(SNY), hadn't been de-classified as such, and was given no reason. Joe said Scaife told him his *"paperwork was too old"* and *"the Mexican Mafia had, in all likelihood, forgotten about you"* despite that there had recently been multiple Mexican Mafia murders at Corcoran. Scaife replied *"It ain't gonna happen"* but also warned him *"**And your people on the outside need to stop writing letters**"* - which I took to be *intimidation* aimed not only toward Joe but also toward me... which prompted my sending yet another letter to Warden Clark and receiving yet another denial back. By December 2020, inmates had been moved from Joe's building to another building at Corcoran, leaving very few inmates in his unit to perhaps reduce his risk of COVID exposure and gain a degree of safety.

October 28, 2020

WARDEN KEN CLARK
California State Prison-Corcoran
PO Box 8800, Corcoran, CA 93212

RE: JOSEPH BELARDE GARCIA, #H-01695, B303, Bed 124

Warden Clark:

On June 30, 2020, you responded to my concern for Mr. Garcia's safety **due to his classification as a Protected Inmate being ignored** (in violation of State law and policy and probably contrary to the federal First Step Act) stating you were referring the matter "to supervisory staff for review."

On August 28, I followed up with further documentation proving Mr. Garcia's Protective status (from the Mexican Mafia at Corcoran) was to be "**for as long as he is incarcerated**."

Thereafter, on October 8, 2020, Mr. Garcia received a visit from **Captain Scaife**, accompanied by a Lieutenant, and reports the following conversation, which not only smacks of **intimidation** of a prisoner who is already forced to live in fear of retribution from the gang he is supposed to be protected from, but also an attempt to **intimidate this writer** (as follows):

> "**Captain Sciafe** asked me how I was doing. I told him 'Not good' and that I wanted to know WHY there is so such *resistance* in having me placed in the Protective Housing Unit. He said '**Your paperwork is too old.**' I said 'What does that mean?' He answered 'The Mexican Mafia has in all likelihood forgotten about you and many others. You'll be just fine on this yard.' I then said 'Mr. Sciafe, I don't want to be a problem to anyone but **I have never been de-classified from being a Protected Custody Inmate, nor do I want to be.** I was here in P.H.U. in the late '70s and been a Protected Custody Inmate ever since. I just can't handle being on a mixed yard; I'm not General Population material. And I fit the criteria for placement in P.H.U. if you read the paperwork. His response was 'That may be so, but I'm giving you a heads up on this. It ain't gonna happen. **And your people on the outside need to stop writing letters.** No one is special around here... Just lay low."

To date you have still not informed me exactly what criteria Joe Garcia does <u>NOT</u> meet for PHU housing, or transfer to a California prison that CAN and WILL protect him as his classification requires. Additionally, retired **LAPD Homicide Detective Frank Tomlinson**, who knows firsthand of Joe's wrongful conviction and safety issue, emailed me that he had spoken to other staff to urge PHU protection or transfer. I don't need to remind you of the number of murders at Corcoran within the past few months, including those involving **Mexican Mafia** members. Just prior to Joe's encounter with **Captain Sciafe**, Joe received a letter from the prison filed **against Corcoran prison staff** (beyond the past "gladiator" suits), and they were getting letters, daily, regarding **CURRENT assaults against inmates by staff**, so Joe is doing his best to <u>avoid</u> clashes with staff, due to what he termed "Corcoran being one of the last holdouts about prison reform as to treatment of prisoners." **Intimidation**, and fear of **retribution** from Guards for *reporting* intimidation, may be the way things have worked in your world, sir, but that time is past.

LORI CARANGELO, Americans For Open Records (4,058 members, https://facebook.com/l.carangelo)
████████████ Palm Desert, CA 92211-1952
<u>cc</u>: Joseph Belarde Garcia, Gov. Newsom Legal Affairs, Congressman R. Ruiz, attorneys, et al

STATE OF CALIFORNIA – DEPARTMENT OF CORRECTIONS AND REHABILITATION   GAVIN NEWSOM, GOVERNOR

DIVISION OF ADULT INSTITUTIONS
CALIFORNIA STATE PRISON - CORCORAN
P. O. Box 8800
Corcoran, California 93212

November 13, 2020

Ms. L. Carangelo
████████████
Palm Desert, California 92211-1952

RE: JOSEPH GARCIA, CDCR# H10696

Dear Ms. Carangelo,

I am in receipt of your letter dated October 28, 2020, addressed to Warden Ken Clark. Your correspondence relates specifically to Mr. Garcia and his perceived protective custody concerns. The issues you have raised have been forwarded to the appropriate supervisory staff for review, to ensure compliance with California Department of Corrections and Rehabilitation (CDCR) policies and procedures.

Rest assured, inmate Garcia is classified and placed appropriately on a facility commensurate with his programming and custodial needs. Inmate Garcia's case factors will not be shared in this correspondence, however, he has had approximately 40 annual classification reviews since the date of your reference. Inmate Garcia has no enemy concerns or case factors precluding him from continuing to safely and successfully program on Facility 3B. The perception of the conversation between Captain N. Scaife and inmate Garcia is not an accurate depiction. Inmate Garcia's safety is paramount to Captain Scaife as well as the institution and will continue to be.

In closing, CDCR has a process set in place for inmate Garcia to address concerns of this nature. I encourage inmate Garcia to address his concerns through the appropriate chain of command. If warranted, utilize the appeal process as the appeal process is intended to provide a remedy for inmates and parolees with identified grievances, and to provide an administrative mechanism for review of departmental policies, decisions, actions, conditions, or omissions that have a material adverse effect on the welfare of inmates and parolees.

KEN CLARK
Warden
California State Prison-Corcoran

140

On November 26, 2020, Joe's Appeal of the Parole Board's denial of his parole as punishment for claiming innocence was Denied by the State Courts and is being appealed to United States Supreme Court.

On December 6, 2020, 8 months after Joe's April 14, 2020 *"Application for Executive Clemency and Commutation of Sentence"* was received by Governor Newsom's Office of Legal Affairs, and despite the July 20, 2020 email from Newsom's Commutation Unit promising "to move forward on Commutations as quickly as possible," it was "returned to sender" with a handwritten note taped to the envelope stating *"RTS Undeliverable, Capitol Not Accepting Incoming Mail."* Offices that had been overwhelmed with mail from inmates and their families demanding their release were shut down due to COVID-19. Direct phone numbers I'd had for Governor Newsom's Legal Affairs Office were no longer in service.

As COVID cases and deaths rapidly increased, Governor Newsom issued an executive "Stay At Home Order" for all of California which was to extend past Christmas. I filled the time by working on completing this book.

And then it happened…

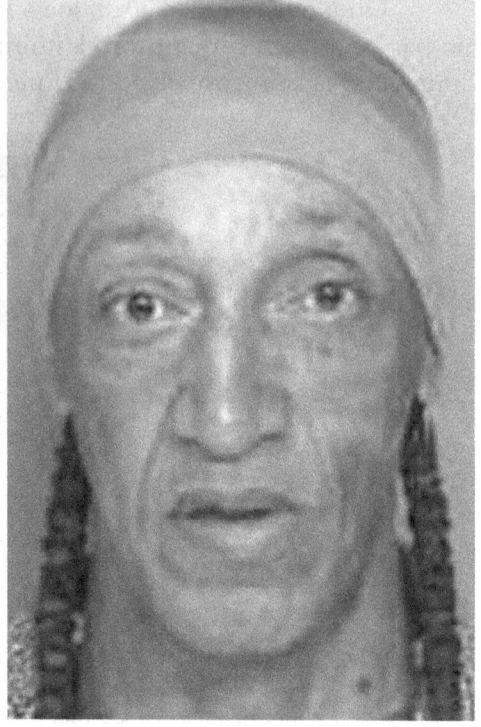

(LEFT): 10-18-1989 Darrell R. Klasey's Composite image of suspect drawn according to Jacqueline D. Brooks' description of her attacker

(RIGHT): 1989 mugshot photo on California's Sex Offender Registry of **RICO GOLDIE TOMAZ**, (alias Rodrecko Tomaz, Hugh Halana Smith, Denis Thompson)

(LEFT): Joe Garcia in 1989;
(RIGHT): Darrell R. Klasey, credited with the 1989 composite image

Chapter 8:
(2021): IT WASN'T JOE

On December 9, 2020, while Googling for further information about **George Felix Levine**, one of the DNA experts who provided his opinion about DNA at Joe's trial and, I discovered, has also analyzed DNA evidence in the case of convicted rapist, **RICO GOLDIE TOMAZ**. Curious, I typed Tomaz's name for a Google Image search, and...

OH MY GOD! I was looking at a face I'd been seeing for 12 years -- the face in the 1989 composite image of the suspect who Jacqueline Brooks stated was the "light skinned Negro" who raped her.

The composite was a mirror image match to the mugshot photo on California's State Sex Offender Registry of RICO GOLDIE TOMAZ -- *same* almond shaped eyes, *same* thinly arched eyebrows (not at all like Joe's bushy eyebrows), *same* nose, *same* lips, *same* head shape. And Tomaz has facial features that could easily be mistaken for African American, even though Registry states Tomaz is "American Indian. "

California's State Sex Offender Registry further describes Tomaz as being "5'8," which matches the height estimated by both Brooks and Archer, and having only one unknown type of tattoo on his abdomen and a non-specific tattoo on one finger. Levine had found a pubic hair on rape victim, Taleia J., 13, that was "inconsistent" with her own pubic hair but "consistent" with Tomaz who he documented as having "curly RED *pubic* hair, one black pubic hair and fine **RED** *head* hair," yet the State Sex Offender Registry states Tomaz has **"BROWN" hair**, just as **Pinard** and Brooks had described the same "Naked Man," and also with **RED** hair thought to have been confused with Alleman's description of the red head covering or beanie cap worn by The Naked Man, perhaps to conceal his easily identifiable RED hair. And Tomaz fit the timetable in Joe's cases – *unless* I was to find that he was in custody on the day he raped Taleia J. There are Indians with red hair, not just those of Peruvian Indian or Spanish lineage, and no American Indian today is a "full blooded" Native American. But Tomaz's mugshot clearly showed his **dark BROWN braids**.

To sort out the Rico Tomaz puzzle, one needs to know that, on July 27, 1989, although Tomaz was brought in for questioning "on suspicion" of raping Taleia J., **he was not taken into custody in 1989** - because Taleia recanted. She refused to accuse Tomaz or even admit she had been raped, despite the medical finding and forensic evidence according to George Felix Levine, that indicated that she had been forcibly raped. Tomaz's 15-year-old daughter was present and witnessed her father rape Taleia J., but also denied it happened. Tomaz's wife (his "common law wife Brenda Fay Magalong," in The Lompoc Record, 7-16-86), also denied it ever happened. That all three denied any rape occurred may have been due to fear of Tomaz and Crips gang members involved in his activities.

Tomaz had previously been convicted, in 1986, for "Attempted Murder, Robbery and Kidnapping" of George Leekins on October 11, 1985, in Santa Barbara County. Before the Taleia rape, Tomaz testified as a state's witness in the unrelated trial of Mitchell Herdman, who was charged with the 1988 murder of Stephanie McHugh, 20. Tomaz was in jail for that crime when Herdman was in jail and told Herdman *We took care of McHugh.* In return for Tomaz being an Informant and testifying against Herdman, and for testifying against Richard Lothery who was convicted in 1987 of murdering Lompoc motel owner Thakorb-hai Patel during an attempted robbery, and *also* for helping to arrest drug dealing Crips gang members, Tomaz and was given a 9-year suspended prison sentence and placed on probation. So **Tomaz was a "free" man in 1989 until June 1990, This is why he did not show up on the radar as a suspect in Joe's case.** He was arrested, and in custody, **in 1990**, convicted of "Sexual Intercourse With a 15-Year Old Girl." Judge Richard St. John added 7 years onto what would have been Tomaz's earlier 15-year sentence for Rape of 13-year old Taleia J. He was sentenced to "up to 22 years" but was released after ten, inY-2000.

Rico Goldie Tomaz not only fits the description given by Jacqueline Brooks of her assailant, but also fits the description offered by Mickie Alleman and Cathy Pinard, and fits the timetable, as follows:
- **July 14, 1989-** Stacia Deane's intruder entered her bedroom;
- **July 26, 1989-** **Taleia J. was raped by Rico Goldie Tomaz**;
- **September 9, 1989-** Carrie Dorgan was attacked;
- **September 17, 1989-** Tyra Wittmeyer was sexually assaulted;
- **October 11, 1989-** Jacqueline Brooks was sexually assaulted;
- **October 12, 1989–** Tracey Archer saw her attacker's face;
- **October 16, 1989-** Cheryl Picco was allegedly assaulted;
- **October 17, 1989-** Catherine Pinard was assaulted

Had "The Central Coast Rapist," who been a figment of an ambitious prosecutor's imagination, suddenly become real?

How else could Jacqueline Brooks have provided such a precise and **honest eyewitness description (of Tomaz) if she hadn't *seen* him?** One thing was certain – *It wasn't Joe.*

Jacqueline Brooks apparently honestly described her assailant, not realizing he could be **Rico Goldie Tomaz.** With regard to cases of Rape, Attempted Rape, or Sexual Assault, when the victim *identifies a person by name* who she knows or thinks was her assailant, that person is usually the prime suspect and the first to be questioned. **In Joe's case, police immediately focused on him, even though Joe was not identified by any victim at the time of his arrest on October 19, 1989, while other potential suspects *had been named* in police reports:**

- **Tyra Dawn Wittmeyer** identified her attacker as **"STEVE" (STEVE BOLT**) who Tyra's mother, Cyndi Wittmeyer also named;

- **Carrie S. Dorgan** identified her attacker as **"TERRY"**;

- **Catherine T. Pinard (Owen)** had a boyfriend, **Dan Machbitz**; she described her attacker as having a red ski mask on top of his head. She and **Mickie Alleman** additionally both described an **unknown "Naked Man"** wearing a **red beanie cap** seen in the neighborhood just before the attack on Pinard (red ski mask "on top of head" could be mistaken for a red "beanie cap" on same man).

Not named was **RICO GOLDIE TOMAZ.**

What about DNA?

Unfortunately, just as the DNA evidence in Joe's case was suddenly "missing" when he requested post-conviction DNA re-testing, Tomaz was informed that, soon after he was convicted, the D.A. in the Taleia J. case discarded Tomaz's DNA evidence. Without the DNA in both Joe's and Tomaz's cases, Joe would not be able to compel testing of Tomaz's DNA against DNA left at crime scenes in Joe's cases. Nor can Tomaz be *eliminated* with regard to allegations by Brooks, Alleman, Archer and the others. I had sent Joe the mugshot of Tomaz, together with the 1989 composite image. Joe wrote back:

"WOW! I could hardly believe what you found! I know we're not saying it's him yet, but his mugshot fits the composite to a "T." Even the eyebrows – one eyebrow is higher than the other. And the eyes and his "look" is so convincing. Could he be the guy? WOW! And the answer to your question is Yes! I've seen lot of guys in prison showers with two colors of hair – red on the bottom and brown on top; and black on the bottom with red hair on top. Many Mexicans in Mexico look "White" with red hair, freckles and blue eyes; they are Mexican Spanish – It's always a "mixed" bloodline... just like mine."

Mistaken and suggestive eyewitness identifications have long been the leading cause of wrongful convictions in more than two-thirds of exonerations. On December 22, 1989, the SLO Times-Press-Recorder reported that San Luis Obispo County Deputy District Attorney Matt Kerrigan, confirmed that his office declined to prosecute Bradley Marvin Teaby, 28, who had been arrested as a rape suspect...because it was a case **of mistaken identity.** Perception and memory itself are inherently incomplete but also unreliable; not only do people have difficulty remembering more than a few characteristics of a person but also expectations tend to conflate incidents, and witnesses have particular difficulty identifying members of **another race. But in the case of Jacqueline Brooks, she was certain her assailant was "Negro," and the composite she helped create reflects an African American, so in that instance, the victim was correct – It was the Prosecution's henchmen who convinced her it must be Joe, who is not at all Black and who did not look at all like the composite she approved.**

I can only theorize about Brooks' "change of mind" about Joe, due to the fact that a witness who must testify about an encounter with a total stranger, under circumstances of emergency or emotional stress, may change their identification if police or prosecutor "suggests" to them that the defendant is the person they saw -- just as Tyra Wittmeyer was adamant *"It wasn't Joe,"* until she was led to believe the unreasonable doubt that *"it had to be Joe because the DNA matched,"* which was a lie told to her.

A jury will tend to place special trust on the reliability of an eyewitness, especially the victim. There is almost nothing more convincing than a live human being who takes the stand, points a finger at the defendant, and says *"He's the one!"*

146

In addition to Rico Goldie Tomaz, other possible suspects in San Luis Obispo County and neighboring counties' cases of rape, attempted rape, and even **serial rapes**, may have been overlooked due to authorities' "tunnel vision" that was focused on Joe Garcia.

Frank Everett Comstock, Jr, 46, was arrested on August 8, 1990 (while Joe was in custody awaiting trial) in connection with at least **five rapes** in 1988 and 1989, including that of a 19-year old woman. On February 13, 1991, the SLO Times-Press-Recorder reported *"three reported rapes in Arroyo Grande, three in Pismo Beach, and five rapes or sex crimes in Grover City."*

Three days before Tyra Wittmeyer, 15, was sexually assaulted on September 17, 1989, and identified her rapist as being 17-to-20 years old," a **17-year old juvenile** was arrested on suspicion of raping a 22-year old woman at her home in Morro Bay (where Jacqueline Brooks was attacked) And an **18-year old** Long Beach man (not named in media because he was a juvenile) was arrested February 6, 1990, on suspicion of raping a 21-year old San Luis Obispo woman.

Richard Wayne Martin, 41, of Grover City, was arrested for rape of a **17-year old girl** in Oceano. On March 3, 1989, **Manuel Luiz, Jr.**, 49, was arrested on suspicion of rape and kidnap of **two girls, ages 13 and 10**, six years earlier on January 9, 1983; there was no followup report as to his activities from 1983 to 1989. **Henry Phillip Matusevic**, 34, was arrested October 11, 1989 on suspicion of raping a **19-year old** Arroyo Grande woman; and **Corbett Wulfing**, 21, was arrested on suspicion of raping a 25-year old victim.

On December 29, 2020, the Lompoc Police Department's Records Clerk left me a Voicemail message confirming that the only archived record of arrest found for Rico Goldie Tomaz was **Case Number 1990-3207 with arrest date June 3, 1990, when he was also taken into custody**. She confirmed that there was no record of his being in custody during the 1989 incidents reported by the eight women in Joe's case, and that **Tomaz was a free man when the October 18, 1989 composite was made at the direction of Jacqueline Denise Brooks**.

As this book went to press, President Donald J. Trump was impeached a second time, this time for inciting thousands of rioters who breached the Capitol Building in Washington, DC, resulting in five deaths – an attempt by White Supremacists and other extremists to overthrow the government and who threatened to murder Democrat leaders as well as Vice President Pence who they perceived as being disloyal to Trump; 20,000 National Guard troops stood watch in expectation of further attacks in DC and at all 50 state capitals. But on January 20, 2020, Joe Biden became President without further incident. President Biden faced multiple monumental challenges, including COVID-19 vaccine distribution,

As if 32 years in prison hadn't inflicted enough on Joe Garcia that he managed to survive, on January 10, 2021, Joe tested Positive for COVID-19. California prisoners were still being moved from prison to prison, increasing risk of exposure to other inmates, instead of releasing elderly prisoners to decrease the spread of COVID. Although not hospitalized, Joe was quite ill with multiple symptoms including permanently scarred lungs, as were many other inmates in the unhealthy, cold, wet conditions at Corcoran Prison, and was forced to wear chains to shower while in quarantine. By March 2021, the United States toll reached:

over 30-million COVID-19 cases,
over 500,000 COVID-19 deaths
with 121-million vaccines distributed
with new COVID strains and anticipated surge in cases

While waiting for Joe to recover, I appealed to Jody Lewen, Mt. Talapais College, San Quentin, who heads an education project for transitioning parolees and who advocates for *release of elderly prisoners*. She never replied. I also sent material to Lompoc Police Detective Magallon to support my request for an investigation of Rico Goldie Tomaz with regard to his whereabouts in 1989. Magallon phoned me stating Lompoc Police Department has had no contact with Tomaz "in over 20 years" and redirected me to police departments in the jurisdictions in which the crimes occurred.

If anyone could help clarify the Rico Tomaz puzzle it was **George Felix Levine,** the FBI's DNA expert who analyzed DNA from Rico Goldie Tomaz in the Taleia J. rape case, and who was also consulted about the DNA in Joe's case. Levine phoned me in response to my inquiry about Tomaz.

Levine provided the answer that explained why Tomaz was described as having RED hair by Levine, but as an "American Indian" with BROWN hair on the State Sex Offender Registry, while Tomaz's mugshot matched the composite image reflecting Jacqueline Brooks' rapist who she described as "Negro." Levine's response: *"Because Tomaz DOES have natural RED hair and he IS African American"* – Levine's analysis of Tomaz's DNA and hair proved it. Levine also felt certain that because Tomaz' curly RED hair made him easily identifiable, a career criminal like Tomaz very likely would be dying his hair to evade the cops. I emailed the Department of Justice office that oversees the State Sex Offender Registry, advising them the description of the error and suggesting they add the information about Tomaz true hair color and ethnicity. DOJ never replied.

According to my notes from Levine's phone call, which he didn't mind my documenting, Levine told me that, in 1993-1994, he had been ordered to return all DNA samples he had saved in small coin collector type envelopes from every case in which he provided analysis. For a time, he resisted doing so, because, he said, police departments typically discarded evidence. It was after the 2004 Federal Innocence Protection Act, that states began requiring DNA evidence in felony cases to be retained indefinitely, just as Joe's prosecutor had requested.

As soon as Levine's call to me ended, I Googled for California cold cases and found the recently solved "cold" case of two Atascadero women, Jane Antunez murdered in 1977, and Patricia Dwyer, murdered in 1978, which a curious local woman researched and brought to the attention of San Luis Obispo County Sheriff's "cold case detective," **Clint Cole**. DNA evidence **saved in the Sheriff's evidence room for 41 years** solved the case (reported in the Washington Post, 4-18-19). Arthur Rudy Martinez was proven to be the perpetrator in both crimes, even though Martinez was deceased when his familial DNA was matched to the DNA from the 1977 and 1978 victims or crime scenes. I explained to Detective Cole that I needed to know if Joe's "missing" DNA could be in his Evidence Room the past **32 years**, and needed someone to pursue the matter of the composite image matching Tomaz, but he referred me back to Atascadero Police Department as having handled "the primary case." I replied that, in 2006, Atascadero's Police Department's Property Technician reported to Attorney Raymond Allen that he found "no evidence listing" and so *"theorized* the file was purged," and that Joe's DNA evidence reportedly had been *"returned to the DA on or about February 15, 1994."*

I asked Cole if he would try using Joe's two Evidence Box DOJ Numbers, SBC-035-91 and 144-89 to *visually check* his log or his boxes to see if Joe's evidence ended up there and who to contact about the composite and Tomaz. His email reply: *"I have my own cases. I can not help you! I apologize."*

On the other hand, **Ryan Enfantino**, Atascadero Police Department's current Senior Evidence Specialist, not only had many old cases still stored but also offered to actually search for Joe's DNA evidence boxes with the information I provided. When I asked what to do about Rico Goldie Tomaz and the composite, he told me what I already knew - that, unlike unsolved Murder cases, California has a Statute of Limitations on Rape cases (revised in 2020) depending on age of the victim, DNA, etc., and Joe's case is considered closed; the San Luis Obispo Court had ruled that it would not hear Joe's further requests for DNA testing, nor anything else.

While awaiting any results from Enfantino's search, my next call was to **Terry O'Farrell**, Chief Investigator to San Luis Obispo's current **D.A., Dan Dow**, who informed me that Joe had a Sheriff's Case Number (9001-01007) and referred me to the ladies who actually run the SLO Sheriff's Evidence Room. While Detective Cole had refused to initiate a search of the Sheriff's Evidence Room, **Stephanie Ross**, Property Officer at the facility, initiated a search for Joe's DNA evidence, later referred to **Sergeant Davish ("Dave") Menghrajani**, who, for months, did not return my calls. In May, when I finally reached him directly, he informed me there was "no digital record" of Joe's evidence and they would not do a physical search, contrary to Ms. Ross assurances. And at one point in our lengthy conversation, he suddenly defensively stated *"It's not a coverup."*

Concurrently, Joe's jailhouse lawyer claimed a *"coverup,"* citing that hundreds of California prisoners' COVID petitions for release were intentionally being ignored. And Republicans were attempting to recall Governor Gavin Newsom for mandating restrictions to reduce COVID-19 cases and deaths in California to the displeasure of political and business interests. Joe's Application for Commutation of Sentence was not going to be a priority. But Newsom, confident that the recall would fail, announced his intention to unilaterally "release 79,000 more prisoners" as California began to emerge from the pandemic and was again open for business. All we could do is wait and wonder if it's finally time to release Joe Garcia.

""A censor is a man who knows more
than he thinks you ought to."
-Laurence J. Peter

Chapter 9:
CENSORSHIP OF "EYEWITNESS"

As if his wrongful imprisonment hadn't inflicted enough injustice on Joe Garcia, Joe informed me that the published copies of this book, "EYEWITNESS," which public libraries nationwide have begun ordering, and which was sent directly from Amazon to Joe at Corcoran Prison, were confiscated by Corcoran's censors, citing California Code Regulations Title 15 ("Contraband") § 3006(d):

"Anything in the possession of an inmate which is **not** contraband but will, if retained in possession of the inmate, present *a serious threat to facility security or the safety of inmates and staff,* shall be controlled by staff to the degree necessary to eliminate the threat"…

and 3006(c)(4): "Plans to *escape* or assist in an escape."

… a totally bogus premise and citing the specific pages "not allowed": page 25 (regarding Tyra Wittmeyer's rape kit); and pages 121, 122, 123,124, 125,128,129,130,131,132,129,140 in Chapter 7 that clearly do not contain an "escape plan," nor does this story of Joe's 32-year quest for legal exoneration and legal release even remotely suggest an "escape plan."

What is clear to this writer is that the pages cited were not in **Warden Ken Clark's** best interests because they include his correspondence evidencing his indifference to Joe's long held protected inmate classification, and the circumstances under which Corcoran became overpopulated and a petrie dish for spread of COVID-19 in defiance of court orders and mandated policies. Not one to give up or give in easily, I printed and mailed a few dozen pages of "EYEWITNESS" at a time to Joe which got thorough uncensored. "EYEWITNESS" was also delivered to Warden Ken Clark without problem. My second attempt to provide Joe with "EYEWITNESS" also resulted in the book being confiscated.

Joe filed a Grievance form asking prison officialdom the "reason" for censoring his book even from him. The Denial simply cited California Code Regulations Title §3134.1, which states that the book "must be mailed directly from a book store, book distributor, or publisher." This book *was* ordered from and mailed directly from Amazon – the largest "book store, book distributor *and* publisher" in the world, and which sells, distributes and exclusively publishes "EYEWITNESS."   Section 3134.1 also states that the prison, within 15 days of the Denial, must send *the publisher* a letter that "must include the *reason* why the book was denied."   As there is no record of any letter being sent to Amazon, nor the original publisher, Access Press, the prison is in violation of California Code of Regulations, Title 15, Section 3134.1. And so the aforementioned was basis for Joe's appeal of the Denial.

In *"Censorship in Prison and Jails: A War on the Written Word,"* (by Christopher Zoukis, for *Prison Legal News*, December 4, 2018), Zoukas cites the landmark ruling in *Citizens United v. Federal Election Commission*, 558 U.S. 310 (2010), which held political campaign spending is a form of "protected speech" – the U.S. Supreme Court noted the First Amendment is "premised on mistrust of government power." **The Court also held that such mistrust extends to bans on books** and other reading materials, since "freedom of speech is not merely freedom to speak; it is also "**freedom to read**" (King v. Federal Bureau of Prisons, 415 F.3d 634, 7th Cir.2005).

Yet restrictions on books and magazines have become commonplace in prisons and jails.   Texas Department of Corrections banned 15,000 titles including Oprah Winfrey's biography and Utah State Prison banned *"Harry Potter"* as being "manipulative" but Kurt Vonnegut's *"Slaughterhouse Five"* is allowed. In February 2018, the Human Rights Defense Center (HRDC), the parent organization and publisher of *"Prison Legal News"* filed suit against the Illinois Department of Corrections (among other similar suits in other states) after prison officials refused to allow prisoners access to *"Prison Legal News"* and the news it contains about the criminal justice system. The ruling granted the Federal Bureau of Prisons "broad discretion" when it came to upholding a regulation that permitted censorship of any publication it "determined detrimental to the security, good order, or discipline of the institution or if it might facilitate criminal activity." But courts have used a "four-pronged test" (in "Thornburgh") **to strike down bans** on publications sent from "unauthorized organizations" and total bans on reading materials with sexual content "that also have literary value."

As it was still unclear why "Eyewitness" book was termed "unauthorized," and why specific pages of this book are prohibited under Title 15, so Joe filed a Grievance form on the matter. It was Denied citing California Code Regs Title 15 Section 3341 which requires that inmates can receive books if the book is mailed directly from "a book store, distributor or publisher," and Amazon, who processed my order and mailed the book to Joe, certainly qualifies under all three of those designations. So Joe filed an appeal of that Denial, also Denied.

(L-R): Steven Spielberg, Barbara Streisand, Jeffrey Katzenberg, and Rob Reiner were among Hollywood Elites Throwing Mega Cash Behind Democrat Governor Newsom ahead of September 14, 2021 Recall Election

"Know thy enemy and know yourself;
in a hundred battles, you will never be defeated."
-General Sun Tzu

Chapter 10:
(2021-2022) GOVERNOR NEWSOM and CALIFORNIA ROARS BACK-
D.A. DAN DOW REMAINS SILENT, PAROLE REVISITED
and CONTINUING EFFORTS TO SAVE JOE GARCIA – 153

Some of the things that define Governor Gavin Newsom's legacy include having had the balls to place a moratorium on the Death Penalty in California by his Executive Order, which also withdrew the legal injection protocol and closed the Execution Chamber at San Quentin. Innocent people had been sentenced to death in California, and since 1973, 164 condemned prisoners, nationwide, including five in California, have been freed from Death Row after they were found to have been *wrongfully convicted.*

Newsom also enabled release of thousands of California prisoners who met specific conditions and he promised to release more.

Newsom's COVID-19 prevention protocols resulted in California being the first state able to re-open businesses and return a degree of normalcy to its 39.7 million residents But on September 14, 2021, a Republican instigated Recall Election threatened to undo all the good Newsom had done for California. And if Newsom had been recalled, Joe Garcia's last hope for release via Commutation of Sentence by Newsom would be gone. Fortunately for Joe, and for California, according to ABC News on September 15, 67% of California voters voted "No" on the Recall while 33% voted "Yes." But we still have an uphill battle as we continue to seek a response of any kind from Newsom and his Legal Affairs staff handling Commutations. And so both Joe and I, and one of his other supporters, are resuming a letter campaign to Newsom, Legal Affairs, and all the powers that be, with follow up phone calls, and my attempt at a media blitz to alert all to Joe's current situation – that his wrongful conviction, wrongful imprisonment, and having twice been infected by COVID-19 in prison, has resulted in his "long haul" side effects and injuries from a fall during a heart attack *that now confines him to a wheelchair.*

Dated:	June 19, 2021
To:	GAVIN NEWSOM, GOVERNOR OF CALIFORNIA 1303 - 10th Street, Suite 1173, Sacramento, CA 95814
From:	LORI CARANGELO, Founder, Americans For Open Records (AmFOR) ██████████ Palm Desert, CA 92211-1952;
Ref:	JOSEPH BELARDE GARCIA #H-01695 4B2L, Cell 8, Corcoran State Prison, PO Box 3481, Corcoran, CA 93212 DOB: 7-20-1948
Re:	**Enclosed** book as Exhibit to Applications(s) for Commutation by a Wrongfully Convicted Man, whose 2020 Application for Commutation was Returned Unprocessed due to COVID short staffing, then refiled and acknowledged in 2021 yet now cannot be found by Legal Affairs staff for the purpose of including the enclosed proof of innocence in further support of Commutation/Release per *"EYEWITNESS: The Case of the Carefully Crafted Central Coast Rapist,"* now being considered ████████████████████████ for ████ documentary on Garcia and others wrongfully convicted **being passed over during mass releases.**

Dear Governor Newsom,

The matter of JOSEPH BELARDE GARCIA, now age 72 and wrongfully incarcerated 32 years to date, warrants your direct attention, as there is a statutory limit on the number of Applications for Commutation within a certain time frame by this (proven) Wrongfully Convicted Man. His 2020 Application for Commutation (a copy of which is **enclosed**) was returned in 2020, *after several months, unopened and unprocessed*, due to COVID/understaffing, when Loyola Project for the Innocent, who had taken up his matter, similarly abandoned him.

Mr. Garcia was also illegally denied parole in 2015, despite his eligibility, and illegally prohibited by the Parole Panel from seeking a new hearing "for 10 years" due ONLY and expressly (according to the Parole Panel testimony in the hearing transcript) to his consistent claim of factual innocence since his 1989 arrest and 1991 trial. As result, Mr. Garcia, already disabled, contracted COVID-19 and now has permanently scarred lungs and other after-effects. His COVID appeal for release, like others' similar appeals, was denied (per pending class action by Attorney Dejon Lewis re California inmates' petitions similarly denied or ignored). We fear that Mr. Garcia, who never killed anyone but whose Rape conviction was based solely on the disproven circumstantial case without evidence, and victims' misidentifications (changed from the police reports), and with DNA that did NOT match/was not ruled on and is now alleged "lost," will be similarly passed over when you release "76,000" more inmates. Even ignoring his innocence, Garcia has "done his time."

THEREFORE, **enclosed** is proof of this father's innocence. Please do not let him get passed over again. Respectfully,

LORI CARANGELO
cc: Joseph Belarde Garcia);
enclosures: 2020 Application for Commutation (copy); book as Exhibit in support

156

Meanwhile, Dan Dow, Republican elected in 2014 as District Attorney for San Louis Obispo County, never replied to my July 19, 2021 letter requesting that he authorize a physical search for Joe's DNA evidence denied him by the Court and by the San Luis Obispo County Sheriff's and Atascadero Police Department's Evidence Managers. Perhaps his silence is due to feeling conflicted by his "mission," as stated on his profile page at https://www.slocounty.ca.gov/District-Attoney/OurTeam.aspx, as follows:

> "As a career prosecutor, Dan has focused on prosecuting domestic violence, **sexual assault** and child abuse crimes where he seeks to bring justice for victims of particularly devastating crimes that are committed against those least capable of protecting themselves. He considers it **a high calling** and a privilege to serve victims and to hold offenders accountable for their actions."

Perhaps that mission prevents him from seeing a man wrongfully convicted of Rape as being a "victim." Yet, Dan Dow *refused* to charge former Paso Robles Police Sergeant Christopher McGuire with *Sexual Assault* **(aka Rape),** despite that the San Luis Obispo County Deputy, who handled the initial investigation, recommended that the D.A.'S office file *"forcible sex act"* **(aka Rape)** charges against McGuire. Both Dow and Assistant D.A. Eric Dobroth publicly *confirmed* that DNA evidence found at the scene of the contacts *did match McGuire.* Yet Dow denies that a "Rape" occurred, saying *"there wasn't enough evidence"* and that there were *"other ways the office is able to support* **victims** *including their Victim and Witness Assistance Center."* If Dow denies a Rape occurred, why is there a *"victim?"* It's not known whether McGuire quit or was fired from the Paso Robles Police Department over the matter. What *is* known is that 3 other women subsequently filed complaints against McGuire for "sexual misconduct and harassment," also reported by media:

- *"D.A. Won't File Charges Against Police Officer Accused of Forcible Sexual Acts,"* by Lindsey Holden and Matt Fountain, reporters, The (San Luis Obispo) Tribune, 11-1-18;
- *"DA Declines to Charge Former Police Officer Accused of Sexual Assault,"* by Chris McGuire, New Times, 11-8-18;
- *"No Charges Against Former Paso PD Sergeant Accused of Sexual Assault,"* by KSBY-TV Local News, KSBY.com;
- *"Woman Who Accused Police Officer Sues City for Damages,"* by Chris McGuinness, New Times, 11-8-18;
- *"Attorney General's Office Reviewing Decision Not to Prosecute Police Officer Accused of Rape,"* by Paso Robles News Staff, 11-26-19

Dan L. Dow, Republican, District Attorney of San Luis Obispo

July 19, 2021

DAN DOW, District Attorney for San Luis Obispo County
1035 Palm Street, San Luis Obispo, CA 93408

REF: People v. Garcia, SLO Sup Ct Case No. 15883 (1991 trial), arising from 1989 Arrest
in Atascadero of Defendant, **Joseph Belarde Garcia** (DOB: 7-20-48), re Rape of 2 victims
Jacqueline Denise Brooks (then age 18, in1989 **Atascadero** Police Report No. 89-5944) and
Tyra Dawn Wittmeyer (then age 15, in **San Luis Obispo** Police Report No. 89-2807) and for
"Attempted Rape" of others, per detailing in the book, *"EYEWITNESS: The Case of the
Carefully Crafted Central Coast Rapist"* (paperback copy **enclosed**).

RE: **Request that you Acknowledge receiving and Respond to this Request to Authorize
San Luis Obispo County Sheriff's and Atascadero Police Property Officers to conduct a
physical search of Evidence storage,** for DNA and Other Evidence (per "**Evidence List,**" on
Page 74 of book **enclosed**), in Compliance with the 2004 Innocence Protection Act and CA Penal
Code Section 1404-1405; and to provide any discovered DNA evidence to the FBI's National
Criminal Information (NCIC) Database to match or eliminate formerly convicted and released serial
rapist, **Rico Goldie Tomaz** who was never investigated in the Garcia case, now identified from
mugshot matching 1989 composite) and other suspects never fully investigated).

Dear D.A. Dow,

I am a non-fiction true crime writer of over 20 books on Amazon. I compiled the **enclosed** book
as a comprehensive detailing of this *circumstantial* case, with sources noted, proving that Joseph
Belarde Garcia was wrongfully convicted. Another supporter of Mr. Garcia may have sent you an
un-edited draft copy in error – **Enclosed** is the actual, edited, updated, published book.

In 2005, Garcia filed his Motion for Post-Conviction DNA Testing and a lame effort by court-
appointed Attorney Raymond Allen, and then-District Attorney Labarbera, consisted only of phone
calls suggesting that Garcia's 2 boxes of DNA and other evidence was "missing" so "presumed
destroyed," but this is doubtful because (1) the Court had Granted the request of then-Prosecutor
at trial, Teresa Estrada-Mullaney's, request to **"preserve the evidence** *indefinitely* **in case
additional victims later come forward."** And (2) no "Notice of Destruction" was ever issued.
SLO Sherrif's Detective, Clint Cole, confirmed that evidence in unsolved murder and "high profile
cases" like Garcia's, are still stored at his evidence facility, as far back as the 1970s; and (3) the
chain of evidence documented the DNA being returned to the former SLO D.A. as late as 1994,
and (4) no one checked the sign-in log to determine who last handled the DNA evidence .
Terry O'Farrell, your **Chief Investigator, in early 2021,** referred me to SLO Evidence Officers
who promised to search their evidence storage facilities for Garcia's DNA evidence, which would
not have been on computer in 1989. After months of my calls for followup not being returned, I
finally reached **Sergeant Davish ("Dave") Menghrajani** (SLO Sherrif's) who informed me *he
would not allow a physical search, and alleging no such case existed,* yet **Terry O'Farrell** provided
the SLO Sheriff's Case #, and I provided the 2 Evidence Box #s etc. Menghrajani also stated that
a court order was needed for a physical search, which I cannot obtain because **the Court
CLOSED GARCIA'S CASE upon receiving Garcia's 2005 "Motion to Compel" a physical
search for said evidence and the Docket has a notation indicating that no further Motions
regarding the DNA evidence will be heard by the Court and that anything further must be file
"elsewhere."** Mr. Garcia has exhausted all Appeals, Denied without reason.

–1– (of 2 pages)

Mr. Garcia, a Native American, was convicted in 1991 by an all-White jury, despite that the victims' descriptions did not match Mr. Garcia (per chart of Dissimilar IDs and M.O.s on page 35 of book), and despite that his alibis in every instance were verified (per Trial Transcripts). The 10-18-89 composite sketch on the front cover of the enclosed book, was on the front page of SLO area newspapers, generated by victim **Brooks** who described the suspect as "*Negro,*" as reflected by the features in the composite *which does not match Joe Garcia* (left of composite on the cover; full faces on page 142) but DOES match **Rico Goldie Tomaz** (at right on composite on the cover), convicted serial rapist and redheaded African American with "hair dyed brown to evade cops," according to FBI DNA expert, George Felix Levine who analyzed Tomaz's DNA and opined re Garcia's DNA evidence as being discredited.

Victim **Wittmeyer,** on the other hand, not only described her rapist as being *White*, and physically different than Garcia, but also *named* teenager **Steve Bolt** as her assailant, and insisted "*It wasn't Joe Garcia*" who was well known to her and was a friend of her family. At trial, she stated only that "the Prosecutor told her the DNA *matched* Garcia" but still did not identify Garcia as her rapist despite the coercion. **The DNA evidence itself was discredited by the FBI and both the Defense and Prosecution DNA experts, and so was never ruled on, per Transcripts.**

Anyone empowered to assist in exonerating Mr. Garcia – has declined to even look into the matter, based solely on the "number of victims" – 8 women, 2 of whom were actually raped, and the rest that were unsolved "Breaking and Entering" type cases, some mis-categorized as "Attempted Rapes" and lumped into one trial, when the FBI did not yet have an adequate DNA database and this was the First DNA case in SLO.

Mr. Garcia, now 73, was recently twice infected by COVID-19 in prison, which permanently damaged his lungs and heart. He remains in prison for someone else's crimes for 32 years, his requests for Commutation ignored, while killers are being released, and in 2015 was denied Parole **solely and expressly (per Transcript) due to his consistent claim of factual innocence**; the **panel** even alleged "the DNA matched.

Therefore, you are hereby requested to reopen this matter by authorizing a physical search of Atascadero and San Luis Obispo evidence storage facilities, for Mr. Garcia's evidence per **ATTACHED list,** and to have any DNA evidence found be entered into the FBI's NCIC Database for the purpose of solving this still unsolved case and correcting a wrongful conviction that has robbed Joe Garcia (and his wife and son) of most of his adult life and health, essentially imposing a Death Sentence.

Respectfully,

LORI CARANGELO

Palm Desert, CA 92211-1951

cc: JOSEPH BELARDE GARCIA, #H-01695, 4B2L, Cell 8,
    Corcoran State Prison, PO Box 3481, Corcoran, CA 93212

–2– (of 2 pages)

160

Months passed without response to my appeal to D.A. Dan Dow's *"humanity"* and it was apparent that such appeal weren't going to get us anywhere -- not because D.A.s lack *humanity*, but because D.A.s manage to rationalize a "conflict of interest" between convicting the guilty and freeing the innocent. I "get" it. Politicians "woo" voters with "tough on crime" rhetoric, so any resulting wrongful convictions must be kept from the public conscience, even though the travesty of justice did not occur on their watch. Opening that can of worms exposes the *fallibility* of the justice system that pays Dan Dow's mortgage and lifestyle so he can advocate for "victims"... *as long as he can't see Joe Garcia as a victim.* Neither does helping to correct a wrongful conviction enhance the reputations of the still-living players who invented a "Central Coast Rapist" in order to instill fear in Joe's jury ... a jury who were shown multiple "victims" ... implying that Joe must have done *something* for there to be *so many* victims - despite their unrelated victimology according to suppressed police reports that Joe's attorney did not present at trial.

Media producers, contacted about Joe's plight, seem to have preferred stories about those wrongfully convicted and exonerated of *Murder*, to avoid the messiness of Joe's Rape conviction that might upset someone, even though the real perpetrator has been free to enjoy his life

Since it had been 6 years since Joe was denied parole *for claiming innocence,* on October 13, 2021, we re-visited the prospect of parole with a letter addressed to Jessica Blonien, Chief Counsel for California's Board of Parole Hearings. The letter stressed Joe's changed circumstances as result of his injuries and his severe Long Haul COVID ailments. While waiting for Attorney Blonien's reply that never came, a letter with a copy of this book also was mailed to Linda Candelaria, the Gabrielino Tribe Co-Chair and Councilwoman, inquiring whether the Tribe currently has funding and will agree that it's time to free Joe Garcia. Again, no reply.

Meanwhile, Joseph Belarde Garcia v. California, Case No. 205835 in California's Fifth Appellate Court on November 23, 2020, was Denied. And so Joe's jailhouse lawyer elevated the case to the United States Supreme Court which was docketed as Joseph Belarde Garcia, on Habeas Corpus, Case No, 2688 on April 22, 2021 and, as of January 10, 2022, the U.S. Supreme Court Docket indicated the status as "Pending."

Joe's Dungeon-like Cell #8 at California State Prison-Corcoran

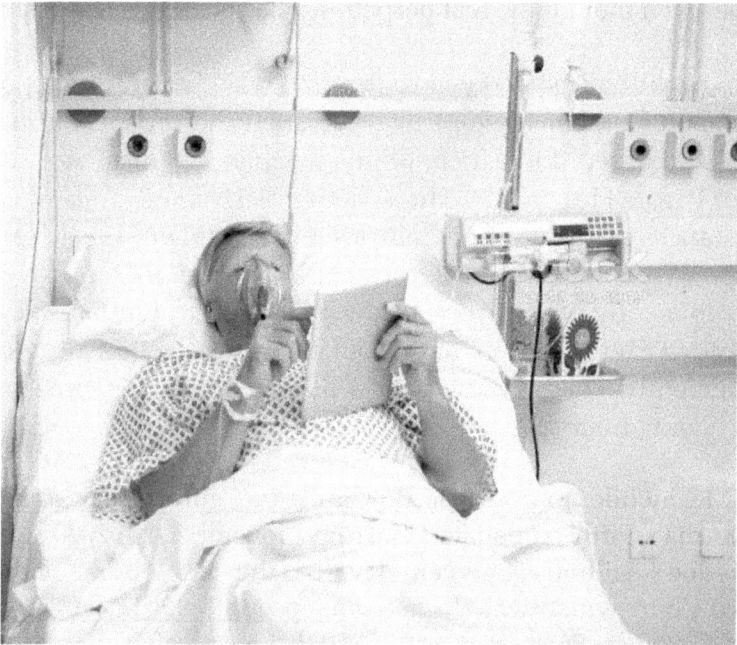

Patient Hospital Room at California Health Care Facility-Stockton

On January 29, 2022, CDC's Inmate Locator website, which I had checked daily, finally informed me that Joe had been moved to California Health Care Facility at Stockton, CDC's prison medical center for care of severely medically ill and mentally ill inmates. I immediately wrote Joe I was aware of his new location and am glad he would at last receive better treatment. On February 1, 2022, Joe wrote back, and subsequently he provided his medical records detailing injury to his heart, brain, liver, ongoing effects of a concussion and more...

"Hi, Lori. It's been awhile since I last wrote. Please be patient. My body and memory have not been good lately but I am determined to overcome and get better.

I'm now at the California Health Care Facility in Stockton Hospital. It is 100 times better than any prison I have ever been in. I have a giant room and a big hospital bed. I will never give up. They say I am a Long Haul COVID patient with complications. The headaches are horrible and [I have] many dizzy spells going on. I am experiencing shortness of breath and soon they will be giving me a CPAP machine [to assist breathing] and a hearing aid for my right ear... And soon, maybe next month, they are providing tablets so I can text you. Will try to write again. Cheers, Joe."

In 2022, the UnCommon Law firm that previously required a $2,000 "consultation fee" and $5,000 for parole hearing representation, was now offering "pro bono" help, according to their website, promoting the concept of *humanity* to combat discretionary and unreasonable parole decisions. I phoned Jonas Steckler at UC who stated the best they could do was put Joe on a "waiting list" for his 2025 parole hearing but *"no guarantee of representation."* Joe continued to wait for court decisions as he struggled to breathe with COVID-scarred lungs, and his COVID-damaged heart and brain are monitored, while his faith, hope and friends sustain him.

Throughout the first half of 2022, Joe's health and strength gradually improved – and then there was another mass outbreak of COVID-19 among the inmates and staff, including those who had been vaccinated, he, too, again tested Positive. But even as his health and energy again fought to rebound, that was not his only concern.

As California Health Care Facility's inmate population increased, so did the likelihood that Joe would be moved to a mixed population unit where he would be vulnerable to young gang-bangers and perhaps older enemies. At Joe's request, I shared his concerns with CHCF Warden Gena Jones and he was subsequently moved to a "safer" section. He also informed me that an attorney is working on resentencing toward his parole, perhaps by late Fall 2022. On July 26, 2022, Joe wrote:

> "Hi, Lori- Just wanted to thank you for your letter to the Warden, Ms. Jones... They recently moved me to another yard with higher level of care... for inmates on their last leg, so to speak, but I agree with you that I will live to be over 100. Thank you for typing up the list of my medical issues for my new doctor. He says he's going to help me get better and I believe he will. The attorneys are being paid to take me back to court for Re-sentencing under AB-2942. It will take them 3 to 5 months. They read 'Eyewitness' and were impressed by all the work you did... I still tire easily so this is brief. Love and a lot of appreciation, Joe"

In May, 2022, Joe was informed by Attorney Aaron Spolin, Esq., that he will be representing Joe. But it was unclear for what specific purpose the attorney was hired, until Joe copied me with Attorney Spolin's March 9, 2023 cover letter to Governor Gavin Newsom, again seeking Commutation of Joe's Sentence. But unlike the Petition for Commutation I submitted to Governor Jerry Brown in 2014, and unlike the Petition for Commutation I submitted to Governor Gavin Newsom on April 14, 2020 together with a copy of "EYEWITNESS" stressing Joe's innocence, Attorney Spolin's material sent to Governor Newsom avoided mention of Joe's innocence, apparently in the belief that any claim of innocence would be a detriment, and instead Spolin emphasized Joe's "rehabilitation." At this writing, it's been over a year since Attorney Spolin's notice of representing Joe and I suspended further efforts in Joe's behalf to avoid conflict, while Joe can only continue to wait to be free.

SL SPOLIN LAW P.C.

11500 W. OLYMPIC BLVD., SUITE 400, LOS ANGELES, CA 90064
PH: 310-424-5816 | FAX: 310-312-4551
WWW.SPOLINLAW.COM

March 9, 2023

Governor Gavin Newsom
1303 10th Street, Suite 1173
Attn: Legal Affairs/Clemency
Sacramento, CA 95814
Sent via email to:
commutations@gov.ca.gov

Re: Application for Commutation of Sentence for Joseph Belarde Garcia, CDCR #H01695

Honorable Governor,

On behalf of my client, Joseph Belarde Garcia, please find the enclosed application requesting the commutation of Joseph's sentence. We are respectfully requesting that this package be added to any previously submitted applications.

Your office has taken admirable steps to provide many criminal offenders with a "second chance" through its clemency powers. Joseph is reformed and rehabilitated, he has a strong network of support, and he has thoughtfully considered and prepared his plans for the future. Joseph is truly worthy of a commutation.

At nearly 75 years old, having served almost 34 years of incarceration, Joseph has dedicated himself to his rehabilitation. Joseph's conduct, character, achievements, and the fact that he has a loving and caring family and support network that is prepared to assist him in his transition from prison, warrant the commutation of his sentence.

Thank you in advance for your consideration of Joseph's application. Please do not hesitate to contact the undersigned with any questions.

Respectfully submitted,

Aaron Spolin

Aaron Spolin, Esq.
Attorney for the Defendant/Applicant

BIBLIOGRAPHY

Alleman, Mickie J., *"Report of Naked Man,"* San Luis Obispo Police Department
 Crime Report #89290021, taken by Dale E. Stockbridge, 10-17-89; and
 Testimony in *"People v. Garcia,"* pages 1952-1966

Anderson, Devanie, *"[Judge] Duffy Takes Plea Bargain, Avoids Facing a DUI
 Charge,"* 6-30-95

Associated Press (AP), *"California Inmates Detail Prison Conditions of Maggots, Mice
 Falling in Dining Hall,"* (Sacramento) 4-7-19

Atascadero News, *"Deputy DA Teresa Estrada-Mullaney Wins Recognition,"* 4-26-91

Atascadero Police Department, *""Property and Evidence Policy 802,"* Atascadero
 Police Department Policy Manual, pages 554-668

Baker, Peter, an Maggie Haberman, *"Trump Tests Positive for Coronavirus,"* New
 York Times, 10-2-20.

Bassin, Margarita Leticia, *"Report of Rape,"* Simi Valley Police Report #79-1164,
 6-4-79; and Testimony in *People v. Garcia,"* San Luis Obispo County
 Superior Court Trial Transcript, 1991, pages 01009-01024 and 2932-2948;
 and California Department of Corrections Parole Hearing Transcript re
 Joseph Belarde Garcia, 9-16-2015

Blajos, Art, and Nicky Cruz, *"Blood In, Blood Out,"* Monarch Books 1996

Bradford, Senator Steven, in *"Gavin Newsom, Sacrament Bee, 8-21-18*
 Wants to Close Prisons As Coronavirus Shreds California's Budget,"

Senator Steven Bradford, quoted in Sacramento Bee, 8-21-18; and in *"Gavin Newsom
 Wants to Close Prisons As Coronavirus Shreds California's Budget,"*
 San Francisco Chronicle, 5-28-20

Brian, Beverly Joan, Testimony in *"People v. Garcia,"* San Luis Obispo County
 Superior Court 1991 Trial Transcript pages 2932-2948; *"medical
 transcriptionist from Santa Margarita running for seat on County Board of
 Supervisors,"* The Lompoc Record, 6-4-82

Brooks, Jacqueline D., *"Report of Rape,"* Atascadero Police Report #895944, taken by
 M. Silva, 10-11-89; and Testimony in *"People v. Garcia,"* San Luis Obispo
 County Superior Court Trial Transcript, 1991, pages 1849-1944

Butte Miner, *"Mistaken Identity,"* Butte Montana, 9-24-03, page 4

Carangelo, Lori, *"Prisoner Shopping by Lawyers,"* and *"After 24 Years in Prison, Man
 Has Reason to Smile,",* in Lawyers and Business Executives In the News,
 11-2-05 and 12-12-05 newsletter editions

Chaffee, Kevin, *"Natural Parent Crusades for Human Right, "* The Desert Sun,
 10-13-87 upon 1987 founding Americans For Open Records (AmFOR);

Chappell, Bill, *"CA Will Release Up to 8,000 Prisoners Due to Coronavirus,"* NPR
 News, 7-10-20

Clarke, Matt, *"California Court of Appeals Vacates Parole Denial for Claiming
 Innocence,"* California Court of Appeals, PrisonLegalNews.org, 12-14-17

Deane, Stacia Michelle, Testimony, *People v. Garcia*, 1991 San Luis Obispo County
 Superior Court Case Nos. CR15883, Trial Transcript pages 1921-1944

DeAtley, Richard K., *"A Car Caravan Protest Passes Outside Chino Prison Main Entrance,"* The Press-Enterprise, 5-24-20; and *"3 Inmates From California Institution for Men in Chino Die From Coronavirus Complications,"* The Press Enterprise, 5-24-20; and *"700 Chino Inmates to be Transferred As Coronavirus Sweeps Prisons,"* Los Angeles Times, 5-28-20

Denkmann, Libby, *"As COVID Decimates Budget, LA City Council Weighs Plan to 'Stop the Bleeding,'"* LA List Repost, 12-20-10

Denny, Maureen N., Defense Investigator's Interview of Witness as follow-up to Catherine Pinard case, San Luis Obispo Police Report #89291002

Dorgan, Carrie S., *"Report of Attempted Rape,"* San Luis Obispo Police Department Report 9-9-89 Case #8908-15980; and Supplementary Report, 10-11-89; and Testimony in *People v. Garcia,"* 1991 San Luis Obispo County Superior Court Trial Transcript pages 1628-1684

Ellis, Ralph, *"33 Million in California Under Stay-at-Home Order,"* Web MD, 12-7-20

Femer, Matt, *"These Panels Could be the Best Hope for the Innocent,"* HuffPost Politics, 3-24-16

Fitzsimmons, Matt, *"Flyers on Drinkers Draw Fire,"* (objecting to public humiliation of drug addicts and alcoholics), The Desert Sun, 6-27-98

Five Cities Times-Press Recorder, Arroyo Grande, CA, *"Deputy DA Receives Public Safety Award from Governor,"* 5-1-89; and *"Convicted Rapist Gets 72-1/2 Years To Life In Jail,"* 7-19-92, page 16

FOX News/ AP, *"California Denies First Medical Parole,"* 5-24-11, updated 11-3-15

Gajdos, Detective John, *"Police Bulletin,"* Morro Bay Police Department WANTED Poster, Case #895844, 1991 Trial Transcript pages 3410-4553

Garcia, Joseph Belarde, *"People v. Joseph Belarde Garcia,"* San Luis Obispo County Superior Court, Case No, 15583; *"Garcia v. People,"* California Appellate Court, 2nd Appellate District Case Nos.B164679, B253004, B253636, B255203, B293491, S261772; *"Garcia v. People,"* California Appellate Court; *"Petition for Writ of Certiorari,"* U.S. Supreme Court, Case No. 20-585 2-18-20, Denied; S259872; S216611; S122971

Garrett, Brandon L, *"Innocence, Harmless Error, and Federal Wrongful Conviction Law,"* Wisconsin Law Review, 2005:35

Gersham, Bennet L., Professor of Law, *"Where Were the Prosecutors?"* Huffington Crime, *Huffington Post,* 3-17-16

Griffy, Leslie, *"Teen Killer Sent to State Lockup,"* (quoting Judge Teresa Estrada-Mullaney), *San Luis Obispo Tribune,* 5-6-06

Griswold, Lewis, *"Inmates Collude in Knife Attack on Guard at Corcoran,"* Fresno Bee, 1-7-19

Hanes, Edward, *"The DNA Wars: Touted as Infallible Method to Identify Criminals, DNA Matching Has Mired Courts in a Vicious Battle of Expert Witnesses,"* Los Angeles Times, 11-29-92

Hoeffel, Janet C., *"The Dark Side of DNA Profiling,"* Stanford Law Review, Vol. 42, No. 2 (Jan. 1990)

Holden, Lindsey and Matt Fountain, *"D.A. Won't File Charges Against Police Officer Accused of Forcible Sexual Acts,"* The (San Luis Obispo) Tribune, 11-1-18;

Hollingsworth, Gerald, MD, *"Psychiatric Evaluation of Joseph Belarde Garcia,"* California Department of Corrections, 5-24-94

Investigation Discovery TV, *"Don't Turn On Me,"* 12-8-16 (based on the book, *"Blood Relatives,"* by Lori Carangelo)

Johnson, Gloria L., Obituary, Santa Maria Times, 11-23-10

Kamin, Eugene, *"Study on False Accusations of Rape,"* Purdue University, 1994

Koseff, Alexi, *"CA Lawmakers Move to Cap Prison Time for Felons,"* (Senate Bill 1279,

KSBY TV Staff Reporters, *"No Charges Against Former Paso PD Sergeant Accused of Sexual Assault,"* KSBY Local News, KSBY.com

Larmer, Jana R., PsychD, *"Comprehensive Risk Assessment of Joseph Belarde Garcia,* California Department of Corrections, 8-20-15

Lee, Henry K., *"Highest Court Thwarts Governor On Prison Overcrowding,"* Los Angeles Times, 5-24-11

Levenson, Eric, *"Pennsylvania Supreme Court Pointedly Questions Use of Prior Bad Acts Witnesses in Bill Cosby's Trial,"* CNN, 12-1-20

Levin, George Felix, (DNA Expert for the Prosecution), Testimony in *"People v. Garcia,"* San Luis 1991 Obispo County Superior Court trial Transcript pages 2341; 5111-5117

Lewen, Jody, Mount Talapais College, San Quentin, CA, 1-10-21

Li, David K., *"Black Man in New Jersey Misidentified by Facial Recognition Tech and Falsely Jailed, Lawsuit Claims,"* NBC-News, 12-29-20

Libby, Randell T., (DNA Expert for the Defense), Testimony in *"People v. Garcia,"* 1991 Trial Transcript pages 1211-1277; 3457; 4051-4093

Loevy, Debra, *"When Innocence Isn't Enough,"* (Altering Convictions), Advocacy for Justice, 9-15-15

Los Angeles Times Editorial Board, *"Eyewitness Testimony is Often Unreliable and Police and Lawmakers Know It,"* Los Angeles Times, 5-8-18

Luis, Joseph, *"CDCR Investigating Inmate Death at Corcoran As Homicide,"* KGET.com, 6-12-20

Magee, Jack, *"Tomaz Gets Prison Sentence for Rape,"* The Lompoc Record, 12-20-91

Marx, Jan Dean Howell, *"Teresa Estrada-Mullaney- Breaking the Mold & Making a Difference,"* San Luis Obispo County Bar Bulletin, March-April 2020

Masuda, Andrew, *"Teenager Given Maximum Sentence in Murder Case,"* (quoting Judge Teresa Estrada-Mullaney), KSBY TV Transcript, 5-5-06

Matherly, Susan, Court Executive Officer, Denial of *"Motion for Post Conviction DNA Testing,"* signed by, Susan Matherly
Deputy Clerk, in behalf of Judge Dodie A. Harman, 10-9-13

Mauer, Marc, *"Is the Tough On Crime Movement On It's Way Out?"* MSNBC, 5-22-14

McCurdy. Jesselyn, *"How the First Step Act is Actually the Next Step After Fifteen Years of Successful Reforms to the Federal Criminal Justice System,"* Cardozo Law Review, Vol 4, Issue 1

McGuinness, Chris, "*DA Declines to Charge Former Police Officer Accused of Sexual Assault*," New Times, 11-8-18; and
"*Woman Who Accused Police Officer Sues City for Damages*," New Times, 11-8-18;

McFadden, Robert D., "*Reliability of DNA Testing Challenged by Judge's Ruling*," New York Times, 8-15-89

McLaughlin, Michael, "*Shocking Number of Innocent People Sentenced to Death Study Finds*," HuffPost, 5-28-14

Middlecamp, David, "*The First Woman Judge in San Luis Obispo Court, Teresa Estrada-Mullaney*," San Luis Obispo Tribune, 10-28-11

Morris, Leslie, "*Judge Comments on Longest Trial in County's History*," Santa Maria Times, 7-19-91; "*Trial Could Cost $500,000*," SLO Telegram-Tribune, 1-23-90; "*Case Was Longest, Most Expensive*," Times-Press-Recorder, 7-19-91

Morse, Nancy, "*Accused Rapist Finally to Have Trial*," Santa Maria Times, 4-14-91; "*Lompoc Man Says He's Innocent of Rape*," Santa Maria Times, 7-29-90

Open Record, The, (newsletter of Americans For Open Records-AmFOR) "Californians For Open Records," July 1989 issue

Nipomo Adobe Press, "*Deputy DA Received Award From Governor*," May 10,1991

Oleary, Tim, "*Trial Slated in Shooting Incident*," The Lompoc Record, 11-7-85; "*Beck Convicted of Attempted Murder*," The Lompoc Record, 1-12-86

O'Neill, Ciara, "*Prisons and Politics: Profiling the Pecuniary Persistence of Private Prisons*," FollowTheMoney.org, 1-24-27

Ormseth, Matthew, "*Danny Roman, Mexican Mafia Member and South LA Gang Chieftan is Stabbed to Death at Corcoran*," Los Angeles Times, June 11, 2020

Paso Robles News Staff, "*Attorney General's Office Reviewing Decision Not to Prosecute Police Officer Accused of Rape*," Paso Robles News, 11-26-19

Peltz, Jennifer, "*Fund Raises Thousands for Exonerated NYC Man*," AP, 4-17-04

Picco, Cheryl Ann, "*Attempted Kidnap Report*," Atascadero Police Report #896030 by Al James; and Supplemental Report, and Witness Interviews, 10-17-89 and Testimony in "*People v. Garcia*," 1991 Trial Transcript pgs 2011-2088

Pinard, Catherine T., *San Luis Obispo Police Report* #8291002, 10-17-89; and Testimony in "*People v. Garcia*," San Luis Obispo County Superior Court 1991, Trial Transcript pages 1011-2088

Queally, James, "*Sentenced to Life, as a Teen, Compton Man to be Freed After Evidence in Question*," {re EmmonBarnes], Los Angeles Times, 9-4-20

Raphael, Michael, "*Investigative Report, Juror #3, Arthur Charles 'Archie' Kuentzel*," 6-20-91

San Luis Obispo Telegram-Tribune staff reporters, "*Defense Musters Evidence in Preliminary Hearing*,"1-23-90

Santa Maria Times Staff, "*San Luis Obispo: Beverly J. Brian*," June 9, 1982"; "*SLO Attorney Gets State Award*," 4-25-91; "Rapist Gets Life Sentence," 7-19-91

Scheck, Attorney Barry T., with Peter Neufeld and Jim Dwyer, "*Actual Innocence When Justice Goes Wrong and How to Make It Right*," NL Trade, 2003

Schumaker, Erin, *"Prisons Should Be COVID-19 Vaccine Priority: Health Experts,"* ABC News, 12-4-20

Stahl, Leslie, *"Eyewitness: How Accurate Is Your Visual Memory?"* CBS-60 Minutes, 7-12-09

Sex Offender Registry, State of California Department of Justice Megan's Law website, https://www.meganslaw.ca.gov

St. John, Paige, *"U.S. Supreme Court Refuses to Hear Brown's Prison Appeal,"* Los Angeles Times, 10-15-13

Swanson, Scott, *"Convicted Rapist Gets 72-1/2 Years To Life n Jail,"* Times-Press-Recorder, 7-19-91

Swenson, Kyle, *"Two Murders Stumped Police for 40 Years. The Key Was Sitting in a Bathroom Cabinet,"* The Washington Post, 4-18-19

Tchedmedyain, Alene, and Richard Winton, *"LA County Jail Inmates Trying to Infect Themselves with Coronavirus, Sheriff Says,"* Los Angeles Times, May 11, 2020

Thompson-Cannino, *"Picking Cotton: A Memoir of Justice and Redemption,"* St. Martin's Griffin, 2010

Times-Press-Recorder, Arroyo Grande; *"Arrest Made in 1983 Sex Assault,"* 3-3-89; *"Rape Suspect is Identified, Sought,"* 7-14-89 *"Sex Crimes Charged in Grover,"* 9-20-89; *"GC Man is Suspected in Rape,"* 10-11-89; *"Movie: 'False Witness' Premiere,"* 10-20-89; *"Police Beat: Rape Charges Were Not Filed,"* 12-22-89; *"Rape Suspect Arrested in GC,"* 11-24-89; *"Arrest Made for Alleged Rapes,"* 2-9-90; *"Suspect Nabbed for Rape Attempt,"* 5-16-90; *"Police Seeking Suspect in Rape,"* 7-27-90; *Police Investigate Possible Rape,"* 2-6-91; *"San Luis Obispo: "Jury Finds Garcia Guilty On All 19 Counts,"* 6-14-91; *"Police Are Investigating Rape,"* 9-9-91 *"Arroyo Man Charged With Rape,"* 10-1-91; *"Rape Suspect Arrested"* 10-2-91; *"Arroyo Man Arrested After Rape,"* 12-4-91

Tomaz, Rico Goldie, *"California Sex Offender Registry,"* www.meganslaw.gov; www.city-data.com; Lompoc Police Report Case # 1990-3207; *"People of the State of California vs. Rico Goldie Tomaz,"* (re Rape of Taleia J.) Case No 1135693, Superior Court of Santa Barbara County, 2-26-04; *"Eric T. Brown vs. Rico Goldie Tomaz,"* Superior Court of Santa Barbara County, Small Claims Case No. 1111702, 2-11-03; *"People vs. Rico Goldie Tomaz,"* (re Murder and Attempted Kidnapping), Superior Court Case No. SM51006 *"People of the State of California vs. Rico Goldie Tomaz, Appellant's Petition for Review,"* (re Rape of Taleia J.), Supreme Court of California, Case No. B061764, 2-9-93

Troughout.org, *"What Do Private Prisons Have in Common with the Upcoming Election?"* HumanRightsDefenseCenter.org, 10-28-14

Wilcox, David, *"Defense Musters Evidence in Rape Case Preliminary Hearing,"* San Luis Obispo Tribune, 1-23-90 p. A-5; *"Cost of Garcia Trial May Hit Half a Million,"* San Luis Obispo Telegram-Tribune, 4-26-91

Wilson, Nick, *"Judge Teresa Estrada-Mullaney to Retire from Superior Court,"* San Luis Obispo Tribune, 10-19-11; and *"In a Career of Firsts, 'Last' Approaches for Superior Court Judge,"* San Luis Obispo Tribune, 10-26-11; and *"Barry LaBarbera Chosen to Be SLO County's Presiding Judge,"* San Luis Obispo Tribune, 10-19-01

Winton, Richard, "*12th Inmate at Chino Prison Dies After Testing Positive for COVID-19*," Los Angeles Times, 6-3-20; and "*700 Inmates to be Transferred as Coronavirus Sweeps Prison*," Los Angles Times, 5-28-20.

Wittmeyer, Travis W., Testimony in "*People v. Garcia*," 1991 San Luis Obispo County Superior Court Trial Transcript pages 2136-2163

Wittmeyer, Tyra Dawn, "*Report of Rape*," by M.P., Atascadero Police Report #89-280, 9-7-89; Testimony in "*People v. Garcia*," San Luis Obispo Superior Court, Case No, 15883, Trial Transcript pages 171-222-.

Yuhas, Alan, "*Nearly Three People a Week in U.S. Exonerated of Crimes Last Year*," The Guardian 2-3-16

Zoukas, Christopher, "*Censorship in Prisons and Jails: A war on the Written Word*," Prison Legal News, 12-4-18

INDEX

accusations of rape,
    --and alcohol, 52
    --honest false memory, 52
    --study, 17,150
accusers,
    -Alleman, Mickie J., 18,33-
       34,42,143-146,151
    -Archer, Tracey Denise, 18
       31,35,143-144,146
    -Brian, Beverly Joan 18-20
       43,60,151-152
    -Brooks, Jacqueline D., 2,
       18-28-31,42,74,82,
       95-96,142-147,151
    -Deane, Stacia Michele,18
       21,35,60,144,151
    -Dorgan, Carrie Suzanne,
       18,22,28,32,35,144-
       145,151
    -Picco, Cheryl Ann, 18,32,
       35,144,153
    -Pinard, Catherine T., 18,
       33-35,96,143-145,
       151,153
    -Wittmeyer, Tyra Dawn,
       12-13,17-18,23-26,
       35,41-42,48,57,59-
       60,64,74,95-96,144-
       145,147,155
Adams, Dwight (DNA expert), 49
Administrative Discretion,
    -abuse of, 99
Affidavit of Innocence, 83
"all-White jury," 60,88
Alleman, Mickie J., 18,33-34,42,
    143,146,151
Allen, Attorney Raymond H., 73,
    76-80

Allen, Susan ("Ki,"), 92
Alternate reality, 96
American Indian, 48,50,143,149
    -see also Native American
Americans For Open Records
    (AmFOR), 72,82,165
Application for Clemency and
    Commutation of Sentence,
    -Governor Brown, 87-88
    -Governor Newsom, 117,
       134,141,150,164-165
Archer, Tracey Denise, 18,31,35,
    143-144,146
Armstrong Schroeder Café
    (Schroeder's), 9
banned books, 151-152
Barrick, John (Ventura County
    DA's office, 89,93
Bassin, Leticia, 52-55,151
Bassin, Margarita (Maggie,
    Megan), 51-58,89,91-
    93-96,105,151
beebee gun, 32,60
Bergantzel, Detective, 76
Beverly Hills, 9
"beyond a reasonable doubt,"47,
    59 (see also reasonable
    doubt)
Bolden, Xina (Ombudsman for
    Corcoran prisoners), 121
Bolt, Steve, 17,23-25,41,43,48,97
    146
Bonien, Jessica, Chief Cousel, CA
    Board of Parole Hearings,161-162
bootstrap (multiple cases), 59
Brian, Beverly Joan, 18-20,42,60,
    145-146,149

Brooks, Jacqueline Denise, 2,18, 28-31,42,74,82,95-96,142-147,149-151

Brooks, Professor Justin (California Western Innocence Project), 82

Brown, Governor Jerry, 73,86-89, 133,143,145-146,154

Burson, Donald A., 28

California Health Care Facility163

California Institution for Men at Chino ("Chino"), 118-120, 151,155

California State Prison-Corcoran, ("Corcoran"), 70-71,119, 121,123,126,137-138,149, 152-153,151
-book censors, 151
-coronavirus,"COVID-19," 13,117-119,120,123-124, 136-138, 141,149,151,155
-leaking roofs, 137
-maggots, mice ,137,151
-wet cell walls 137

Candelaria, Linda, 161

censorship of "EYEWITNESS" by Corcoran Warden, 151-152

Central Coast Rapist 6,41-2,71,145

Change of Venue, Motion for, 41

charges against Joe Garcia,
-(in 1979), 47
-(in 1989), 65,96

Chart of Dissimilar Victim IDs, 35

circumstantial case, 6,17,105

Clark, Warden Ken, 123-126,128, 132-133,138,151

CNN, 71,152

Cole, Detective Clint, San Luis Obispo County Sheriff's Department, 149-150

Commutation of Sentence (see Application for Clemency)

composite of suspect, 28-29,31,95-96,142-143,145-147

conflict of interest, 107,112

Conner, Anita May, 92,103

Conviction Integrity Unit-CIU 107

Corcoran Prison (see California State Prison-Corcoran)

COVID-19, coronavirus, 117-120, 136-138,141,148-149,151-152,154-155,
-COVID cases in U.S., 148
-COVID deaths in U.S.,148

De Priest, Thomas R., (police officer), 11,21

Deane, Stacia Michele, 18,21,35, 60,144,151

Deane, William "Bill," 21

Deluca, Samuel, process server 25

Denny, Maureen Nelly, 12,33-34, 151

Deuel Vocational Institution for Men ("Tracy"), 10

Deukmejian, Governor George,45

"Dissimilarities of Victims' Identifications" (chart), 35

DNA, 6,17,26,32,47-50,59,60,73-75,80-83,87,95-97,102,143-146-147,149,152-153
-database, 48-50,146
-expert(s), 26,48-50,107, 143,152
-first DNA case in San Luis Obispo County, 47
-inconclusive and flawed, 26,95
-missing, destroyed. 73, 76-79,146
-no uniform standard," 48-49
-Post-Conviction DNA Testing, Motion for, 48-49,73,82,87,95,146

174

-RFLP- Restriction Fragment Length Polymorphism 48-50

Dorgan, Carrie Suzanne, 18,22,28, 32,35,144-145,151

Dow, Dan, District Attorney for San Luis Obispo, 150, 152-161

Duffy, Judge Michael,73,76,80,151

Dutra, Mr. (Property/Evidence Technician, Atascadero Police Department), 76

early release, 89,113,117,119
-AB 1812; AB 2942, 11
-"elderly release" (due to COVID risk) criteria, 113

Enfantino, Ryan, Atascadero Police Senior Evidence Specialist, 150

Enhancement(s), sentencing,57,60 63,94,136

Espino, Robert (police officer), 31

Estrada-Mullaney, Teresa (see Mullaney)

exoneration(s), 4,107,113,146
-National Registry of, 4

evidence, 12,23,32,42,44,48-50, 54,57,60,6,75,81-83,106
-Evidence List, 73,74,76
-Notice of Intent to Destroy Evidence, 75,89, 146
-"planted," 32

eyewitness identification, 5,145-147,153-154
-mistaken, 5,143,145-146
-suggestive, 146

Fasano, Tony, 47

Feirabend, Conrad, 25,45

fingerprint(s), 33,54,94

First Step Act, 115,153

Ford, Simon (DNA expert), 50

Fredman, Judge William R., 39,41 46-47,50,60,62-64

Gabrielino Tribe, 161

Garcia, Joseph Belarde,
-abused physically and sexually in childhood by mother, 10
-Affidavit of Innocence, 83
-bail, $400,000, 41
-heroin addiction, 7,9-10
-psychiatric assessment/ evaluation,55,102,113,152
-suicide attempts in childhood, 10
-U.S. Supreme Court, 163

Garcia, Jordan, 15-16,70,85,87-88, 110,113,113

Garcia, Judith Emily, 6-7,10-12,14 -16,19,70,85,133

Garcia, Raymond Apodaca Sr., 9

Garcia, Rose Carmel Belarde Cueva, 9-10

Gates, LAPD Police Chief, 130

Gearhart (Knuckles), Karla, 24,57

Gudmunds, Attorney, (Steinthor) Jon, 20,22,25,28,34,40-42, 44,46-49,52,58-59,60,62,82

"Guilty on all Counts," 60-61,96

gun, 35,49,52,58-59,62,67-68,83

Harman, Judge Dodie Ann, 83-84, 153

Heller, Jack, Bailiff, 46

heroin, 7,9-10

"hit list," 128

Hobson, Larry, 109-112

Holguin, Robert, 64

Hollingsworth, Gerald, MD, 102, 152

honest false testimony, 52

Human Rights Defense Ctr,152

Indian (see American Indian, Native American)

identification, mistaken 143,
145-146
-suggestive, 146
Innocence Project(s), 5,72-73,80,
82,111,137
Innocence Protection Act (aka
Innocence Act),73,80,82
intimidation, 138-139
*"It doesn't add up; it makes no
sense,"* 59
"It wasn't Joe," 23,41,60,96,142,
145,147
Johnson, Gloria L., 17,152
Jones, Warden Gena, 164
jury, 18,28,34,39,41,43-44,46-48,50,
58-60,64,88,112,147,154
-"all White," 60,88
-Keuntzel, Arthur, 151
"juvie" (Juvenile Hall), 9,55
Klasey, Darrell R. (San Luis
Obispo Police Fingerprint
Tech; composite image)
2,28-29,95,142-144
Kovacs, Bruce W., (DNA expert),
49
Kuentzel, Arthur Charles, (juror),
64,68-69,154
Krebs, Rex Allan, 57,63,109
Kulick RN, Jane, 25,74
Kushner, Jared, 115
LaBarbera, Barry T., 28,40,42,63,82
155
Larmer, Jana R.,PsychD, 93,97,103
157
Lascher, Attorney Wendy Cole,
105-108
Levin PhD, Daniel T., *"Race As A
Visual Feature,"* American
Psychological Association,
Journal of Experimental
Psychology: General,
Y-2000, Vol. 129, No. 4,

599-574
Levine, George Felix (DNA
expert), 50,143-144,148-149
Lewd Act on a Child Under 14,
143
Lewen, Jody, 148,157
Lewis, Attorney Dejon Ramone,
89-90,93,97,105,107
Lewis, Johnny W., Transition
Clinic Network, 135
Libby, Randell T. (DNA expert),
50,151
Lifers Support Therapy Group, 71
Lighthouse Bible Church and
"transition" team, 102
Lompoc Police Department, 147-8
Luxor, Trevor, (Case Manager,
California Western
Innocence Project), 82
Machbitz, Dan, 33-34,145
Magallon, Detective, Lompoc
Police Department, 148
Malone, Attorney Joe T., 44
Manson, Charles, 71
Marcy's Law (PC § 3043(3)(b)
(1), 105
Medina, James, 34
Megan's Law, 55,154
Menghrajani, Sgt. Devashish
("Dave"), 150
Mentally Disordered Sex
Offender, 55,63
Mexican Mafia, 91,120-124,126,
128-130,132,138-139,153
Miller, William "Bill," 44-45,47,
91,95-96
Miranda Rights, 13-14
misidentification(s), 6,18 (see also
"identification')
"Mistaken Identity" (1903), 5
modus operandi ("M.O."), 95-96
Morro Bay, 28,32,147,152

-Police Department, 77
Motion to Sever, 44
Mount Talapis College, 148
Mueller, Laurence W. (DNA expert), 49
Mule Creek Prison, 70-71
Mullaney, Teresa Estrada, 18,28, 34,40-42,44,47,52,57-59,62-64,75,82104,151-153,155, 149
"Naked Man, The," 18,33-34,42 143,145,151
National Registry of Exonerations, 4
Native American, 6,9-10,15,17,29, 46,48,59,143,145-146
-full blooded, 49,143
Newsom, Governor Gavin Christopher, 63,115-117, 119,133-134,136-137, 141,150,152,155-156
Notice of Intent to Destroy Evidence, 75,89,146
Observer, parole hearing, 89
O'Farrell, Terry, D.A.'s Chief Investigator, 150
Ogilvie, Sandee, 133
Ostini, Ed and Marietta, 134
parole, 89,92,94,97,102,105,161,163
parole panel (2015),
    -Barrick, John (Ventura County DA). 89,93
    -Chang, Helen (San Luis Obispo Victim Support) 91
    -Dunn, Linda (San Luis Obispo County DA) 89, 91,93,95
    -Jallins, Richard (Deputy Commissioner/ Observer), 89
    -Lam, Nga, (Deputy Commissioner), 89,97,104
    -Miller, James, (Victim Support Advocate), 91
    -Miller, William "Bill" (ex SLO DA investigator) 91,95-96
    -Roberts, Brian (Commissioner), 89,91, 93,96
P-Gabrielino Band of Mission Indians, 48
Pantangelo, Attorney Frank J., 44
past bad acts, 60,152
"past mistake(s)," 2,7,52,85,93-94
PCR (Polymerase Chain Reaction) 49
"People v. Garcia," San Luis Obispo County Superior Court Case No. 15883, 35, 41,72,74,151-152,155
Picco, Cheryl Ann, 18,32,35,144, 149,153
Pinard, Catherine T., 18,33-35,96, 143-145,151,153
Pinard, "Peg," 95
"planted" evidence, 32
polygraph test, 13,112
    -denied, 13
Power,Attorney Richard,70,81,146
Prison Legal News, 151-152
Pueblo Tribe, 9
Raike, Fred "Mike, 6-7,11-12,24,71
Rape, definition of, 52
    -date rape, 6,52
rape kit , 25,28,55
    -Bassin, Margarita (Maggie, Megan), 55
    -Brooks, Jacqueline D., 28
    -Wittmeyer, Tyra Dawn 25
rape suspects, other, 39,145,147
Raphael, Michael, 47,63,151
reasonable doubt, 5,43,47,50,55,

59,60,63-64,111
-unreasonable doubt, 5,43, 50,55,59-60,63-64,80,147
Reid, Cynthia P.(police officer),20
Robinson, Bert, 19-20
Roman, Danny (murder of), 121-122,153
Ross, Stephanie, San Luis Obispo Sheriff's Property Officer, 150
Rowlands, Ted (CNN), 71
Saint. Sebastian's Church, 9
San Quentin Prison, 10,55,63,138
Sbarro's Pizza (alibi), 10,26
Scaife, Captain Nathan, 138-139
Schwarzenegger, Arnold, 80
Scoles, Cindy (DA's office who assumed evidence that old "was purged"), 79,150
Scott, Michael, (investigator), 25
sex offender, 26,55,63-64,85,105, 143-145,154
Sex Offender Registry, State of California, 143, 154
Shapeiro, Attorney Martin (DNA expert), 50
Simms, Gary (police investigator) 12-13,23,26,76,80
Simpson, Harvey, 53-55,58,94,96
Simpson, O.J., 9,32
Singer, Cathy (Producer, NBC Dateline), 106,109
Smith, Margarita Lucille,18,43,61
sodomy, sodomized, 55,58-59,61,
Spolin, Attorney Aaron, 164-165
Starr, Linda (Innocence Project Santa Clara, CA), 82
statistical group (DNA), 49
-"questionable," 81
Stephens, Linda, 92
suggestive eyewitness, 146
"Super Lawyer"(Wendy Lascher), 105-108

support letters (re Joe's release) 92
suspect (see rape suspects, other)
Swanigan, Fred, (Parole denial for claiming innocence, vacated), 98
Szabo, Richard, 91
Taleia J., 143-144-,146,154
Tarborch RN, Sharon (Margarita Bassin rape kit), 55
"Three Strikes Law," 57
Tilley,William D, police officer, 20
Tinoco, Ollie Rayshawn, 64
Tomlinson, Frank, 53-56,91-92,97, 129,136
Tomaz, Rico Goldie,142-145,148-150,157,159
Tracy Prison (Deuel Vocational Institution), 10
Transition Clinic Network, 92,135
Trapp, Kara Elizabeth, 31
Trump, President Donald J., 112, 115,117,137-1378,147-8,151
Umhofer, Judge Donald G., 37
UnCommon Law, 163-164
unreasonable doubt, 5,43,50,55, 59-60,63-64,80,147
Watson, Charles "Tex," 71
Willis, Roger D., Pastor, 93
Wilson, Governor Pete, 45,47,57, 59-60,63,70
Wittmeyer, Cynthia (Cyndi), 12, 23-25,27,47-48,145
Wittmeyer, Travis, 12-13,17,23-25 57,60,145-146,159
Wittmeyer, Tyra Dawn, 12-13,17-18,23-24,35,41,48,57,59-60,74,96,144-45,147,151,159
Wittmeyer, William "Bill," 25
"Writ of Mandate," 87
Zuchelli, Officer Patrick L., 11,21

*"That ye be not slothful, but follow of them who, through **faith and patience** inherit the promises."*
-Hebrews 6:12, The Bible

Joe Garcia, 1989-2022, now age 74, half of his life stolen, confined to a wheelchair due to "long haul" COVID-19 side effects including a heart attack

CONTACT JOE

Joe welcomes *supportive* letters and cards. You can contact him directly. Media must contact the facility's administration for in-person interview or a phone interview can be arranged.

JOSEPH BELARDE GARCIA - #H-01695
CALIFORNIA HEALTH CARE FACILITY – D3B, 128
PO BOX 213040
STOCKTON, CA 95213

THE WISDOM OF MY PRISON
by Joseph Belarde Garcia, 2010

Prison is my brother which contains my lonely heart.
It maintains my soul, cold as its walls.
The chains, which at times I must wear
are my jewelry, like the scars on my hands.

The high cement walls are like blankets
protectively surrounding me through the night.
And they are the first thing I see when I awake,
along with iron and steel,
as impenetrable as my emotions and feelings
that I am not allowed to honestly express.
To do so would be viewed by those around me
as a sign of weakness.

Prison is my teacher of many of life's lessons,
including the price one has to pay for not being free.
An obedient student, I have been taught to be strong.
Despite the cacophony of noise all around me,
my solitude helps me maintain my sense of
identity and sanity,
as I remind myself not to cry
lest I begin to slowly die.

For tears are useless in this place,
a luxury which my soul may one day taste.
Prison has, through all these years,
played the roles of my father and mother,
but I call prison my teacher and brother.

When I am hungry, prison feeds me.
When I act out, prison punishes me.
When I am ill, prison eventually provides medicine.
Yet my heart remains injured because of this injustice.

180

ABOUT THE AUTHOR

LORI CARANGELO was born and raised in Connecticut and is retired from administrative positions in Santa Barbara and Palm Desert, California, where she now writes true crime stories. For 20 years, her national network of volunteers, Americans For Open Records (AmFOR), helped thousands of separated families to reconnect without fee, including adoptees, some of whom were behind bars. With that experience and research, she served as Data Source to the United Nations *Rights of the Child* Project and the Hague Intercountry Adoption Conference *Sale of Children* Report.

Lori has authored over 600 published articles on family rights and justice issues and 20 unique non-fiction books. Her "ripped from the headlines" true murder stories endeavor to answer the question as to WHY they did it, in part by providing the killer a voice. She has also devoted many years to providing a voice to those who are wrongfully convicted, as in the case of Joe Garcia.

MORE BOOKS by LORI CARANGELO:

SCHOOL SHOOTERS
Why They Did It – and America's War on Guns

ADOPTED KILLERS
430 Adoptees Who Killed –How and Why They Did It

SERIAL KILLERS ON THE INTERSTATE
200 Highway Killers by State

KILLERS ONLINE
100 True Stories

KONDRO - *The "Uncle Joe" Killer*

JAMES MUNRO - *And the Freeway Killers*

RAGE! - *How an Adoption Ignited a Fire*

BLOOD RELATIVES
A True Story of Family Secrets and Murders

ESPOSITO – *The First Mafioso*

THE ULTIMATE SEARCH BOOK- U.S. & World Editions
Adoption, Genealogy & Other Search Secrets

CHOSEN CHILDREN 2021
*Children As Commodities in America's
Failed Foster Care, Adoption and Immigration Systems*

THE ADOPTION & DONOR CONCEPTION FACTBOOK
*The Only Comprehensive Source for U.S. and Global Data o the Invisible Families
of Adoption and Donor Conception*

THE 8 BALL CAFÉ
Adoption, Addiction and Redemption

ADDENDUM

JOE'S 2025 PAROLE HEARING - "EYEWITNESS" BOOK IS TO BE "INVESTIGATED"

Data from 2024 suggests a parole denial rate of approximately 69% (derived from a 31% grant rate). For the first 5 months of 2025 (up to May 31, 2025), California's Board of Parole Hearings reported 8,250 denials and 3,739 grants of parole, resulting in a denial rate of around 68.7% for those hearings.

On August 12, 2025, a parole suitability hearing was held with regard to Joe Garcia, age 77, now confined to a wheelchair, unable to walk as result of strokes, heart attacks, blind in one eye, hearing problems, taking pain medications and diagnosed with Dementia, after being wrongfully incarcerated 36 years based on alleged DNA "matching" evidence in 1989 that would exonerate him if retested under today's DNA testing techniques and standards -- DNA evidence that the District Attorney's office claims they could not find when I filed a request for retesting with the Court. Nor did I get a response as to who was the last person on a sign in sheet who removed Joe's evidence box. The 2025 hearing was attended by his 1991 prosecutors, including now-retired Judge Teresa Estrada-Mullaney and retired District Attorney's Investigator, James William "Bill" Miller who read victim statements. Christine Veronica Morse Fitch, a bankruptcy attorney, was appointed to represent Joe.

In order for readers to understand how both Joe Garcia and the alleged rape victims had been, and continue to be, manipulated, and how feeding him leading questions resulted in repeated denials of parole, I have included the 100 page transcript of his August 12, 2025 parole suitability hearing as Addendum to his story for readers to compare the 2025 statements of Joe's accusers and Joe himself, to the actual 1989-1991 police reports and trial transcript pages cited and photocopied in this book, particularly statements by the alleged victims, then and now.

For example, Tyra Dawn Wittemeyer, on pages 23-27, is documented in police report pages and trial transcript page numbers cited as identifying her assailant as being "White, age 17-20"...and *"It wasn't Joe"- "It was Steve*

Bolt,"including in the photocopied police report on page 27 – yet no written report of that prime suspect, Steve Bolt, was made.

On page 28, Jacqueline Denise Brooks' 1989 description on her assailant by page numbers identified in 1989 police reports and 1991 trial transcripts and the 1989 police composite sketch (on the cover of this book and on page 29) that she verified was a "*Negro* with a Southern accent" who attacked her and her ID in a flawed lineup was based on "His eyes *reminded me somehow of the man who raped me,*" never a positive identification of Joe Garcia, and the police sketch was later identified by this author as matching a mugshot of Rico Goldie Tomaz, *a convicted rapist,* about whom no written report was made or found in connection with the 8 alleged rapes and attempted rapes Joe was charged with. And phone records proved Joe was talking by phone with Carrie Dorgan, not at Brooks' location, at the time of the Brooks incident. Page 29 is a photocopy of page 2920 of Joe's trial transcript documenting that *Brooks changed her story* about having had consensual sex with her boyfriend on the day of the alleged "intent to rape." On page 76 of the parole hearing, Brooks stated "*I may not have been raped but I was violated.*" Nor was there a *DNA match* and the control sample of semen for even ethnicity of her assailant was flawed. But the DA convinced the alleged victims there had been a" DNA match" so it "had to be Joe" even though the women could not describe their masked intruders as matching Joe's appearance. And yet Joe was charged with Intent To Rape Jacqueline Brooks, and, 36 years later has convinced himself that he must have raped her, when even Brooks stated she was never "raped" but believed *someone* had "*intent.*" What about Joe's admission after 3 decades that he "raped"Brooks despite that Brooks continues to state she was never raped? Do the alleged victims feel so tortured by having mistakingly convicted an innocent man that it's easier to continue to support the lies that are now mixed up in Joe's Dementia?

The coverup has now extended to a call for an "investigation" into this book, "Eyewitness" which Joe's prosecutors waved at the presiding Commissioners and a video camera, never citing even one passage in the book nor that they nor the Commissioners had read the book (on page 99 of parole hearing Decision transcript, addressing Joe): "*...ordering investigation into what this book is, what your participation in thus book has been* *in this book..."* and) on alleging (page 100 of Decision): "...so that the results of the investigation will be ***available to the next panel at your next hearing"* – (not at the current hearing when it could exonerate him).* *"And the investigation will be into,* ***what this book is****, what your participation in this book has been, Mr. Garcia, who else has participated in this book. Is this -- are* these your support people that are helping you claim your innocence, and who, if anyone, has reached out to the victims or other people 10 connected with this case in connection with this book and what have they been saying to them, um, because this does 12 raise real issues, uh, real questions around, uh, current dangerousness that are, are necessary to explore. And, it is gravely concerning that the victims would 15 potentially continue to be harassed, traumatized, and 16 harmed in this way so many years after the offense."

Clearly, by suggesting a negative context without specific, defamatory allegations, only by *insinuation*, Joe's prosecutors have added yet another threat of denial of his NEXT parole hearing, in 5 years, if he lives to age 82 in his present condition, for the "crime" of continuing to assert his innocence of the 1989 crimes which he has the legal right to do without penalty. Now they also threaten by insinuation this author who has dared to question all that stinks about the case of the carefully crafted Central Coast Rapist. My having informed Joe's prosecutor, and the alleged victims, of the book's existence and to request their input, as any non-fiction author would want to document all sides, is not "harassment." It's conscientious reporting. Unspecified retaliatory threats without teeth, against a helpless prisoner who is given a Bankruptcy attorney for a lawyer, about a book documenting the problems with Joe Garcia's conviction, tells me they are scared that the truth will spoil their legacy.

Joe Garcia is not dangerous. The truth is dangerous.

Bring it on!
-The Author

PAROLE SUITABILITY HEARING

STATE OF CALIFORNIA

BOARD OF PAROLE HEARINGS

In the matter of the Parole   CDCR Number: **H01695**
Consideration Hearing of:

JOSEPH GARCIA

CALIFORNIA HEALTH CARE FACILITY

STOCKTON, CALIFORNIA

AUGUST 12, 2025

10:45 AM

PANEL PRESENT:
EMILY SHEFFIELD, Presiding Commissioner
MICHAEL METTE, Deputy Commissioner

OTHERS PRESENT:
JOSEPH GARCIA, Incarcerated Person
JESICA CURLEY, Deputy District Attorney
CHRISTINE MORSE, Attorney for Incarcerated Person
JACQUELINE GUY, Victim
JANE DOE, Victim
KELLY TRAUGHBER, Victim Advocate
BILL MILLER, Victim Support
THERESA ESTRADA-MULLANEY, Victim Support
C.P., Victim
UNIDENTIFIED, Correctional Officers

Transcribed by:

PETER NEUBAUER

INDEX

		Page
Proceedings		3
Case Factors		--
Pre-Commitment Factors		21
Post-Commitment Factors		46
Parole Plans		--
Closing Statements		59
Recess		44,70,88
Decision		89
Adjournment		101
Transcript Certification		103

1   **PROCEEDINGS**

2   **DEPUTY COMMISSIONER METTE:** We are on record.

3   **PRESIDING COMMISSIONER SHEFFIELD:** Good morning.

4 Today is August 12, 2025. The time is 10:45 a.m. We are

5 conducting this hearing by video conference. Mr. Garcia,

6 can you see me and hear me?

7   **JOSEPH GARCIA:** I can see everybody with my left eye.

8 I don't see out of my right.

9   **PRESIDING COMMISSIONER SHEFFIELD:** Sir, I just asked

10 you a yes or no question.

11   **JOSEPH GARCIA:** Yes. Yes.

12   **PRESIDING COMMISSIONER SHEFFIELD:** If that changes at

13 any time, please let me know, we'll make the necessary

14 adjustments. This is the --

15   **JOSEPH GARCIA:** Yes, ma'am.

16   **PRESIDING COMMISSIONER SHEFFIELD:** -- first

17 subsequent parole suitability hearing for Joseph Garcia,

18 who is present in the BPH hearing room at California

19 Health Care Facility. Uh, he is with his attorney and all

20 other people are participating remotely. We will identify

21 ourselves for the record. And, uh, Mr. Garcia, you are

22 qualified for elderly parole consideration, so we will

23 give special consideration to those factors today. Uh,

24 the hearing is being audio recorded. So, for the purpose

25 of voice identification, I will go around and identify

1   each person. When I do, please state your full name and

2   spell your last name. Uh, with the exception of we do

3   have a number of people who prefer not to go by their full

4   names on the record. So, just state, um, you know, how

5   you would prefer that we reference you for the record.

6   Um, so, I'll start with myself. I am Emily Sheffield, S-

7   H-E-F-F-I-E-L-D, commissioner for the Board of Parole

8   hearings. Commissioner.

9   **DEPUTY COMMISSIONER METTE:** Thank you. Michael

10 Mette, M-E-T-T-E. I'm a deputy commissioner with Board of

11 Parole Hearings.

12   **PRESIDING COMMISSIONER SHEFFIELD:** And Mr. Garcia,

13 can you please state your full name, spell your last name,

14 and also provide your CDCR number.

15   **JOSEPH GARCIA:** Uh, Joseph Bilare Garcia. And my

16 number is, uh, H-0-1-6-9-5.

17   **PRESIDING COMMISSIONER SHEFFIELD:** Great. And Garcia

18 is G-A-R-C-I-A. Um, and Ms. Morse.

19   **ATTORNEY MORSE:** Good morning. My name is Christine

20 Morse, M-O-R-S-E. I am counsel for Mr. Garcia, appearing

21 in person.

22   **PRESIDING COMMISSIONER SHEFFIELD:** Ms. Curley.

23   **DEPUTY DISTRICT ATTORNEY CURLEY:** Jesica Curley, C-U-

24 R-L-E-Y, San Luis Obispo County Deputy District Attorney.

25   **PRESIDING COMMISSIONER SHEFFIELD:** Thank you. And we

1   do have a number of, uh, victims and supporters today.

2   So, I will go through each of you. When I do, uh, please

3   state again your name as you would prefer to be

4   referenced, as well as whether you're a victim or the

5   capacity in which you will be appearing today. So, I'll

6   start with you, uh, Ms. Guy.

7   **JACQUELINE GUY:** Yes, it's Jacqueline Guy, G-U-Y, and

8   I'm a victim.

9   **PRESIDING COMMISSIONER SHEFFIELD:** Thank you. And we

10   have Jane Doe one.

11   **JANE DOE:** Jane Doe, D-O-E. Jane Doe one, victim.

12   **PRESIDING COMMISSIONER SHEFFIELD:** Thank you. Uh,

13   Ms. Traughber.

14   **KELLY TRAUGHBER:** Kelly Traughber, T-R-A-U-G-H-B-E-R,

15   San Luis Obispo District Attorney's Office, and support

16   person for Jane Doe one.

17   **PRESIDING COMMISSIONER SHEFFIELD:** And Mr. Miller?

18   **BILL MILLER:** I am Bill Miller, M-I-L-L-E-R. I'm a

19   retired district attorney investigator. I'm here to read

20   statements from, uh, two victims.

21   **PRESIDING COMMISSIONER SHEFFIELD:** Thank you. And

22   Judge Estrada-Mullaney.

23   **THERESA ESTRADA-MULLANEY:** I'm Theresa Estrada

24   Mullaney. I was the prosecutor in the inmate's case. I'm

25   a retired judge now, working in the assigned judge

1   program. And I'm speaking for Jane Doe two, reading her

2   statement.

3   **PRESIDING COMMISSIONER SHEFFIELD:** Thank you. And

4   can you, uh, spell your last name for the record too,

5   please?

6   **THERESA ESTRADA-MULLANEY:** E-S-T-R-A-D-A, hyphen, M-

7   U-L-L-A-N-E-Y.

8   **PRESIDING COMMISSIONER SHEFFIELD:** Thank you. And we

9   have C.P.

10   **C.P.:** I'm going by the initial, C.P., and I'm a

11   victim.

12   **PRESIDING COMMISSIONER SHEFFIELD:** Thank you. And,

13   uh, Mr. Garcia, were you able to hear everyone who

14   identified themselves?

15   **JOSEPH GARCIA:** Yes. Yes.

16   **PRESIDING COMMISSIONER SHEFFIELD:** Also present in

17   the room are correctional officers. They may be relieved

18   from time to time throughout the hearing. The proceeding

19   is being recorded as mandated by penal code section 3042B.

20   It will be transcribed as the official record of this

21   hearing. And, commissioner, would you like to take a

22   break to check the recording?

23   **DEPUTY COMMISSIONER METTE:** No. I've been checking

24   the audio quality as we have been going along, and we are

25   coming in clearly.

PRESIDING COMMISSIONER SHEFFIELD: So, Mr. Garcia, we
are not here to reconsider the findings of the trial and
appellate courts, and we are not here to retry your case.
The purpose of today's hearing is to find out who you are
today and whether you would pose an unreasonable risk of
danger to society if released. So, we are going to look
at a number of factors. We'll look at your criminal
history, your institutional behavior, your programming in
prison, your parole plans if you are released, as well as
your testimony that we hear today. Um, after we, the
panel members, have asked you our questions, then the
attorneys will have the chance to ask clarifying
questions. Then they will each give a closing statement
for up to 10 minutes a piece. Uh, then if you would like
to give a closing statement on your own behalf, you may do
so as well. Um, and then we'll have the, uh, victims and
representatives speak last. And to those of you who are
speaking, you may speak for as long as you wish. Uh, the
only requirement is that you just direct your comments to
the panel and not to Mr. Garcia. So, Mr. Garcia, I do
strongly encourage you to be completely honest with us
today. I'm going to swear you in. So, can you please
raise your right hand. Raise your right hand. Do you
solemnly swear or affirm that the testimony you give at
this hearing will be the truth, the whole truth, and

1 nothing but the truth?

2   **JOSEPH GARCIA:** Yes.

3   **PRESIDING COMMISSIONER SHEFFIELD:** Thank you.

4   **JOSEPH GARCIA:** Yes.

5   **PRESIDING COMMISSIONER SHEFFIELD:** You can put, you

6 can put your hand down. You can put your hand down.

7 Thank you. So, Mr. Garcia, I have your birthday as July

8 20, 1948, and that you are 77 years old, is that correct?

9   **JOSEPH GARCIA:** I think I'm 78, but that's okay. I

10 think I'm 77 or 78.

11   **PRESIDING COMMISSIONER SHEFFIELD:** All right. And

12 you were between the ages of 39 and 41 when you committed

13 your crimes. Uh, you've been in prison for 35 years and

14 nine months. That sound about right to you?

15   **JOSEPH GARCIA:** How many years?

16   **PRESIDING COMMISSIONER SHEFFIELD:** 35 years and nine

17 months.

18   **JOSEPH GARCIA:** I think so. I think that's right.

19   **PRESIDING COMMISSIONER SHEFFIELD:** All right. So,

20 before proceeding further, we will conduct a review under

21 the Americans with Disabilities Act. I did review the

22 1073 from July 10, 2025. Um, and it looks like you

23 completed your GED a while ago. Is that right?

24   **JOSEPH GARCIA:** I, I think it was about, uh, 10 or 12

25 years ago. Oh, no, wait a minute, I'm -- that's my 12.9,

```
 1   right?  What's it --
 2        PRESIDING COMMISSIONER SHEFFIELD:  Uh, that's --
 3        ATTORNEY MORSE:  He's mixing up his TABE.
 4        PRESIDING COMMISSIONER SHEFFIELD:  That's your
 5   reading level, we have is a 12.9.  Is that accurate?
 6        ATTORNEY MORSE:  Uh, she asked you about your GED.
 7        JOSEPH GARCIA:  Oh, yeah.  Yeah, you're right.
 8   You're right.
 9        PRESIDING COMMISSIONER SHEFFIELD:  Okay.
10        JOSEPH GARCIA:  That's right.
11        ATTORNEY MORSE:  And yeah, the 12.9 is what is
12   listed, although I think it's not accurate anymore.
13        PRESIDING COMMISSIONER SHEFFIELD:  All right.  Um,
14   so, according to the 1073 you're in EOP right now, so you
15   have your attorney there as an accommodation.  Um, it also
16   says that you use a wheelchair.  Are you sitting in a
17   wheelchair right now?
18        JOSEPH GARCIA:  For about three or four years, yeah.
19        PRESIDING COMMISSIONER SHEFFIELD:  Okay.
20        JOSEPH GARCIA:  A permanent wheelchair.
21        PRESIDING COMMISSIONER SHEFFIELD:  And then you have
22   a disability vest on, I see that you're wearing.  Um, says
23   that you use --
24        JOSEPH GARCIA:  I, I have three vests.
25        PRESIDING COMMISSIONER SHEFFIELD:  Sir, please don't
```

1 | interrupt me.

2 | **JOSEPH GARCIA:** Oh, I'm sorry. I'm sorry.

3 | **PRESIDING COMMISSIONER SHEFFIELD:** Um, it says that

4 | you wear a helmet. So, do you have that with you?

5 | **JOSEPH GARCIA:** No, they left it in the room. They

6 | told me I didn't need it, as long as I didn't stand up.

7 | **ATTORNEY MORSE:** If he is in the chair, he doesn't

8 | need the helmet, although he's always in the chair now, so

9 | I don't know why he has a helmet.

10 | **PRESIDING COMMISSIONER SHEFFIELD:** Okay. Uh, back

11 | brace. Are you wearing that today?

12 | **JOSEPH GARCIA:** No.

13 | **PRESIDING COMMISSIONER SHEFFIELD:** No. Do you need

14 | that to sit comfortably?

15 | **JOSEPH GARCIA:** I need it, but they rushed me out of

16 | the room. They said I got to go to a board or something,

17 | a hearing board or something like that.

18 | **PRESIDING COMMISSIONER SHEFFIELD:** All right. So, do

19 | you know where you are right now?

20 | **JOSEPH GARCIA:** Uh, yeah, I'm in, uh, the visiting

21 | room. The old visiting room.

22 | **PRESIDING COMMISSIONER SHEFFIELD:** Do you know who

23 | you're speaking to right now? Do you know what my job is?

24 | **JOSEPH GARCIA:** Yeah. You, you're, uh, the board

25 | member, a commissioner or something like that. Yeah, the

1 commissioner.

2 **PRESIDING COMMISSIONER SHEFFIELD:** Okay. That's

3 right. So, you understand you're at a board hearing right

4 now?

5 **JOSEPH GARCIA:** Yeah. Yes.

6 **PRESIDING COMMISSIONER SHEFFIELD:** All right. Um,

7 so, you said you -- do you use it to sit -- if, if you're

8 feeling uncomfortable during this hearing, physically, if

9 you need to take a break, uh, let us know. All right.

10 Uh, we don't want the pain to be too distracting for you.

11 Okay.

12 **JOSEPH GARCIA:** Thank you so much.

13 **PRESIDING COMMISSIONER SHEFFIELD:** So, just speak up.

14 **JOSEPH GARCIA:** Thank you.

15 **PRESIDING COMMISSIONER SHEFFIELD:** Um, you also have

16 compression stockings, uh, knee braces, orthotics. Are

17 you wearing all of those?

18 **JOSEPH GARCIA:** I got the stockings on, yes. And my

19 hearing aid.

20 **PRESIDING COMMISSIONER SHEFFIELD:** All right. You

21 have your hearing aids, um, and those work all right for

22 you?

23 **JOSEPH GARCIA:** Yes.

24 **PRESIDING COMMISSIONER SHEFFIELD:** Okay.

25 **JOSEPH GARCIA:** Yes.

1   **PRESIDING COMMISSIONER SHEFFIELD:** And what about

2 glasses? Do you have your glasses with you?

3   **JOSEPH GARCIA:** No, I, I don't -- glasses don't work

4 for me. I see out on my left eye blurry, but my right eye

5 is gone. They operate on them for five times.

6   **PRESIDING COMMISSIONER SHEFFIELD:** So, the answer to

7 that question is no. Is that right?

8   **JOSEPH GARCIA:** Yeah, no glasses.

9   **PRESIDING COMMISSIONER SHEFFIELD:** Do not have

10 glasses, okay.

11   **JOSEPH GARCIA:** No.

12   **PRESIDING COMMISSIONER SHEFFIELD:** Do you have a

13 magnifier with you?

14   **JOSEPH GARCIA:** No. I do have one on my bed though.

15   **PRESIDING COMMISSIONER SHEFFIELD:** All right. Um, if

16 you do have any -- there should, um, be a, a magnifying

17 plate there for you if you need it. If you are having

18 issues with sight, again, let us know. All right. We

19 want to make sure that you're able to communicate properly

20 with us --

21   **JOSEPH GARCIA:** Thank you.

22   **PRESIDING COMMISSIONER SHEFFIELD:** -- and understand

23 what we're talking about, okay?

24   **JOSEPH GARCIA:** Yes. Thank you.

25   **PRESIDING COMMISSIONER SHEFFIELD:** All right. And

1   if, um, again, if you do ever want to take a break, let us

2   know for any reason. Um, are you taking any medications

3   that might affect your ability to understand or answer

4   questions to?

5   **JOSEPH GARCIA:** Uh, I just took 16 pills about an

6   hour ago, but they help me. They help me.

7   **PRESIDING COMMISSIONER SHEFFIELD:** Do they --

8   **JOSEPH GARCIA:** For dementia.

9   **PRESIDING COMMISSIONER SHEFFIELD:** They're for

10 dementia?

11   **JOSEPH GARCIA:** Yeah. And other pills for other

12 things.

13   **PRESIDING COMMISSIONER SHEFFIELD:** All right. Do

14 they make it more difficult for you to understand what

15 people are saying to you or to respond to people?

16   **JOSEPH GARCIA:** I think they're helping me. I've

17 been taking them for years, so I think they're helping me.

18   **PRESIDING COMMISSIONER SHEFFIELD:** All right. Great.

19 All right. Um, Ms. Morse, anything further for

20 accommodations?

21   **ATTORNEY MORSE:** No, I'll just say that, um, this is

22 par for the course. I've actually met with him five times

23 and spoken at length with one of his support members to --

24 because I was worried about some of his cognitive decline.

25 But what you're getting is, is who he normally is. So, I

think we're ready to go forward.

PRESIDING COMMISSIONER SHEFFIELD: Okay. Thank you.
Uh, then we will proceed with the hearing. And so, any
additional documents, preliminary objections or motions?

ATTORNEY MORSE: Um, I just have a few things to say.
First of all, yes, on the documents. They should have
been sent. They were just scanned about 20 m -- 25
minutes ago.

JOSEPH GARCIA: It went to my counselor.

ATTORNEY MORSE: Um, yeah, well, no, the -- but we
gave them to the officer and he did scan them in, so that
that email should be coming. There are additional letters
and things. Um, and then, um, I wanted to say that, um,
Mr. Garcia, as you've seen in the CRA, has, um, admitted
guilt to one of his crimes. And then there was a, a
former one that he admitted last time, and he will be
speaking to those today, and I'll let him do that. But
the others, he's continuing to maintain innocence and
therefore he's not testifying to those. Um, and then I
also wanted to say that I, I was hoping the panel would
not hold against him, that he did not stipulate today,
because I, I just have -- we've received training on this,
we panel attorneys, that if we don't feel that somebody
thoroughly understands the concept of something that we
shouldn't push it. And I, I did meet with him for an hour

1 and 20 minutes, my first meeting, discussed waiver. I

2 thought he wanted it. The next time I followed up with

3 him because I followed up after my waivers. He didn't

4 know what I was talking about, and I had to rescind it.

5 So, I got nervous about -- I did talk with him about the

6 possibility of stipulating, but I got nervous that he, he

7 was just going to, the next time I saw him say, why aren't

8 we going to the hearing? So, it is because I did not push

9 that issue, and not because I feel he understands

10 stipulation and said no. So, I just wanted that kind of

11 clear. And then in terms of the, um, recent RVRs, there

12 was -- he's accused of behavior, I think just last month

13 in July. And that one, as far as I understand, has not

14 been adjudicated yet. And, and he's adamant that he

15 didn't say what is being alleged. And he says, there's an

16 officer that says, yeah, I, I didn't hear you say that.

17   **JOSEPH GARCIA:** It's on camera.

18   **ATTORNEY MORSE:** So, I -- and, and it was on camera.

19 So, I am thinking that the fair thing to do is to not

20 discuss the one that has not -- has yet to be heard.

21 However, there is one from June that he is prepared to

22 talk about and take responsibility for and explain. And I

23 think that's all I have to say, <laugh>. Thank you.

24   **PRESIDING COMMISSIONER SHEFFIELD:** All right. Okay.

25 Thank you. Let me just address those, um, briefly. So,

1   with respect to maintain, you know, not wanting to speak

2   about the crimes, I think there -- you said there's eight

3   of them that you are not willing to speak about because

4   you're maintaining your innocence. Um, Mr. Garcia, I want

5   you to understand what that means. What that means is

6   that we just have the paper record in front of us to

7   consider. So, we will be looking at that when we are

8   assessing, um, you know, your understanding of the crime

9   and your, you know, whether or not that you take

10   responsibility for things. We -- we're just going to be

11   reading what we have in front of us, all right?

12   **JOSEPH GARCIA:** Yes.

13   **PRESIDING COMMISSIONER SHEFFIELD:** Okay. Um, with

14   the, you know, with respect to the stipulation, our

15   assessment of current dangerousness has nothing to do with

16   whether or not he stipulates. So, um, you know, that's

17   neither here nor there for us. Uh, the RVR we will be

18   asking about -- I'm not sure if I understood you. We, we

19   will be asking about the behavior in the RVR, unless

20   you're saying that he's refusing to speak to it, is -- I

21   wasn't clear.

22   **ATTORNEY MORSE:** He's not refusing, but it hasn't

23   been adjudicated yet. In other words, the, um, they

24   haven't played back the camera to here, if he did say the

25   things being alleged.

1   **PRESIDING COMMISSIONER SHEFFIELD:** Right, we -- okay,

2 we understand that. So, we'll give it the appropriate

3 way, uh, given the fact that --

4   **ATTORNEY MORSE:** Thank you.

5   **PRESIDING COMMISSIONER SHEFFIELD:** -- it has not been

6 adjudicated, but we will speak to it. Um, and then, um,

7 okay. And then I understand you're going to speak to the

8 other RVR as well from June. So, and we will look out for

9 the documents that you sent. So, uh, that being said,

10 we'll go ahead with the hearing then. Um, Mr. Garcia, the

11 panel has reviewed your central file and your

12 Comprehensive Risk Assessment. You are encouraged to

13 correct or clarify the record as we go through the

14 hearing. The panel has also reviewed the confidential

15 portion of your file, and we will let you know if we are

16 going to rely on that for our decision today. We are not

17 going to be spending time going over all the documents in

18 our record. Instead, we will focus our discussion on the

19 issues the panel has determined to be particularly

20 relevant to determining who you are today and whether your

21 personal change has sufficiently mitigated your risk to

22 the public. So, that means we might not have questions

23 about every factor in our guidelines, but we are going to

24 give you the chance to comment and clarify your record,

25 uh, as we go through the hearing. So, I will note a

1 couple things for you before we begin. Uh, the panel

2 members do use multiple computer screens. Uh, we have

3 documents that we're looking at when we're talking to you,

4 so don't be concerned if we look away. Sometimes it just

5 means we're looking at our documents in front of us. Um,

6 also, there may be times, and I think I've already done

7 this, but when you're answering a question and we stop you

8 or we interrupt you, please understand we don't mean any

9 disrespect when we do that. We are just really trying to

10 focus you, so that we can get the information we need to,

11 uh, make our decision today. So, I want to first ask you

12 about your CRA. You have a Comprehensive Risk Assessment.

13 Um, I understand from your attorney that potentially your

14 capacity to understand is, is somewhat limited. Um, but

15 this was a recent CRA from June 27, 2025. You were rated

16 a high risk for violence. Have you had the opportunity to

17 look at that document?

18   **JOSEPH GARCIA:** Oh, the, the, the evaluation report?

19 The, the --

20   **PRESIDING COMMISSIONER SHEFFIELD:** Correct.

21   **JOSEPH GARCIA:** -- lady that came to -- yes.

22   **PRESIDING COMMISSIONER SHEFFIELD:** Okay.

23   **JOSEPH GARCIA:** It was read to me like five times

24 already.

25   **PRESIDING COMMISSIONER SHEFFIELD:** All right.

1   **JOSEPH GARCIA:** It was read to --

2   **PRESIDING COMMISSIONER SHEFFIELD:** So, you've been

3 able -- you've been able to speak about it with your

4 attorney?

5   **JOSEPH GARCIA:** Yes.

6   **PRESIDING COMMISSIONER SHEFFIELD:** Okay. Is there

7 anything in there that you do not agree with or that you

8 would like to clarify for us right now?

9   **JOSEPH GARCIA:** Uh, no. I, I agree with the whole

10 thing.

11   **PRESIDING COMMISSIONER SHEFFIELD:** All right. So, I

12 mean, I will say a high risk rating in your late 70s is

13 pretty unusual. Uh, do you have any understanding as to

14 why the clinician is so concerned about you? Uh, what

15 risk factors they're really worried about?

16   **JOSEPH GARCIA:** Well, I think, I'm not sure, but I

17 think it's because I was more honest than I was years ago.

18 And I told her that, uh, back then I was, uh, I had

19 problems with my own control and I was very impulsive.

20 And, uh, back then, not now, but back then, I sort of --

21 because of what happened to me with my mother and me when

22 I was a kid, I was, uh, I began to look at women as a

23 young child, as nothing but sexual objects. But that

24 changed year later on when I got married, I was married

25 for 30, for 34 years, and then I got divorced.

1   **PRESIDING COMMISSIONER SHEFFIELD:** All right. So,

2 you're saying you think the clinician was, found you to be

3 a high risk because you were honest with them?

4   **JOSEPH GARCIA:** I don't think it was because of

5 honest, because she, uh, she was a very nice lady. And sh

6 -- uh, well, just to be quite honest, I, I really don't

7 know why I got a high risk. Uh, I'm not a perfect human

8 being, but I know I've, I've changed over the years and,

9 uh, I'm sorry for -- I'm just sorry for being that person

10 back then, you know, because I was a horrible person back

11 then. But, uh, I, I can't look into her mind, and, but

12 she was very nice to me. She helped me understand a lot

13 of things.

14   **PRESIDING COMMISSIONER SHEFFIELD:** Okay.

15   **JOSEPH GARCIA:** But I think it's --

16   **PRESIDING COMMISSIONER SHEFFIELD:** That's fine. I --

17 you don't have to look into her mind. She wrote it all

18 out for you. So --

19   **JOSEPH GARCIA:** Yeah.

20   **PRESIDING COMMISSIONER SHEFFIELD:** -- um, the risk

21 factors are listed there. You do have a number of them, a

22 number of things she was concerned about. Um, as, as your

23 attorney mentioned earlier, I mean, you do have many, many

24 sex crimes on your record. Um, you were found guilty of I

25 think 10 very similar, um, sex crimes, very violent, just

1 really awful crimes or, or attempted sex crimes, um, with

2 various assaults of women. And I understand you're not

3 speaking to eight of those, and that's because you are

4 maintaining your innocence on those, is that right?

5 **JOSEPH GARCIA:** Uh, the ones that were just the

6 knocking on the door and the guy tried to go and then he

7 took off, those are the ones I didn't do. So, I'm not

8 talking those -- I've been advised not to talk about

9 those. But I did do the rape in Morro Bay and the rape in

10 1979 Simi Valley, I did do that. The other ones were just

11 knocking on doors, attempted rape or something like that.

12 **PRESIDING COMMISSIONER SHEFFIELD:** All right. Um, do

13 you -- I'm not asking you about the facts of the crimes

14 here. Do you have any thoughts as to why you would've

15 gotten wrongly accused and convicted of eight separate,

16 um, offenses?

17 **JOSEPH GARCIA:** I can -- I can only tell you that --

18 first of all, I'm sorry that whole trial took place, but,

19 uh, my lawyers, I had two ex-judges out of Santa Maria,

20 Don, uh, Goodmans. And he told me, he kept telling me it

21 was a six month trial. He tell me they're trying to clean

22 up a bunch of sexual crimes in this, in the city here.

23 So, don't be, uh, don't be -- don't feel odd if they throw

24 them on you. And I said, yeah, but, uh, I -- back then I

25 said I wasn't guilty, but I was guilty of, of something,

1 and I played it off. And I, I went through the trial and

2 the next thing I know, they started putting these cases, I

3 mean, where people were knocking on people's doors and

4 then putting a mask on. And before they could get in the

5 house, the girls pushed them out. And I think there was

6 four or five of those. And then there was also one of my

7 friend, uh, a young lady named, uh, uh, she was -- she got

8 molested by her brother's brother, uh, John, uh,

9 Whitmeyer. Whitmeyer, I think it was Whitmeyer.

10 **PRESIDING COMMISSIONER SHEFFIELD:** Okay.

11 **JOSEPH GARCIA:** Because her mother was working with

12 us. Cindy was working with us.

13 **PRESIDING COMMISSIONER SHEFFIELD:** Thank you. My

14 question was, was specific, and then I think you sort of

15 answered it. Why do you think that you have been falsely

16 accused of so many, uh, sex crimes or attempted sex crimes

17 and, and convicted of them. And you said that you think

18 they, the office was just trying to clean up unsolved sex

19 crimes and unsolved assaults and just put them on you?

20 **JOSEPH GARCIA:** No, I don't, I don't think that, uh,

21 my lawyers told me that the <crosstalk> --

22 **PRESIDING COMMISSIONER SHEFFIELD:** Okay, well, what

23 do you think?

24 **JOSEPH GARCIA:** I really can't speak on that. I, I

25 don't know why they would do that, but, uh, it was, uh, it

1 was a horror. It was just a horror. It was like a

2 nightmare. But I went through it and, uh, I should

3 admitted guilt to certain things that I didn't back then

4 because, uh --

5 **PRESIDING COMMISSIONER SHEFFIELD:** All right. What,

6 what was a nightmare? You said it was a nightmare. Do

7 you mean the trial?

8 **JOSEPH GARCIA:** Well, my wife had to testify for five

9 days on the stand, and she was with me on the rape out of

10 being out of town with the Whitmeyer. We just came back

11 from Salinas and she had to testify, and she broke down on

12 the stand all the time.

13 **PRESIDING COMMISSIONER SHEFFIELD:** All right. Uh --

14 **JOSEPH GARCIA:** She's a vice principal.

15 **PRESIDING COMMISSIONER SHEFFIELD:** -- how do you

16 think the victims felt during that trial?

17 **JOSEPH GARCIA:** They felt horrible. They felt they

18 were traumatized, and I was responsible for some of that.

19 And, and all I can do is live a different life now for

20 that which I have been doing because I got no violence

21 whatsoever in prison all these years.

22 **PRESIDING COMMISSIONER SHEFFIELD:** Okay. What --

23 you've said -- you have admitted to, to two of these

24 rapes, right?

25 **JOSEPH GARCIA:** Yes.

1   **PRESIDING COMMISSIONER SHEFFIELD:** Okay, <crosstalk>

2 --

3   **JOSEPH GARCIA:** The one in 1979 -- 1979 -- yeah, the

4 one in 1979. It wasn't 1989, it was 1979. But in the

5 trial, the DNA proved there was no match. So, that helped

6 me.

7   **PRESIDING COMMISSIONER SHEFFIELD:** I'm not interested

8 in that.

9   **JOSEPH GARCIA:** Okay.

10   **PRESIDING COMMISSIONER SHEFFIELD:** What is your

11 understanding today, looking back, why do you think you

12 made the decision on those two days to go out and commit

13 these horrible rapes, these horrible violent sex crimes?

14   **JOSEPH GARCIA:** Can I speak on that?

15   **PRESIDING COMMISSIONER SHEFFIELD:** Yes, <crosstalk> -

16 -

17   **ATTORNEY MORSE:** Yes, she's asking you to speak.

18   **JOSEPH GARCIA:** Oh, do you want me to speak on the

19 1979 or the 1989?

20   **PRESIDING COMMISSIONER SHEFFIELD:** Um --

21   **JOSEPH GARCIA:** Which one should I speak?

22   **PRESIDING COMMISSIONER SHEFFIELD:** -- you can speak

23 to --

24   **ATTORNEY MORSE:** Whichever one.

25   **PRESIDING COMMISSIONER SHEFFIELD:** -- both of them.

1   **JOSEPH GARCIA:** Okay. The one on the -- the one on

2   in the 1989, uh, her name, she was out of Morro Bay. I

3   met her at a post office and we started talking over --

4   looking at our -- looking at her mail. I didn't have no

5   mail. I was just there to meet somebody. And, uh, and

6   the discussion led to, uh, uh, me asking her if she was

7   willing to, uh, go around to -- I was a -- I was an

8   account executive, I was a photographer for my company,

9   Homes and Mans, uh -- Homes and Man --

10   **PRESIDING COMMISSIONER SHEFFIELD:** Okay. I don't

11   need -- I don't -- I don't need these specific details. I

12   --

13   **JOSEPH GARCIA:** Oh, okay.

14   **PRESIDING COMMISSIONER SHEFFIELD:** -- you, you have

15   been incarcerated for a very long time for these crimes,

16   right?

17   **JOSEPH GARCIA:** Yes.

18   **PRESIDING COMMISSIONER SHEFFIELD:** So, you've had a

19   long time to think about why, why did I do these things,

20   right?

21   **JOSEPH GARCIA:** I think it was because I started

22   drinking that day, and I was driving around drinking a

23   little bit. I started drinking because my boss, I started

24   drinking with him a little bit. And when I got -- when I

25   got drunk, I just forgot about all my, uh, inhibitions or

1 what do you call it?

2 **PRESIDING COMMISSIONER SHEFFIELD:** All right. Let's

3 just focus here. So, you think alcohol played a part in

4 that? Is there anything else? Because a lot of people

5 <crosstalk> --

6 **JOSEPH GARCIA:** But I don't want --

7 **PRESIDING COMMISSIONER SHEFFIELD:** -- and they're

8 not, and they're not --

9 **JOSEPH GARCIA:** Yeah, I don't want to --

10 **PRESIDING COMMISSIONER SHEFFIELD:** Sir, please don't

11 interrupt. We, we have to keep a clean transcript,

12 otherwise, it's just going to say crosstalk, crosstalk.

13 And no one's going to know what anybody said today.

14 **JOSEPH GARCIA:** Yes.

15 **PRESIDING COMMISSIONER SHEFFIELD:** Okay?

16 **JOSEPH GARCIA:** Yes. Yes.

17 **PRESIDING COMMISSIONER SHEFFIELD:** All right.

18 **JOSEPH GARCIA:** First, first of all, I don't want to

19 blame the alcohol, but I think it was my def -- defects I

20 had back then. I was somewhat callous. I was mean, and I

21 was selfish. The world revolved around me back then, and

22 I think I took advantage of her because, uh, she was

23 vulnerable and susceptible to my words. I didn't have no

24 weapon or nothing, but I was still in her house. I still

25 went home with her, and I took advantage of the situation.

1　But I don't want to blame the alcohol, even though I'm

2　Native American, they say that alcohol messes us up.　I

3　don't want to blame that.

4　　　　**PRESIDING COMMISSIONER SHEFFIELD:**　Okay.　Why do you

5　think that all your victims are women?

6　　　　**JOSEPH GARCIA:**　Can you repeat that, please?

7　　　　**PRESIDING COMMISSIONER SHEFFIELD:**　Sure.　Why do you

8　think that your victims are women?　Do you understand the

9　question?

10　　　　**JOSEPH GARCIA:**　Uh, why do I think that the women are

11　victims?

12　　　　**PRESIDING COMMISSIONER SHEFFIELD:**　That, that you

13　have chosen as your victims, women.　When you, you said

14　you're a callous person, you're going out there, you're

15　hurting people.　The people you are choosing to hurt are

16　women, specifically, right?　So, why do you think women,

17　specifically you have targeted as victims?

18　　　　**JOSEPH GARCIA:**　Well, it, it was just one woman, the

19　one in Morro Bay.　I didn't, I didn't go around hurting

20　any other women.　But, uh, I think also, uh, it was my

21　thoughts, my thought patterns, my -- uh, my thought

22　patterns about women.　When I drink, I started seeing them

23　as sexual objects instead of seeing them as a person with

24　a name and with their own identity.

25　　　　**PRESIDING COMMISSIONER SHEFFIELD:**　And why do you

1 think that is?

2 **JOSEPH GARCIA:** Because when I was a kid, my mother

3 was a prostitute, used to stick me in the, in the closet

4 every time she had sex. And I would listen to the sex

5 going on. But after a while, I started seeing my mother

6 and other women just as a sex object. But I think I

7 overcame that when I got married to my wife, Judith Emily

8 Garcia.

9 **PRESIDING COMMISSIONER SHEFFIELD:** Okay.

10 **JOSEPH GARCIA:** I thought I overcame it.

11 **PRESIDING COMMISSIONER SHEFFIELD:** Well, it's one

12 thing to see women as a sex object, and it's one another

13 thing to, you know, violently sexually assault them.

14 Right? Those are two pretty <crosstalk> --

15 **JOSEPH GARCIA:** That is very true. That is very

16 true.

17 **PRESIDING COMMISSIONER SHEFFIELD:** Okay. So, so, why

18 do you think the violence, the sexual violence?

19 **JOSEPH GARCIA:** Well, first of all, I think it's

20 violent because there's no consent and it's an invasion of

21 the person's privacy.

22 **PRESIDING COMMISSIONER SHEFFIELD:** Why do you think

23 you were -- you chose to be sexually violent with women?

24 **JOSEPH GARCIA:** Well, as I, as I said, I think I was

25 self-centered. The world revolved around me, and when I

1 would drink, I become selfish. And I became somewhat

2 mean. And even though I didn't use a weapon on the girl

3 in Morro Bay, it was still, it was still, uh, uh,

4 offensive, it was an invasion of her. I should have never

5 did it. And it was horrible that it happened. And I wish

6 I could change the whole thing, but I can't. All I can do

7 is become a better person. That's why I'm in prison.

8   **PRESIDING COMMISSIONER SHEFFIELD:** Do you feel like

9 you should be in prison if you didn't commit most of these

10 crimes?

11   **JOSEPH GARCIA:** Yes. Yes.

12   **PRESIDING COMMISSIONER SHEFFIELD:** Why is that?

13   **JOSEPH GARCIA:** Because it was horrible. I had, I

14 had no, I had no right to do what I did. And, uh, I'm

15 paying for it, but since I've been in here, I haven't had

16 no violence, and I've got like a 100 self-help groups, and

17 I'm trying to change. I'm, I'm -- I think I'm a different

18 person.

19   **PRESIDING COMMISSIONER SHEFFIELD:** All right. Have

20 you been following the rules in prison?

21   **JOSEPH GARCIA:** Up until the last year, I'd never

22 gotten a 115, until the last year I started unraveling.

23 And I did get 115s for, for -- they were minor, but I was

24 still guilty. I was still, I was still guilty of not

25 keeping my mouth shut. And --

Dictate Express Transcription

1   **PRESIDING COMMISSIONER SHEFFIELD:** I, I would, I

2 would agree with that. I, I mean, you didn't have a

3 perfectly clean record before, but it did seem like

4 something happened this past year and you've really, you

5 know, gone downhill. So, what's going on with you? Why,

6 why do you think that you've been ha -- because you have

7 so many write-ups, um, for, what they call it, um,

8 disrespect without the potential for violence, right.

9 Just within the past year, you have a number of those.

10 Um, and you have the conspiracy to damage state property,

11 which has not been fully adjudicated. But, um, we can

12 discuss, uh, we do have the pending RVR as well. You have

13 two false reports of criminal offenses from 2024. So,

14 really this past year, year and a half has been pretty bad

15 for you. So, what's been going on?

16   **JOSEPH GARCIA:** Well, I respect my clinicians and my

17 psychologists, which I meet one-on-one for many years now,

18 20 years of mental health. And they tell me, and I

19 believe them, they say, I have dementia, and that's why I

20 forget a lot of stuff. And also, I forget, uh, I lose, I

21 lose control of myself. I become impulsive. And they say

22 it's because you're getting triggered. You're, you're

23 getting triggered. The last year you've been, you've been

24 doing good, but the last year you've been getting

25 triggered by people and you can't be doing that.

1   **PRESIDING COMMISSIONER SHEFFIELD:** But why do you

2 think -- why do you think that is? Why do you think

3 you've been so triggered, uh -- more easily triggered this

4 past year?

5   **JOSEPH GARCIA:** This last year?

6   **PRESIDING COMMISSIONER SHEFFIELD:** Mm-hmm

7 <affirmative>.

8   **JOSEPH GARCIA:** I think it has to do something with

9 my memory, because when I'm talking to the officers or

10 talking to the lieutenant or the sergeant, I sort of, I

11 sort of, uh, lose what they're saying. But then I come

12 back a couple seconds later, I come back and I ask them to

13 repeat what they're saying, and they help me. And I'm

14 taking medication for my dementia. But also, I feel, I

15 feel bad about all of this, you know. I do feel bad

16 because I never got 115, a bunch of, 115s, and just this

17 last year, and I was thinking of coming to board. I knew

18 I got a 10 year denial, and I just -- it's been bothering

19 me a lot, you know, lately.

20   **PRESIDING COMMISSIONER SHEFFIELD:** Yeah. Well, these

21 are not just im -- impulsive, um, you know, moments that

22 can really be accounted for by dementia. I mean, first of

23 all, dementia doesn't make you inherently violent or

24 aggressive. Uh, these RVRs about disobeying or disrespect

25 have been adjudicated. They consider your, your mental

1 state and your mental issues when looking at those. Um,

2 but generally just looking at the facts of them, I mean,

3 this one I'm looking at now, and you're yelling racist

4 slurs at staff, right?

5 **JOSEPH GARCIA:** Oh, you're talking about the one

6 about the nice Indian girl from India, the nurse, and they

7 said that she, she squat down behind the ch -- uh, behind

8 the, uh, cart for a minute to get my medication. There

9 was a big line behind me. And, and, and she said, what

10 did you just say, Garcia? And I said, I -- it was -- came

11 from the back of the line. They yelled out to go back to

12 India and just stick the pills up your, you know, and I

13 didn't say that, I said, the officer's standing right

14 here. And the officer told her, he didn't say that it

15 came from the back, but I feel guilty for it because to

16 have her go through that, because she's a nice nurse and

17 everything, and these guys in the line, they make a bunch

18 of foolish comments, you know? But she said, you sure it

19 wasn't you? And I said, no, it wasn't me, but I'll tell -

20 - I'm going to plead guilty anyway. And I plead guilty.

21 **PRESIDING COMMISSIONER SHEFFIELD:** Why would you

22 plead guilty?

23 **JOSEPH GARCIA:** Because they said, if we plead

24 guilty, we won't take your canteen away and you can use

25 the phone. Otherwise, we can take one or the other. And

1   I said, I just don't want to be involved --

2   **PRESIDING COMMISSIONER SHEFFIELD:** Stop. When we

3 started speaking about this, you said, yeah, I have been

4 impulsive. Yeah, I have been, you know, lashing out at

5 staff. So, I mean, it doesn't sound like that's really

6 something that you disagree with, right?

7   **JOSEPH GARCIA:** Not at all.

8   **PRESIDING COMMISSIONER SHEFFIELD:** Okay.

9   **JOSEPH GARCIA:** But if I did say it, I don't remember

10 saying it, but I don't remember saying it. I never -- I

11 don't talk to nurses like that. There's nothing in my

12 record saying that. I talked to nurses like that, you

13 know.

14   **PRESIDING COMMISSIONER SHEFFIELD:** All right. So,

15 you do have this very recent, um, RVR that is pending.

16 So, it has not been adjudicated. I understand there may

17 be video of this that has not yet been viewed. So, we

18 just have the --

19   **JOSEPH GARCIA:** Uh-huh <affirmative>, yes.

20   **PRESIDING COMMISSIONER SHEFFIELD:** -- <crosstalk>

21 report from July 26, 2025. Um, and it's a DVS staff. So,

22 is this a janitorial staff?

23   **JOSEPH GARCIA:** Oh, the -- oh, you're talking about

24 Mo -- you're talking about Mo, the cleaning girl. Mo, her

25 name's Mo. Her last name, I don't know, starts with an A

1 or something. I don't know her last name.

2   **PRESIDING COMMISSIONER SHEFFIELD:** All right. So,

3 she says while she was cleaning the observation cell, she

4 was approached by you. You mentioned that your magnifying

5 -- you mentioned your magnifying glass, and proceeded to

6 talk about how it could zoom in while pointing his tablet

7 in my direction. This immediately made me feel

8 uncomfortable. And I asked Garcia if he could step to the

9 side. Garcia refused my request and made the following

10 spontaneous statement, quote, oh, did I make you nervous,

11 end quote. And then another, quote, women in the outside

12 world would enjoy a man looking at a woman, end quote.

13 And then it says, these comments made me feel extremely

14 uncomfortable. So, what is your response to that?

15   **JOSEPH GARCIA:** The last one, she's a very nice

16 person. She cleans our dorm out. A whole bunch of them.

17 There are 50 of them. They come every day, two of them,

18 they clean our dorms.

19   **PRESIDING COMMISSIONER SHEFFIELD:** Okay, stop. Let

20 me ask you something more specific. Did you make those

21 comments?

22   **JOSEPH GARCIA:** Not the last two things about women,

23 like being looked at when they're in the movies and all

24 that -- or not in the movies, uh, when they're, uh, on the

25 outside, the outside world. I didn't say that. What I

1 did, I said, I, I showed her my magnifying glass. I held

2 it up. I go, look, they just gave me this about a month

3 ago, and it helped me to read a lot. And she says, I just

4 cleaned your room and, uh, can you go back to your room?

5 You're, you're in my way. And there was two nurses

6 standing next to us, and there was an officer and officer

7 said, Joe, go back to your room because she doesn't want

8 you making her nervous. And, uh, I said, okay. I said,

9 I'll see you, Mo, and I left. And since then, I talked to

10 her two times and she told me, don't worry about that

11 incident. The officer said, that's good that you guys are

12 talking, but do me a favor, don't go to a room when she's

13 cleaning. So, I said, I won't go no more.

14 **PRESIDING COMMISSIONER SHEFFIELD:** All right. Um,

15 are you pleading guilty or not guilty to that one?

16 **JOSEPH GARCIA:** Not guilty. When it comes time to

17 it, I want to plead not guilty because I'm not guilty.

18 She said I was guilty of, of flirtation, was it flirtation

19 or something like that?

20 **PRESIDING COMMISSIONER SHEFFIELD:** Overfamiliarity.

21 **JOSEPH GARCIA:** Flirtation or over -- yeah, and I

22 said I did not flirt with her at all. And I wasn't, I

23 wasn't like trying to -- she's a nice person. She talks

24 to us all the time. So, I don't know what happened, uh,

25 that day, you know.

1   **PRESIDING COMMISSIONER SHEFFIELD**: Okay. You have a

2   couple of false reports of criminal offenses on there.

3   Um, you lied about, um, laying on the floor in urine and

4   blood and being neglected by staff, that -- so you just

5   made up?

6   **JOSEPH GARCIA**: No, that really happened. I, I

7   blacked out, I hit the floor, I peed on myself, and there

8   was blood on my head. I still got the scar here. They

9   took me to Sims, which is the clinic. They cleaned me up

10 and they brought me back. And this friend of mine told

11 me, you should, you should 602 this, because they left you

12 on the floor for like 20 minutes. So, I let him do a

13 grievance on it, and then the grievance came back saying

14 that never happened. And I said, well, I got all the

15 medical reports from the doctor right here that it

16 happened. And they, and they said, well, I'm just telling

17 you, says they, they de -- they denied the allegations.

18 **PRESIDING COMMISSIONER SHEFFIELD**: All right. Um,

19 I'm just going to ask you maybe a couple more questions

20 and then I'm going to turn it over. Um, you have a

21 fiance, is that right?

22 **JOSEPH GARCIA**: Yes. Anita.

23 **PRESIDING COMMISSIONER SHEFFIELD**: Okay. So, I saw a

24 letter from Anita. Um, what does Anita know about your

25 criminal history?

1   **JOSEPH GARCIA:** Uh, she knows about the 1979. Uh,

2   that's when I met her. And Frank, Frank introduced me.

3   Frank's a homicide detective. He introduced me to her,

4   and that's in 1979. And I got drunk and I did what I did,

5   and then I went to Frank, and -- and then I went to Frank,

6   and he said, well, you came to me, we're going to get you

7   out of this, some kind of way we're going to help. You

8   might have to be in trouble.

9   **PRESIDING COMMISSIONER SHEFFIELD:** Stop. I had a

10   specific question. It was about Anita. What does Anita,

11   what does Anita know about your criminal history?

12   **JOSEPH GARCIA:** She knows that I was a, a, a

13   criminal, that I did that.

14   **PRESIDING COMMISSIONER SHEFFIELD:** What crimes --

15   **JOSEPH GARCIA:** And that I got --

16   **PRESIDING COMMISSIONER SHEFFIELD:** -- what crimes

17   does Anita know that you committed?

18   **JOSEPH GARCIA:** Uh, that one in 1979, but before I

19   met her, she knows I did burglaries and I, I was in

20   burglaries and --

21   **ATTORNEY MORSE:** Just a second.

22   **JOSEPH GARCIA:** Mm-hmm <affirmative>.

23   **ATTORNEY MORSE:** Does she know about both rapes?

24   **JOSEPH GARCIA:** Yes. Yes.

25   **PRESIDING COMMISSIONER SHEFFIELD:** All right. In her

1   letter, she only referenced one. Do you know why that

2   might be?

3   **JOSEPH GARCIA:** Well, she was shocked when I told her

4   that I did the one in Morro Bay. She, she goes -- how

5   come you didn't tell me? She started crying. I said, I

6   was scared to tell you. And she says, well, why didn't

7   you tell me? I said, because the girl identified her

8   assailant as black and painted a picture, which was in

9   court, and it was a black man that was five, eight. And,

10   and, uh, talked like a rapper. I don't know why she said

11   that, because I'm the one that did it and must have been

12   shocked -- she must have been in shock or something. But

13   she painted a picture and they put a bulletin, uh, paper.

14   **ATTORNEY MORSE:** Oh, okay, but --

15   **PRESIDING COMMISSIONER SHEFFIELD:** Stop. Why -- so,

16   why did you, why did you lie to Anita initially about

17   that? That you didn't -- why did you say you didn't do

18   the crime?

19   **JOSEPH GARCIA:** Because I was scared I was going to

20   lose her if I told her I raped the girl in Morro Bay.

21   **PRESIDING COMMISSIONER SHEFFIELD:** Okay. And when

22   did you tell her, when did you confess?

23   **JOSEPH GARCIA:** Uh, I confessed during the evaluation

24   because she was on the monitor.

25   **PRESIDING COMMISSIONER SHEFFIELD:** During the most

1 recent evaluation, the, um --

2 **JOSEPH GARCIA:** Yeah.

3 **PRESIDING COMMISSIONER SHEFFIELD:** -- the 2025 CRA

4 evaluation?

5 **JOSEPH GARCIA:** Yes, and I want to hear -- to hear

6 me. I knew it was going to take a chance. It was risky,

7 but I had to tell the truth because I'm a committed

8 Christian now, and I know I've been lying all these years.

9 **PRESIDING COMMISSIONER SHEFFIELD:** So, you, you have

10 a -- you've had a partner, uh, that you've committed to

11 for life, a fiance who you've been lying to for years

12 about your criminal history?

13 **JOSEPH GARCIA:** Yes, but also another reason is

14 because I didn't want her to think that I was guilty of

15 all these other crimes that she's been supporting me. Uh

16 --

17 **PRESIDING COMMISSIONER SHEFFIELD:** Okay, don't --

18 **JOSEPH GARCIA:** Thinking I <crosstalk> --

19 **PRESIDING COMMISSIONER SHEFFIELD:** -- don't, don't

20 you think that's kind of manipulative?

21 **JOSEPH GARCIA:** In a sense, yes.

22 **PRESIDING COMMISSIONER SHEFFIELD:** Yeah. Why is that

23 manipulative? What's manipulative about that?

24 **JOSEPH GARCIA:** Well, one, because I was lying to her

25 all these years, and because I was a -- well, just not

1 telling the truth is manipulative and being manipulating,

2 you know?

3 **PRESIDING COMMISSIONER SHEFFIELD:** Mm-hmm

4 <affirmative>.

5 **JOSEPH GARCIA:** Because I was like trying to control

6 some of her thoughts about me, that I was a good person.

7 Well, she knows I'm a different person now, but back then

8 I was not a good person. And, uh --

9 **PRESIDING COMMISSIONER SHEFFIELD:** Right. Well,

10 that's, that's a pretty significant fact to omit, right,

11 in a relationship?

12 **JOSEPH GARCIA:** Yeah. Yes. Excuse me. Yes.

13 **PRESIDING COMMISSIONER SHEFFIELD:** Mm-hmm

14 <affirmative>. And it sounds like you were lying about

15 that because you didn't want to lose her.

16 **JOSEPH GARCIA:** I, I, I known her since she was 14,

17 and we separated for 45 years.

18 **PRESIDING COMMISSIONER SHEFFIELD:** That's not what I

19 asked. That -- that's not what I --

20 **JOSEPH GARCIA:** Okay. Yes.

21 **PRESIDING COMMISSIONER SHEFFIELD:** You were lying --

22 you were, you were lying to her about something very

23 serious because you did not want to lose her, right?

24 **JOSEPH GARCIA:** Yes. Yes. Yes.

25 **PRESIDING COMMISSIONER SHEFFIELD:** Do you think

1 that's selfish?

2 **JOSEPH GARCIA:** Uh, yes.

3 **PRESIDING COMMISSIONER SHEFFIELD:** Um --

4 **JOSEPH GARCIA:** But I also think it's being mean to

5 her and being self-centered even then to her.

6 **PRESIDING COMMISSIONER SHEFFIELD:** Yes, I would agree

7 with that. Okay. Um --

8 **JOSEPH GARCIA:** I'm sorry.

9 **PRESIDING COMMISSIONER SHEFFIELD:** Okay. And then my

10 last question for you, you, um, when you spoke to the

11 clinician in the CRA, you said you would be open to sex

12 offender treatment, but you have never admitted to a

13 therapist of being guilty of, of those things. So, I

14 think it means of your crime. So, does that mean that you

15 have never admitted to a therapist that you have committed

16 any sex offenses?

17 **JOSEPH GARCIA:** I think I told her, Dr. Lyle, I had

18 five years of, uh, sexual offender therapy with him in Mu

19 -- Mule Creek. And I told him that I was, that I'm pretty

20 sure I told him I was guilty of, because some of the

21 crimes. He didn't want to know the, he didn't want to

22 know exactly the crimes, but his name is Dr. Lyle for five

23 years in Mule Creek.

24 **PRESIDING COMMISSIONER SHEFFIELD:** Which, which

25 crimes did you tell him you were guilty of?

Dictate Express Transcription

1   **JOSEPH GARCIA:** Uh, the one in, uh, the one in, uh,

2 1979. And also, also, um, uh, I think there was a girl

3 named Bernard -- Kathy Bernard, where I walked into her

4 house, and, uh, sh -- uh, she talked to me about her

5 boyfriend growing plants, and then I, I said, can we, can

6 we make love? And then she told me I'm on my period, and

7 I walked out of the house. I told him I was guilty of

8 trying to take advantage of her too. That was, uh, not

9 Morro Bay, uh, it's a little town over there because I

10 used to cover seven different cities.

11   **PRESIDING COMMISSIONER SHEFFIELD:** I don't, I don't

12 care <crosstalk> --

13   **JOSEPH GARCIA:** I think I told him I was guilty of

14 that too.

15   **PRESIDING COMMISSIONER SHEFFIELD:** All right. So,

16 you spoke about that one as well?

17   **JOSEPH GARCIA:** I think there's another one I spoke

18 about. Uh, but I didn't do no rape, but I still, uh --

19 which one is that? Uh, I think there was -- Dr. Lyle was

20 a good doctor, but I think there's another one I

21 mentioned. Uh, uh, Kathy Bernard, um, Margarita Basin. I

22 know -- I think there's --

23   **ATTORNEY MORSE:** I -- suffice to say he spoke about

24 some crimes with a therapist.

25   **JOSEPH GARCIA:** He was a doctor.

1   **ATTORNEY MORSE:** I, I --

2   **JOSEPH GARCIA:** Dr. -- Dr. Lyle.

3   **ATTORNEY MORSE:** I know. It's fine. You're getting

4   mixed up though.

5   **PRESIDING COMMISSIONER SHEFFIELD:** All right. Do you

6   have anything else to add to that response, Mr. Garcia?

7   **JOSEPH GARCIA:** Well, to that response, or the

8   response in general?

9   **PRESIDING COMMISSIONER SHEFFIELD:** To, to the res --

10   that response. You're talking about your crime.

11   **JOSEPH GARCIA:** Well, first of -- yeah, first of all,

12   with Dr. Lyle, I learned a lot about I need structure. I

13   need to be --

14   **PRESIDING COMMISSIONER SHEFFIELD:** Okay, that's not

15   what I asked you about.

16   **JOSEPH GARCIA:** -- to be accountable to, to people.

17   **PRESIDING COMMISSIONER SHEFFIELD:** Um, all right, Mr.

18   Garcia, I don't have any further questions for you. I'm

19   going to direct your attention now to Deputy Commissioner

20   Mette, and he will have some questions for you. So, thank

21   you for answering my questions.

22   **JOSEPH GARCIA:** Thank you. Thank you very much.

23   **DEPUTY COMMISSIONER METTE:** Thank you very much.

24   Before I begin, I'm going to suggest we take a quick five

25   minute break.

1   JOSEPH GARCIA: Yes, sir.

2   PRESIDING COMMISSIONER SHEFFIELD: Yeah, that's fine.

3   DEPUTY COMMISSIONER METTE: Perfect. So, time -- all

4   right, let me just do this. We're going to go off record

5   about five minutes, and then we'll be back.

6   [RECESS]

7

8   DEPUTY COMMISSIONER METTE: We are back on record.

9   PRESIDING COMMISSIONER SHEFFIELD: Back on the record

10   at 11:36 a.m. All parties have returned. And, uh, Mr.

11   Garcia, you said you have something to say, so please go

12   ahead.

13   JOSEPH GARCIA: Yeah, you asked me something about

14   why would they accuse me of so many crimes. Well, I

15   already had a record of the 1979 rape, and now I'm being

16   accused of another rape. So, of course they're going to

17   see me as this person that's out there attacking a bunch

18   of women. And besides that, in my own way, I was a, I was

19   like a monster in my own way, I mean. You know, being

20   selfish and cruel and callous towards women. And when

21   the, the drinking didn't help me, you know, not to be

22   that. So, that's why I think they put so many crimes on

23   me, because they already had a record. 1979, they said I

24   fit the perfect picture, so why not put a bunch of

25   knocking on the doors trying to rape the girls.

1   **PRESIDING COMMISSIONER SHEFFIELD:** All right. Okay.

2 All right, Mr. Garcia, um, I don't have any further

3 questions for you, so I'd --

4   **JOSEPH GARCIA:** Okay.

5   **PRESIDING COMMISSIONER SHEFFIELD:** -- going to, uh,

6 now again, direct your attention to Deputy Commissioner

7 Mette.

8   **JOSEPH GARCIA:** Thank you very much.

9   **PRESIDING COMMISSIONER SHEFFIELD:** He'll have some

10 questions.

11   **JOSEPH GARCIA:** Thank you very much. Thank you.

12   **DEPUTY COMMISSIONER METTE:** All right, Mr. Garcia, do

13 you think in your life you had a problem with sexual

14 offending?

15   **JOSEPH GARCIA:** Can you repeat that again?

16   **DEPUTY COMMISSIONER METTE:** In your life, did you

17 ever have --

18   **JOSEPH GARCIA:** My whole life.

19   **DEPUTY COMMISSIONER METTE:** -- in your whole life,

20 did you ever have a problem with sexual offending?

21   **JOSEPH GARCIA:** As a kid, you're talking about as a

22 teenager and all that?

23   **DEPUTY COMMISSIONER METTE:** I'm talking about in your

24 entire life, at any point in your entire life, did you

25 have a problem with sexually offending?

1   **JOSEPH GARCIA:** Yes, I think I did.

2   **DEPUTY COMMISSIONER METTE:** Do you currently --

3   **JOSEPH GARCIA:** I'm pretty sure -- I'm pretty sure I

4 did.

5   **DEPUTY COMMISSIONER METTE:** Do you currently have a

6 problem with sexual offending?

7   **JOSEPH GARCIA:** Does that mean -- are you asking me

8 if I want to offend somebody sexually?

9   **DEPUTY COMMISSIONER METTE:** I'm saying right now, do

10 you think you have a problem with sexual offending?

11   **JOSEPH GARCIA:** Uh, I have sexual thoughts, but I

12 know how to deal with them. Uh, my coping skills kick in.

13   **DEPUTY COMMISSIONER METTE:** Okay.

14   **JOSEPH GARCIA:** But do I have a, uh, uh -- what's --

15 I'm trying to understand what you're -- you -- what you're

16 saying.

17   **DEPUTY COMMISSIONER METTE:** Let me -- let me ask this

18 --

19   **ATTORNEY MORSE:** You understand it.

20   **JOSEPH GARCIA:** Huh?

21   **DEPUTY COMMISSIONER METTE:** Let me ask --

22   **ATTORNEY MORSE:** You're getting it.

23   **DEPUTY COMMISSIONER METTE:** Okay.

24   **JOSEPH GARCIA:** I'm not a, I'm not a perfect person,

25 but I do have sexual thoughts, but I deal with them now.

DEPUTY COMMISSIONER METTE: Okay.

JOSEPH GARCIA: I, I use my coping skills to eradicate those thoughts from my mind, because I know it is not healthy for me to have fantasy thoughts and all that.

DEPUTY COMMISSIONER METTE: Why is it not -- why is it not a good idea for you to have fantasy thoughts?

JOSEPH GARCIA: Because they can lead to an action eventually if you let them, if you let them have free rent in your brain for a long time, they can become an action. And there's guys here -- there's guys right here that attacked the nurses, and it's horrible.

DEPUTY COMMISSIONER METTE: Okay.

JOSEPH GARCIA: You know, because they don't know how to control their thoughts, you know?

DEPUTY COMMISSIONER METTE: Okay. All right. Uh, when was the last time you had a sexual fantasy?

JOSEPH GARCIA: Uh, a fantasy, well, sometime when, uh, the nurses are talking to me, and I don't want to blame them at all for nothing, but, uh, if they're a good looking woman, sometimes I have a thought, you know, she's a beautiful woman, you know, and, uh, I like to take her out, you know, like that. And that's a sexual thought, you know.

DEPUTY COMMISSIONER METTE: Do you think --

1   **JOSEPH GARCIA:** But then I get rid of that.

2   **DEPUTY COMMISSIONER METTE:** So, with --

3   **JOSEPH GARCIA:** My coping skills help me get rid of

4   that.

5   **DEPUTY COMMISSIONER METTE:** Okay. We'll get to

6   coping skills in a moment. With those staff members, you

7   think they're attractive, is there ever times where you

8   think they think you are attractive?

9   **JOSEPH GARCIA:** Oh, no, I'm an old man. I'm not --

10   I'm not attractive. I used to be when I was, uh, up till

11   about 55, I think I was pretty good looking, but I lost

12   that look, you know.

13   **DEPUTY COMMISSIONER METTE:** Do you think you --

14   **JOSEPH GARCIA:** I just started --

15   **DEPUTY COMMISSIONER METTE:** Do you think you ever had

16   a problem with believing that someone was flirting with

17   you when in reality they weren't?

18   **JOSEPH GARCIA:** Of course, yes.

19   **DEPUTY COMMISSIONER METTE:** Describe --

20   **JOSEPH GARCIA:** Yes.

21   **DEPUTY COMMISSIONER METTE:** -- describe what the

22   issue was.

23   **JOSEPH GARCIA:** Well, sometimes, they're giving me my

24   medication and they're going, Joey, how you doing today?

25   And I says, I'm doing pretty good. And they go, uh, I

1   seen pictures of you when you were, like, when you first

2   came to prison, you were a nice looking man. You know,

3   you're a pretty big guy and all that. I say, yeah, but,

4   you know, that's -- those are, those days are gone. You

5   know, I'm like a, I'm almost, I'm almost like a shell now

6   for, man, I don't got my muscles no more. I don't got my

7   strength. And, uh, I got dementia and they go, yeah, I

8   know I give you the pills for that. But, uh, uh, anyway,

9   you keep having a good day. So, when I get away from

10 that, I go to my room, I got my own room. I said, this

11 girl was flirting with -- I feel like they're flirting

12 with me. Then I start thinking, wait a minute, they

13 weren't flirting with me. They were just being nice and

14 compassionate. And I'm over here, um, misconstructing --

15 misinterpreting, and then I get rid of that

16 misinterpretation, then I'm okay.

17   **DEPUTY COMMISSIONER METTE:** Did that thought happen -

18 -

19   **JOSEPH GARCIA:** It takes me about --

20   **DEPUTY COMMISSIONER METTE:** Did that thought --

21   **JOSEPH GARCIA:** -- 20 minutes, half hour.

22   **DEPUTY COMMISSIONER METTE:** Did a thought like that

23 happen recently?

24   **JOSEPH GARCIA:** Where somebody -- I thought somebody

25 was flirting with me?

1   **DEPUTY COMMISSIONER METTE:** You just, you just

2   provide -- you just gave a scenario where a nurse was

3   providing you pills. I think you mentioned your dementia

4   medication, and then you went back to your cell and

5   thought, hey, I think they were flirting with me, but you

6   stopped yourself. That scenario, did that happen

7   recently?

8   **JOSEPH GARCIA:** I think so.

9   **DEPUTY COMMISSIONER METTE:** Okay.

10   **JOSEPH GARCIA:** Uh, I think it -- I think it did

11   happen.

12   **DEPUTY COMMISSIONER METTE:** Okay. You've been --

13   **JOSEPH GARCIA:** With the group -- you talking about

14   the nurses?

15   **DEPUTY COMMISSIONER METTE:** Yeah. Okay. I'm going

16   to ask you a -- I'm going to ask you a different question.

17   In the psychological evaluation, you have been diagnosed

18   with other specified paraphilic disorder, coercive type.

19   Do you recall --

20   **JOSEPH GARCIA:** What is that?

21   **DEPUTY COMMISSIONER METTE:** -- do you --

22   **JOSEPH GARCIA:** No, I don't understand that.

23   **DEPUTY COMMISSIONER METTE:** You don't know what that

24   means?

25   **JOSEPH GARCIA:** No. You said -- you -- what did you

1 | call it, Yapa?

2 | **DEPUTY COMMISSIONER METTE:** It's called other

3 | specified paraphilic disorder coercive type.

4 | **JOSEPH GARCIA:** I don't know what para -- whatever

5 | you call it -- means.

6 | **DEPUTY COMMISSIONER METTE:** Okay. Do you think

7 | you've had a problem with raping women in your life?

8 | **JOSEPH GARCIA:** Of course, I did, those two, but that

9 | -- but the last one or two years, I haven't been really

10 | like, thinking like that. Not thinking about rape, but

11 | just flirting.

12 | **DEPUTY COMMISSIONER METTE:** Let's go, let's go back a

13 | little bit, because in that scenario, you talked about

14 | coping skills. What coping skills do you use?

15 | **JOSEPH GARCIA:** I use positive, uh, uh -- uh, uh,

16 | positive thoughts and, uh, yoga. And sometimes -- I know

17 | this may sound silly, but sometimes I even take a shower

18 | just to help me calm down. And, uh, I go to my therapy.

19 | I got pamphlets of therapy, and I, and I also use a lot of

20 | music. I use Christian music, and then that really helps

21 | me a lot to get away from thinking like that.

22 | **DEPUTY COMMISSIONER METTE:** Okay. I believe it's

23 | mentioned in the CRA, you have phone sex with your wife?

24 | **JOSEPH GARCIA:** I'm not with my wife. After 36

25 | years, we got divorced. I'm with Anita now.

1   **DEPUTY COMMISSIONER METTE:** Anita, my apologies. It

2 wasn't your wife. My apologies. You've had phone sex

3 with Anita?

4   **JOSEPH GARCIA:** A few times.

5   **DEPUTY COMMISSIONER METTE:** When was the last time?

6   **JOSEPH GARCIA:** Well, once, uh -- it's been about

7 two, three months, I think. But I didn't -- well, I don't

8 put ...

9   **DEPUTY COMMISSIONER METTE:** Did you masturbate?

10   **JOSEPH GARCIA:** No.

11   **DEPUTY COMMISSIONER METTE:** Do you think phone sex

12 could be problematic for you?

13   **JOSEPH GARCIA:** I think it could be. That's why I

14 told them, we got to stop doing this. We can't be really

15 doing stuff like that because the officers are listening

16 on the -- they got a machine where they can hear us, and I

17 don't want, I don't want them to think, I don't want them

18 to think little of you for opening up this, uh,

19 conversation between us.

20   **DEPUTY COMMISSIONER METTE:** Okay.

21   **JOSEPH GARCIA:** I says, but, uh -- I -- she says --

22 she agreed to that.

23   **DEPUTY COMMISSIONER METTE:** Do you think it's

24 possible --

25   **JOSEPH GARCIA:** But we don't --

1   **DEPUTY COMMISSIONER METTE:** Let me ask you another

2 question. Do you think it's possible that you could

3 sexually offend in the future?

4   **JOSEPH GARCIA:** Do I think it's possible that I could

5 sexually offend in the future?

6   **DEPUTY COMMISSIONER METTE:** I can re -- I can -- let

7 me re-ask the question just to be a little more specific.

8 Do you think it's possible that you could commit a sexual

9 offense against a woman in the future?

10   **JOSEPH GARCIA:** Can I explain that with a few words?

11   **DEPUTY COMMISSIONER METTE:** Yes.

12   **JOSEPH GARCIA:** First, first of all, I sure, I sure

13 hope not. I sure hope I never do, but I'm not a perfect

14 human being, people have triggers and, uh, I can't put

15 myself in those situations around women. Uh, I have to

16 stay with my coping skills. I have to stay with

17 structure. I have when I -- if and whenever I get out, I

18 have to stay with my doctors, and I have to stay with my

19 prescriptions and keep taking all my prescriptions. And

20 when I have a problem, I have to ask for help and not just

21 think I can handle it myself.

22   **DEPUTY COMMISSIONER METTE:** Let me --

23   **JOSEPH GARCIA:** And I love the mental health now

24 because I've been with them 20 years, and it really helped

25 me a lot.

1   **DEPUTY COMMISSIONER METTE:** I'm going to stop you

2   right there. You mentioned as far as not putting yourself

3   in a triggering situation or a triggering place, do you

4   think it's possible that you could put yourself in a place

5   where you could be triggered to sexually offend against

6   another woman?

7   **JOSEPH GARCIA:** Of course.

8   **DEPUTY COMMISSIONER METTE:** What places --

9   **JOSEPH GARCIA:** I can go to night -- I can, I, I can

10   go to nightclubs and the women flirt with me, and whether

11   I get their permission or not, I'm drinking, I might take

12   a few pills and then I give it to my, uh, uh, old way of

13   thinking.

14   **DEPUTY COMMISSIONER METTE:** Well, let me ask you this

15   specifically.

16   **JOSEPH GARCIA:** And I, I want, I want sex, so I just

17   go, okay --

18   **DEPUTY COMMISSIONER METTE:** Mr. Garcia, hold on.

19   Hold on one moment.

20   **JOSEPH GARCIA:** Okay.

21   **DEPUTY COMMISSIONER METTE:** I'm talking about in

22   prison. Do you think there are places that you need to

23   avoid that could potentially trigger you to sexually

24   offend?

25   **JOSEPH GARCIA:** In prison?

1   **DEPUTY COMMISSIONER METTE:** Yeah.

2   **JOSEPH GARCIA:** No.

3   **DEPUTY COMMISSIONER METTE:** Okay.

4   **JOSEPH GARCIA:** I -- I'm always in my room. I'm

5   always in my room or the day room. I go to my 10 groups a

6   week. My EOP groups. I'm not around women, if that's

7   what you're thinking. I'm not around women. The only

8   time I have contact with women is when I take my pills or

9   my -- Ms. Hyatt comes to see me. She, she don't see me in

10   the room. She sees me, uh, in the back of the, of the

11   building with, uh, supervision. That's Ms. Hyatt. She's

12   my psychologist.

13   **DEPUTY COMMISSIONER METTE:** Are you around female --

14   **JOSEPH GARCIA:** Or Ms. --

15   **DEPUTY COMMISSIONER METTE:** -- are you around female

16   correctional officers?

17   **JOSEPH GARCIA:** They sit at their station.

18   **DEPUTY COMMISSIONER METTE:** Okay.

19   **JOSEPH GARCIA:** They don't come and mix -- they don't

20   come and mix with us.

21   **DEPUTY COMMISSIONER METTE:** In 2024 --

22   **JOSEPH GARCIA:** And the only time we talked to them

23   is --

24   **DEPUTY COMMISSIONER METTE:** I'm going to pause. In

25   the year 2024, did you submit requests through CDCR to

1 have a female inmate search policy be conducted on you?

2   **JOSEPH GARCIA:** Yeah, they asked me -- they asked me,

3 because of, of being two-spirit, they said, well, you have

4 an opportunity to either have a man search you or a woman

5 search you. And because I got a, a writeup for falsifying

6 information, which was not falsifying on, on CO Zapata for

7 not wearing my helmet, he gave me a 115 for not wearing my

8 helmet. So, I had a guy help me do a grievance saying

9 that I didn't have to wear my helmet as long as I have it

10 on my chair, and he insisted. So, I wrote him up, and

11 then it came back six months later saying that, uh, my

12 allegation was false and it was a false report. So, I got

13 a 115 for that.

14   **DEPUTY COMMISSIONER METTE:** Okay.

15   **JOSEPH GARCIA:** But, but, but I, I did tell her I'd

16 rather have a female, uh, instead of Zapata searching me.

17   **DEPUTY COMMISSIONER METTE:** Okay.

18   **JOSEPH GARCIA:** Because I can't get off the chair. I

19 can't walk. I can't walk. I can stand up, but I can't

20 walk. And so, they said, well, you got the right to have

21 a female search you. But since I got that paper, no one

22 has ever searched me. No one.

23   **DEPUTY COMMISSIONER METTE:** Okay. But do you think

24 it would be -- do you think it, it would be problematic at

25 all -- and I want to be very pointed with this question.

1   Do you think it --

2   **JOSEPH GARCIA:** Yes.

3   **DEPUTY COMMISSIONER METTE:** -- would be problematic

4   at all for someone with your history to have a female

5   officer do an unclothed search of you?

6   **JOSEPH GARCIA:** They don't do, they don't do

7   unclothed. Three other male officers come with her and

8   they search us right there in front of her. She searches

9   us, she pats us down right in front of three officers.

10   **DEPUTY COMMISSIONER METTE:** Okay.

11   **JOSEPH GARCIA:** That's how it happens here in prison.

12   **DEPUTY COMMISSIONER METTE:** In --

13   **JOSEPH GARCIA:** She's not alone.

14   **DEPUTY COMMISSIONER METTE:** When you, when the -- but

15   you recall making the request for the female search?

16   **JOSEPH GARCIA:** No, I didn't make it. They asked me.

17   **DEPUTY COMMISSIONER METTE:** Okay.

18   **JOSEPH GARCIA:** They go, Joey, Garcia, you have a

19   right to have a male or female search you. Which one do

20   you want, prefer? And I says, well, if it's not to take

21   my clothes off, I'd rather have a female. They go, it's a

22   pat down search. And I said, okay, I'll take a pat down

23   from a female.

24   **DEPUTY COMMISSIONER METTE:** Okay.

25   **JOSEPH GARCIA:** And then I found out that three other

1   males have to be there when she does pat you down in front

2   of them.

3   **DEPUTY COMMISSIONER METTE:** Okay.

4   **JOSEPH GARCIA:** It's for weapons or something like

5   that? I don't know. I don't have no weapons, but it's to

6   carry weapons or something.

7   **DEPUTY COMMISSIONER METTE:** Okay.

8   **JOSEPH GARCIA:** People carry knives around.

9   **DEPUTY COMMISSIONER METTE:** Let me change the topic.

10   Um, did you use methamphetamine in November 2024?

11   **JOSEPH GARCIA:** I have never taken no drugs since

12   I've been in prison.

13   **DEPUTY COMMISSIONER METTE:** Okay. So, very specific

14   question related to this, did you take opiates in either

15   October or November of 2024?

16   **JOSEPH GARCIA:** The only opiate that I know that I

17   take right now is Tramadol. It's within the opiate family

18   is Tramadol for my pain.

19   **DEPUTY COMMISSIONER METTE:** Okay.

20   **JOSEPH GARCIA:** I have pain all day, so I take pain

21   pills.

22   **DEPUTY COMMISSIONER METTE:** Okay. I have no further

23   questions at this time. Thank you very much, Mr. Garcia.

24   **JOSEPH GARCIA:** Thank you, sir. Thank you very much.

25   **PRESIDING COMMISSIONER SHEFFIELD:** All right, thank

1 you. I don't have any further questions either, so, uh,
2 we are going to move on to clarifying questions. Ms.
3 Curley, do you have any questions for the panel?
4   **DEPUTY DISTRICT ATTORNEY CURLEY:** No.
5   **PRESIDING COMMISSIONER SHEFFIELD:** Thank you. And
6 Ms. Morse, any questions for your client?
7   **ATTORNEY MORSE:** No questions. Thank you.
8   **PRESIDING COMMISSIONER SHEFFIELD:** Thank you. Then
9 we'll go ahead with closing statements. Uh, Ms. Curley,
10 you may go ahead.
11   **DEPUTY DISTRICT ATTORNEY CURLEY:** Thank you. It
12 remains the position of San Luis Obispo District
13 Attorney's Office that Mr. Joseph Co -- Garcia remains an
14 extremely dangerous sexual predator and is unsuitable for
15 release into the community. Um, we all heard the
16 testimony today and, um, I will say that it is extremely,
17 um, hard to hear. Uh, and that's even -- that's for me
18 and I'm, I'm considering all of the victims who are
19 attending today. And, um, it's hard to hear on a number
20 of levels, but specifically the fact that he continues to
21 deny so many of these, um, sexual offenses is, you know,
22 it's not unexpected, I suppose, um, given the history, but
23 it's awful and frankly, retraumatizing to the victims.
24 Uh, and I will leave it to them to speak about and not to
25 take, uh, the emotional floor on that one. Although it is

1 very hard to remain professional in that regard. I will

2 do so and leave it to them. I will say that given -- I

3 only have 10 minutes to discuss our position on Mr.

4 Garcia's suitability, and given the plethora of sexual

5 crimes and the plethora of misinformation, uh, that was

6 discussed today, it would be a poor use of my time to go

7 through every single one, um, or even, uh, just a couple,

8 uh, for all that we heard today and straighten the record.

9 So, I will tr -- I will trust the commissioners, um, as

10 Commissioner Sheffield said that they would, um, review

11 the records front of them for the facts and consider

12 those, um, because apparently we are not getting into

13 those facts today, which I understand, uh, on a number of

14 levels. Um, but I, I will, I will just say that I am

15 going to, um, trust that similar to the excellent job the

16 commissioners did today of asking questions of this

17 inmate, that they will also do an excellent job of, uh,

18 reading the record for inconsistencies. Um, aside from

19 that factual, um, what -- you know, what is called static

20 factors, what the, the sexual offenses that have occurred

21 in the past, what we heard to was, you know, basically

22 underscores the CRA doctor's assessment that Mr. Garcia

23 remains a high risk of violence and particularly sexual

24 violence to the community, uh, for a number of reasons,

25 which are also in the CRA, um, for all of us. Uh, but I

1   will just go ahead and read those into the record. Um,

2   that some of the most relevant or salient risk factor

3   considerations are his persistent and social orientation

4   as evidenced by minimizing responsibility for his behavior

5   and deflection of blame. Um, and I would, uh,

6   accelerating pattern of misconduct, which increases his

7   risk for violence, a limited awareness of his sexual

8   violence risk factors, which I believe that, uh, uh, the

9   deputy commissioner, uh, did a, did a good job at least

10   trying to highlight, um, whether or not we were able to

11   get into a meaningful discussion of that. But that -- you

12   know, that's where in the problem lies, uh, limited

13   relapse prevention planning and concerns about

14   availability of true accountability partners in the

15   community. Basically, there's just not much here to go on

16   as far as, um, as far as, uh, an argument for his

17   suitability. I am going to address the one thing that I

18   know that these commissioners will consider, um, um, and

19   that I'm sure that inmate's counsel will highlight because

20   I don't get a chance for rebuttal in these circumstances.

21   And that is the elderly parole consideration, um, and the

22   fact that he is advanced in age and has some, some

23   disabilities, um, and some, uh, at least limited cognitive

24   function at this point, apparently. Um, I will echo and

25   highlight the CRA doctor's assessment on page 17, um, of

1   that document where she's highlighted that Mr. Garcia has

2   continued to engage in misconduct despite their advancing

3   age, suggesting that this factor has not yet fully

4   mitigated risk. So, despite Mr. Garcia's advanced age,

5   and, you know, some of the ailments we heard about today

6   and the wheelchair, it still at this point all of these

7   years later has not fully mitigated the risk, and

8   therefore we do not believe that, uh, the elderly parole

9   factors bode in his favor. And again, I want to highlight

10   the CRA doctor's assessment that one of the most relevant

11   and salient risk factors is his accelerating pattern of

12   misconduct. So, not only is he not a rehabilitated

13   individual, uh, by any means, uh, although he takes

14   classes, there doesn't seem to be an internalization of

15   that. There can't be an internalization if you're not

16   willing to admit, um, what you've done. Um, but you know,

17   there -- you can't change what you don't identify. Um,

18   however, just even recently, the, the misconduct that has

19   occurred has shown a continued, um, and accelerating lack

20   of control and impulsivity, which is gravely concerning.

21   Um, and finally, the rating in the Comprehensive Risk

22   Assessment wherein Mr. Garcia scored higher than 89%

23   individuals, um, on this assessment and making him above

24   average risk for sexual offending even at his advanced

25   age. Um, all of these factors underscore that he remains

1 a high risk for violence and particularly sexual violence.
2 Um, and we respectfully request the commissioners to deny
3 parole once again and to consider the longest possible,
4 uh, period for that as Mr. Garcia remains wholly
5 unsuitable and the victims who have, um, who have shown up
6 today continue to be dismissed and re-traumatized. And,
7 um, and it's not fair, it's not fair to them. Thank you
8 very much for listening.
9   **PRESIDING COMMISSIONER SHEFFIELD:** Thank you. And
10 Ms. Morse, you may go ahead.
11   **ATTORNEY MORSE:** Thank you. Nothing I say today
12 minimizes the pain and suffering of the victims and their
13 loved ones. That pain is real and forever, and I respect
14 that. My role today is to be forward looking. Mr. Garcia
15 has served a long time. He's in his 70s. He can't walk.
16 He's clearly declining cognitively. As I said earlier, I
17 have spent a lot of additional time on this case, ensuring
18 effective communication. I see a man in Mr. Garcia who
19 has gotten into one-on-one therapy for many years who did
20 go to programming, who has admitted to raping. He's
21 remorseful. He has done insight. He's thought about his
22 mom, his past, his trauma. He can list his defects. When
23 people start to cognitively decline, it can be
24 unsatisfying to the rest of us because they can't say what
25 we might want to have them more clearly articulate, but

1 that doesn't make them a future risk. Being confused

2 doesn't make someone a predator. The CRA has in fact

3 listed positive factors. For example, the cessation of

4 overtly violent misconduct for many years, reported

5 sobriety for many years, acknowledgement of sexual

6 offending, consistent emotional support from the

7 community, participation in mental health treatment with

8 positive results. And he's also very compliant with his

9 doctors, with all of his medical staff when we consider

10 his age length of incarceration, his decline, his

11 diminished capacity, the progress he's made in admitting

12 his crimes and the remorse that he obviously has. He also

13 very poignantly talked about triggers and his coping

14 skills. We've seen that he's learned from his one-on-one

15 therapy replacement thoughts. He, he talks about, he

16 talks about the things he does to stay positive, to move

17 away from negative thinking. This is incredible progress,

18 particularly for someone who has such cognitive decline.

19 Mr. Garcia may not fit the perfect picture of what we want

20 to see in a reformed person, however, his risk absolutely

21 has been lowered. And when we think about high risk

22 reports, it can be misleading because we think of high

23 risk as being compared to anyone out in the world. But

24 actually the training that we attorneys have received is

25 that this is high risk relative to other people who go out

1 | and commit crimes and are on parole and are in the system.
2 | And there's the percentages of people who re-offend in
3 | these groups is extremely low. In many cases, it's less
4 | than 1%. And even being high risk, they're -- we're
5 | talking about less than 3%. We're -- we're talking about
6 | very low percentages of people who are this age, who have
7 | served this long and who get released on parole, even with
8 | the higher risk assessments. So, I really think we need
9 | to keep that in mind. And finally, um, I want to
10 | reiterate about holding things against him in turn. And,
11 | and I appreciate what the commissioner said in the
12 | beginning about it doesn't matter if we stipulate or not,
13 | but in terms of if this is not his day to get a grant, and
14 | if this is a denial, and thinking about those denial
15 | periods, I, I think that normally where you might look at
16 | somebody who has no cognitive issues at all, um, and I,
17 | and I have to say that the 12.9 TABE score is, is just not
18 | accurate. And I believe it wa -- this -- the test hasn't
19 | been given in 10 years, so it's old. But when we look at
20 | a normal person who doesn't have cognitive decline, we
21 | might say, well, you should have known you're not ready,
22 | or you shouldn't have gotten confused and gotten into
23 | these confrontations, and you need a longer time to figure
24 | it out. But I, I think we have the opposite situation
25 | here. I think we have somebody who got into the

confrontations in the RVRs because of his confusion. I
think he's clearly on the decline and every day that
passes, he's getting worse. And I, I think it's, it's not
helpful and actually overly, um, punitive to give him a
longer period of denial when we consider everything. So,
I trust that these commissioners will take everything into
consideration. I've been in front of this, uh, panel
before, or at least both of them in different situations
before in different hearings. And I trust in both of your
decision making. I thank you for your compassion that you
showed today and understanding in your questions. And on
that, I submit.

PRESIDING COMMISSIONER SHEFFIELD: Thank you. And
Mr. Garcia, would you like to give a, a statement?

JOSEPH GARCIA: <Inaudible>.

ATTORNEY MORSE: Would you like to give a statement,
a closing statement?

JOSEPH GARCIA: As to my crimes or?

ATTORNEY MORSE: Just, this is your chance to say
anything you want. Remember you told me you wanted to say
you were sorry.

JOSEPH GARCIA: Oh, yeah, yeah. First of all, I feel
pri -- I feel privileged to be given an opportunity to
come before the commissioners today. I feel it's a -- it
is a privilege for men in prison that, that have life

 1   sentence or long sentences who come before you, because I
 2   know you have the hardest job in the world. Like my big
 3   brother, Frank Thomason always says, it's not easy, let
 4   them -- deciding who can come out of prison, who can't,
 5   Joe. So, you just got to hang in there. But I want to
 6   say that I'm sorry, or I am sorry for taking those women,
 7   those -- Margaret and the -- the lady and Margaret, I'm
 8   sorry for offending them. It should have never -- they
 9   should -- this should have never happened to them. If I
10   wouldn't have been -- I -- I'm not blaming the liquor, but
11   if I would've just been working on myself more back then,
12   even though I was married at the time, I was hiding things
13   from my wife and stuff, you know. But, uh, I am sorry.
14   I, I believe that I, I put a lot of work like the, the
15   psychiatrist, psychologist told me, keep doing all your
16   groups, and I, I accumulated, I think I did, uh, like 89
17   self-help groups in five years of college courses long
18   time ago since I've been in. And I, I developed four
19   trades since I've been -- I can't work no more, I'm too
20   old, but I'm just so sorry I can't take it back because
21   those women are going to live with trauma for -- they're
22   going, they're going to live with trauma for the rest of
23   their lives. And, and they got to see psychologists and
24   psychiatrists and take medications just like I do. And
25   I'm just sorry that it happened. I can't, I can't reverse

it. I wish I could reverse it, but I hope that I, uh,
worked on myself a lot never to reoffend because I believe
that anybody can reoffend. I can reoffend if you're not
careful, if you don't use your coping skills, if you put
yourself in situations that are risky and, and you trigger
yourself. And, and, and you got to be careful because out
there and outside, from what I see on TV, it's a lot of
nightclubs and all that crazy stuff going on, drugs. But
I'm not going to put myself in those situations. I never
will. Uh, I'm almost 80 years old and I just think that
if anything, I got to have a changed life, not just for
myself, but for those two women, for they can also hear
how if I was to get a grant -- if they can hear how good
I'm doing in that home, that they accepted me into that
I'll be with a psychiatrist, medication and a psychologist
for the rest of my life. And I'm grateful that, that I --
that that's been offered to me. Not that I'm, I'm not
saying I'm going to get it, but I'm, I'm grateful that
they offered me a home, uh, Freedom through Education.
They, they gave me a bed there in Sacramento. But, uh, I,
I just, I just don't know what else to say except, I'm
sorry. I'm sorry everything -- for everything that
happened. I'm even sorry that I put the DA and Mr. Miller
and all those people through that whole trial because it,
it never should have happened. I should have just pled

1   guilty from the beginning of the rape and, and took a

2   deal. They offered me a deal for 20 years and I didn't

3   take it. I should have just took the deal, but I didn't.

4   I was playing stupid and hard and stubborn, you know.

5   **ATTORNEY MORSE:** That's good.

6   **PRESIDING COMMISSIONER SHEFFIELD:** All right. Thank

7   you Mr. Garcia. Um, at this time, we will turn to, um,

8   the victims and representatives. So, I was, uh, given a

9   list at the beginning of the order. So, I'm going to go

10   down the list that I was given and start with Jane Doe

11   one. Um, you may unmute yourself and speak when you're

12   ready.

13   **DEPUTY COMMISSIONER METTE:** Just in case someone is

14   speaking, we cannot hear you. And I don't know if you are

15   unmuted at this time.

16   **PRESIDING COMMISSIONER SHEFFIELD:** Yeah, we see

17   everyone's on mute.

18   **DEPUTY COMMISSIONER METTE:** Okay.

19   **PRESIDING COMMISSIONER SHEFFIELD:** Do we have Jane

20   Doe one with Ms. Traughber? Am I recalling that

21   correctly?

22   **DEPUTY COMMISSIONER METTE:** I believe you are

23   correct. I believe she is with Ms. Traughber.

24   **PRESIDING COMMISSIONER SHEFFIELD:** Okay. Ms.

25   Traughber, are you there?

1   **DEPUTY DISTRICT ATTORNEY CURLEY:** She's calling me.

2   She may be having an issue. If you could give me one

3   moment.

4   **PRESIDING COMMISSIONER SHEFFIELD:** Yeah, let's just

5   go off the record.

6   **[RECESS]**

7

8   **DEPUTY COMMISSIONER METTE:** We are back on record.

9   **PRESIDING COMMISSIONER SHEFFIELD:** Back on the record

10   at 12:16 p.m. All parties have returned. Uh, so, we are

11   moving on to our victim statements. So, uh, we will begin

12   with you, uh, Jane Doe one, you may go ahead when you're

13   ready.

14   **JANE DOE:** Yes, Jane Doe one, victim. I live with

15   the pain that Joseph Garcia put me through at knife point

16   and raping me at 21. I am here today to stand tall on

17   behalf of all the victims that have endured this

18   horrendous crime of a mentally deranged human who I

19   strongly feel he shall remain in prison forever. I've

20   conquered many things in my life and I continue to have a

21   beautiful and healing and peaceful life, but I live in

22   fear now. I believe strongly in the justice system and

23   hope that you make the correct decision, a strong choice

24   for all of us. I continue to live with God on my side,

25   and no weapon formed against me shall prosper. And the

1 presence -- and I say this in the presence of Jesus

2 Christ. Amen. I know my presence shows here that any

3 words I could ever say will not endure the pain that I've

4 been through all my life. I did not choose this to happen

5 to me. And I want to continue to not live in fear. And I

6 want to thank the courts and the parole board and everyone

7 that's here today to let me live a continuous safe and

8 healthy life, but I'd also like to mention that I've had

9 to live the pain of knowing about a book that was written

10 with all the victims' names in it. And I've had to endure

11 the pain of the harassment letters I would get in the mail

12 all the time from a woman out of Palm Springs, and

13 something should be added for that. It's not right that

14 we have to live in this continuously. It's not fair. I

15 just want to thank you kindly and keep him in prison.

16 Please. If I was your sister, mother, daughter, you

17 wouldn't want me to go through this. I've lost 10 pounds

18 recently because I can't take this anymore. Please keep

19 him where he is. Thank you.

20 **PRESIDING COMMISSIONER SHEFFIELD:** Thank you. Um,

21 and Ms. Guy, you, you may go ahead when you're ready.

22 **JACQUELINE GUY:** Thank you. Thank you, uh, for this

23 opportunity to speak. Um, I've been listening to the

24 testimonies and I'm just appalled at the inmate's lack of

25 true remorse after 30 plus years. Um, what he's been

1 saying during this is not true, and he continues to

2 perpetuate the lies that he did way back then in 1989. I

3 was the victim in 1989 of Morro Bay. Um, and I did not

4 speak to him at a post office. I did not invite him to my

5 home. He followed me home, um, about 11 miles and I no --

6 noticed him following me. And I actually went into the

7 house and picked up the phone to call 911, because I felt,

8 I was afraid, talked myself out of it because it was a

9 small town in Morro Bay with, you know, 4,000 people. Um,

10 talked myself out of it. A few minutes later, there's a

11 knock on the door and he -- I opened the door and he asked

12 me for some person's name and I said, please try

13 downstairs. And he put a mask on and pushed his way into

14 my home. Um, I was not able to identify him because he

15 did wear a mask. I was able to identify him in a voice

16 lineup though. And I can remember certain things about

17 that day that I'll never forget. While I was being raped

18 by Joseph Garcia at 18, I remember looking down from the

19 corner of the room of what was happening and feeling so

20 sorry for that girl. She did nothing to deserve this, and

21 she must be so scared. That's how I survived this attack.

22 I protected myself the only way that I could. We as

23 survivors are forced into the position of having to

24 ferociously and ten -- tenaciously stand up for ourselves

25 and other survivors and make our voices heard. Joseph

1   Garcia should not be granted early parole. He should be

2   held in prison until his original parole, which was

3   supposed to be 40 years at sentencing or even longer.

4   After listening to this man today, he should not be let

5   out. He has told you he will re-offend. He has said, I

6   basically said, I will do it again. Um, the remorse that

7   he is expressing is not true because again, he still tried

8   to turn it around that I invited him to my home. Um, and

9   then the other victims that have all stood strong and

10   stood up against him, he still diminishes that and says

11   that didn't happen either. Um, I do believe he is a

12   danger to society. Is he -- if, if he is released, will

13   there be a guarantee he will not be around children, young

14   girls, young boys, people that are weaker than him, people

15   who he can take advantage of. He's -- he's doing it to

16   people inside prison where they're protected and they're

17   still afraid of him. Um, please review all the past, all

18   the past crimes, all the victims, everyone who has stood

19   up and has gone against them. I do believe there are evil

20   people in this world, and Joseph Garcia is one of them. I

21   do not believe he is remorseful or he has been re

22   rehabilitated or has he tried to be rehabilitated. Um, I

23   hope you were -- oh, sorry. I, I survived the horrific

24   experience and I've been lucky enough to have gone to have

25   an amazing life. Mr. Mar -- Garcia thought he picked a

1   weak girl that didn't have the strength to fight back. I

2   might not have fought back that day, which quite frankly,

3   probably saved my life. However, I am not weak and I will

4   continue to be strong and relentless in using my voice to

5   ensure he stays in prison for as long as possible. Thank

6   you again, and I appreciate everyone's time.

7   **PRESIDING COMMISSIONER SHEFFIELD:** All right. Thank

8   you very much. And, um, next is C.P.

9   **C.P.:** Hi, um, my initials are C.P. I was 18 years

10 old on October 17, 1989, sitting at my home watching the

11 news coverage of the Loma Prieta earthquake when a masked

12 intruder broke into my home. He held a knife to my throat

13 and attempted to rape me. When my fight or flight

14 instinct kicked in, I chose to fight. In that moment, I

15 was prepared to die, if that was the cost of resisting. I

16 had no idea I was up against a violent serial rapist. All

17 I knew was that I had to fight and hope to survive. Due

18 to my tenacity and perhaps his desire for an easier

19 target, I did survive. After the attack, I could not be

20 in crowds. I believed that someone had watched me,

21 followed me home. I avoided people. I tried not to draw

22 attention. I developed severe anxiety and panic attacks,

23 and I dropped out of Cal Poly. My dream of becoming an

24 architect was gone. I could no longer focus or sit in

25 crowded classrooms. I took a self-defense class to try

1   and regain some sense of control and safety just in case

2   there was a next time. Months later, I returned to

3   college, but at a different school in a different major.

4   My life was forever changed. Being attacked in my own

5   home meant nowhere was safe. My body stayed in a constant

6   state of high alert. I didn't realize how constant until

7   last year, I sought therapy for depression and holistic

8   treatment for exhaustion. I learned that my cortisol, the

9   hormone that rises in the morning to give us energy, had

10   been depleted by years of stress. Instead of starting my

11   day energized, my body was already running on empty. I've

12   also struggled with my weight. Through therapy, I

13   realized part of me still believes it's safer to not be

14   what a predator might consider attractive. When I had my

15   daughter, my fear for her safety became part of her

16   upbringing. I taught her how to stay aware of her

17   surroundings, what to watch for, and how to be prepared.

18   At 16, I put her through the same self-defense class that

19   I took. This shows my trauma was still alive in me

20   decades later. Sadly, she has been in therapy for the

21   past two years for anxiety of her own. My intentions were

22   to protect her, but she never really had a chance to grow

23   up, carefree or fully trust the world. I passed along.

24   My fears and hypervigilance contributing to generational

25   trauma. These are only some of the impacts of the attack.

1 Others, I choose to keep private. I strongly oppose

2 parole for Joseph Garcia. His history shows that every

3 time he has been released, he has returned to violent sex

4 crimes. In the past, while fully able-bodied, he used

5 guns, knives, and threats to overpower his victims. His

6 age or reduced physical ability now does not change his

7 methods. Weapons and threats can be used by anyone

8 regardless of strength. I believe he will always be a

9 danger to society if released. I may not have been raped,

10 but I was violated. I may not have been killed, but that

11 night he killed the version of me that could have existed

12 had I not been attacked in my own home. I have lived with

13 the consequences of his actions every single day of my

14 life. He should live with the consequences of his choices

15 for the rest of his life behind bars. Thank you for

16 allowing me to speak today. I respectfully ask that you

17 deny parole and hold Joseph Garcia fully accountable for

18 the pain and trauma that he's inflicted. Thank you.

19   **PRESIDING COMMISSIONER SHEFFIELD:** Thank you. And

20 uh, next is Judge Estrada-Mullaney.

21   **THERESA ESTRADA-MULLANEY:** Turning the microphone on.

22 Can, can you hear me?

23   **DEPUTY COMMISSIONER METTE:** Yes.

24   **PRESIDING COMMISSIONER SHEFFIELD:** Yes.

25   **DEPUTY COMMISSIONER METTE:** Yes, we can.

1   **THERESA ESTRADA-MULLANEY:** My name is Theresa

2   Estrada-Mullaney. I was the -- I was the prosecutor of

3   the defendant's case from arraignment through the jury

4   trial and sentencing, a period of over two years. The

5   DA's office did not prosecute an innocent man. I served -

6   - after my career as an attorney, I served as a judge for

7   20 years in this county, and since my retirement from that

8   position, I continued to work as an assigned judge around

9   the state of California. I submitted a letter for your

10   consideration, and I am here today as the representative

11   for one of the defendant's eight victims, Jane Doe number

12   two, and now I will read her statement. It is my opinion

13   that Mr. Garcia displays no remorse for his actions, and

14   furthermore, until his agenda is to admit what he did to

15   all his victims and ask for forgiveness, then he's where

16   he needs to be until his final living days. About two

17   years ago, I received a letter in the mail at my home from

18   a friend of his that was writing a book and asked me to

19   change my story. He has served many years, but clearly

20   not enough time for him to ask forgiveness from all of his

21   victims. Therefore, until that letter arrives in the mail

22   from him, he shouldn't be given parole. Sincerely, Jane

23   Doe number two.

24   **PRESIDING COMMISSIONER SHEFFIELD:** All right, thank

25   you. And Mr. Miller.

1   **BILL MILLER:** Thank you. My name is Bill Miller.

2   I'm a retired senior district attorney investigator. I

3   was the lead investigator during the prosecution of this

4   inmate, Joseph P. Garcia, number, H01695. I worked on

5   this case with our other officers, deputies, detectives,

6   investigators, and the prosecutor for more than two years.

7   The inmate was convicted by the unanimous vote of a jury

8   based on scientific evidence, victim testimony, witness

9   testimony, other physical evidence, including phone

10   records, and a meticulous law enforcement investigation.

11   All of the inmate's claims that others were to blame for

12   his vicious acts were investigated and invalidated. All

13   of his alibi claims were investigated and invalidated.

14   This inmate exploited every delaying tactic at his

15   disposal during his long court process. He even sought to

16   intimidate one of his victims by insisting on representing

17   himself at one point, which allowed him to question one of

18   his rape victims during her testimony. Joseph B. Garcia

19   is here where he belongs in state prison where he cannot

20   engage in his favorite entertainment, entertainment, the

21   stalking, the attack, planning, the assault, the rape of

22   women and girls. Joseph B. Garcia is intelligent,

23   cunning, charming, and dangerous. Joseph B. Garcia has

24   never admitted responsibility for his life crimes. He has

25   not shown any remorse for these crimes. He has never

taken responsibility for the hurt he has inflicted on his
victims. He has never apologized and has continued to
blame the court, the police, the prosecutor, his attorney,
his jury, and his victims for his predicament. I suspect
he will add the parole board to his blame list after these
proceedings are concluded. I must address a claim the
inmate made at the previous parole hearing 10 years ago,
that there are many 1,000s of innocent men in prison
wrongly convicted, including himself. He is not innocent.
My career goal has been the pursuit of justice, not the
pursuit of convictions. The inmate is not innocent of
these crimes. He was lawfully convicted in a jury trial
based on overwhelming evidence and sentenced to state
prison. Thank you for your time, and I will now read the
written statements of victim, Tyra, and Victim, Cheryl. I
was able to speak with Tyra prior to this hearing. Tyra
remains terrified of this inmate. She lives in fear that
he might someday be released and would then be able to
find her and hurt her again or hurt her family or other
victims. Tyra and Cheryl wrote the following statements,
and these are their voices. To the parole board, my name
is Cheryl, and I'm a victim in the case involving Joseph
Garcia. I am submitting this statement to describe how
this crime has affected my life and to request that parole
be denied at this time to protect my safety. The

1 | consequences of the crime go far beyond the moment of the

2 | offense. I have experienced emotional distress, emotional

3 | effects, fear, anxiety, irritability, depression, PTSD,

4 | physical effects, sleep disturbance, headaches, changes in

5 | appetite, and these symptoms persist months and years

6 | later. I have difficulties with sleep and concentration,

7 | which have impacted my work performance and ability to

8 | engage in daily activities I used to enjoy. I often feel

9 | on edge, startled by sounds or situations that remind me

10 | of what happened, and I avoid certain places or activities

11 | to reduce triggering memories. The impact extends to my

12 | family as well. My partner, children and other relatives

13 | have witnessed my changes and have had to adjust their

14 | routines to support me, which has created strain in

15 | relationships. I continue to fear for my safety if the

16 | offender is released. The potential for recontact or

17 | retaliation, even if managed by supervision remains a real

18 | and persistent source of anxiety for me. Without

19 | assurances and effective risk reduction me -- measures, I

20 | do not feel safe in the community with Joseph Garcia being

21 | released. I am asking the parole board to deny parole at

22 | this time or to impose conditions that will reliably

23 | protect the public and reduce the risk of revictimization.

24 | If parole is granted, I urge the board to require ongoing

25 | risk assessment of verified treatment program tailored to

1 this offender, strict supervision restrictions on contact

2 and resources to ensure my safety and access to support

3 services. Thank you for your careful consideration of my

4 experience and for prior -- prioritizing community safety.

5 And that was from Cheryl. This statement is from Tyra. I

6 don't want to do this. I don't want to do this. I

7 thought it was over. I've moved on. I don't want to

8 think about any of these memories. It makes me physically

9 ill. When I found out that he was up for parole again, I

10 started to burn up. I could feel my emotions shaking,

11 unthinkable, unfathomable, how terrible and dangerous,

12 what harm is he going to inflict as soon as he is able?

13 I'm so angry because I'm terrified still. I'm scared for

14 myself and what harm he might wish on me. I'm scared for

15 his next victim, so I'm compelled beyond myself to speak

16 up. It's the only power I have left to protect the next

17 woman or child. My name is Tyra and I was raped as a

18 teenager by Joseph Garcia, who was a middle-aged adult

19 man. I didn't know anything about the world or evil, but

20 I was trying to be a righteous and praiseworthy young

21 woman who could someday be married in the temple of my

22 church. I was happy. I had great friends, good,

23 excellent parents, and I had plans for my future. When

24 Joseph raped me, it changed my life. I became

25 disconnected from friends and family and church for many

years. I was extremely depressed. For many years, I had
horrible flashbacks and terrible scary feelings. I had
stopped planning for the future. I became reckless and
careless of my life and safety. I had slipped into risky
behavior with little regard to reality or safety or common
sense. I could easily have severely hurt myself or gotten
myself into terrible situations. At some point, I
realized that I behaved the way I did because I had been
raped and had left me feeling worthless, and I had stopped
caring for my life. Now, Joseph Garcia is up for parole.
He writes lies and makes up stories. It makes my stomach
churn. It makes my bones shake. I feel my teeth
grinding. How terrifying, how horrible. Woe was me with
all my sorrow and all my fear and my tears. It's
unthinkable, a travesty. I hurt to think of what would
happen this very moment happened the very moment the
opportunity presented itself to this dark and putrid soul.
During the time that Joseph Garcia was free in the central
coast, multiple women were subjected to rape with a knife
or gun or brute strength by Joseph Garcia. Just like me,
he found a way into their lives by becoming, becoming part
of their life, watching and observing and planning to rape
his chosen victim. Some of his victims, forgiving
friends. I don't forgive him. How dare he even think
about me. It's gross that he touched me and stared at me

1   with sexual desire. It makes me want to puke. I was the

2   end of my freshman year of high school when I met Joseph

3   Garcia. I had just gotten home from school and I was

4   alone. Joseph showed up at my door right after I had

5   gotten home and told me he was a friend of my mom's from

6   the gym, asking where she was and if anybody, anybody else

7   was home. When he found out no one was else was there.

8   He walked inside and asked me to lay on the ground so he

9   could instruct me with hand weights. He was creepy, and

10   he looked over my body and he was commenting on my body.

11   I felt so uncomfortable. I got up and he walked -- I got

12   up and he wanted to walk around my house and talk about my

13   church. He got really religious and was <inaudible> my

14   church. It was so weird. I didn't understand why he was

15   talking to me. It was unusual behavior. He left before

16   anyone else in my family got home. Somehow he tricked my

17   parents into thinking he could be a helpful mentor to my

18   brother and came over to our house sometimes. I would

19   always hide in my room because he would stare at me in an

20   unsettling manner. He would stare at me and smile like he

21   had a secret. He got me a job at Homes and Land Magazine

22   and just inserted himself into our lives, taking advantage

23   of my good Christian parents' kind and gullible nature.

24   When my parents went out of town, he knew -- he knew the

25   front door had been broken and he knew that my brother was

1 supposed to have it fixed and didn't. He knew my brother

2 was always at his friend's home on the coast, and he knew

3 that Carla, a lady from Homes and Land magazine, was

4 staying with me while my parents were out of town. He met

5 me at the end of my freshman year. He planned all summer

6 and then he raped me in my bed at gunpoint. He woke me up

7 in the middle of the night. He was standing over me in my

8 bed, had he been looking in my windows, he was terrifying.

9 He hit me with his gun. He told me I had to be quiet so

10 that I had to whisper. He wants to know where my brother

11 was. I said, I didn't know. At first, I thought he was

12 going to hurt my brother. I was so worried and I didn't

13 want him to know where my brother was. He said he did

14 drugs with needles. He told me he needed help. I didn't

15 know how I could help. He told me Carla was tied up and

16 he made it seem as though there was someone else there. I

17 believed him. I was so worried. I wondered if the same

18 thing was happening to Carla. He made me take off my

19 shirt. I said, oh no. And that's when I knew he was

20 there to rape me. He told me my breasts were small. I

21 told him I was 15. He made me take off all my clothes.

22 He made me rub his penis. I was grossed out. He hit me

23 all around my neck with his gun. I had bruises. He got

24 up on the bed. I sort of checked out while he did things

25 to me. I still don't remember everything clearly,

1 although some of it I remember perfectly. I think he was

2 trying to arouse me as though I was his lover. Hours went

3 by. I could see a digital clock, hours of molesting me,

4 and I didn't even know what happened. I think he was down

5 between my legs because then he climbed up on top of me.

6 He began to enter me and I yelled. He hit me with his gun

7 and told me to be quiet. He had just taken away my

8 virginity. Then he ejaculated on my chest. He told me

9 not to move for a while or he would shoot me. I waited

10 for the amount of time he told me then I called 911. He

11 actually had the audacity to show up at my house the next

12 day or so. I was asleep in the living room. He had

13 ruined my sanctuary. My dad answered the door. I saw him

14 looking at me. He was leery at me. I am horrified and

15 terrified at the thought of him going free. He wanted

16 this. He wants to rape women. He plays a game where he

17 is there to help, to be family, friends, a mentor to young

18 people. He gets to know everything he needs to, needs to

19 so that he can rape who he wants to. It's his goal, his

20 plan, his game. He studies how not to get caught. He's

21 sneaky. He told my brother and his friends about he, how

22 he had learned how not to get caught committing crimes.

23 He used my t-shirt to wipe his fluids off of me. He was

24 thorough. He missed some of my arm though. Later at the

25 doctor's office, right after the rape, the nurse used a

black light to look me over for evidence. We saw it, we
celebrated, we had evidence. Do you understand me? Do
you want him back out in the world just so he can rape as
many beautiful women and young girls as he can. He wants
to seduce women and rape their children. He wants to come
into good people's lives and make himself useful, so that
he can plan to rape someone in the family. He will kneel
down with his victims and bow his head and pray for people
to let him get away with his crimes. He thinks he's
special. He thinks he's right. He thinks he's so great
and that women want him. I'm not making this stuff up.
He wrote a book. He's just over there offending me and
attacking us, my sister victims, like it's no big deal.
Like, I should just, just get over that. He changed the
course of my whole life. I'm so sick of trying to explain
that this inmate, this criminal is rotten to the court.
He exact -- he is exactly where he should be. He lives in
the world he carved out for himself with his hard work of
planning for months and obsessing over his victims and
living out his heinous fantasies. He's glad he did it. I
don't want to write these things. I certainly never want
to see him again or hear his voice and his lies. I never
want to look into his eyes again and see his smug
expression. I don't want to talk about how despondent I
felt for so many years. I don't want to think about all

1 the horrible things he did to me. I don't want to feel

2 all stirred up and angry and worried and depressed that

3 this is being asked of me by all who I could save. But,

4 but how can I not? What if I didn't and he got out and

5 hurt my mom or found me and raped a new victim? What if I

6 just let it go? How could I be happy? How could I be

7 old? How could I feel brave or proud? I've been stalling

8 on out on this letter. I didn't want to write it, but how

9 could I face myself if I, if I didn't protect myself and

10 my mom? How could I face myself if I didn't speak up for

11 all the women he raped? The worst is how could we face

12 ourselves knowing in our gut he will gladly rape again

13 with no remorse or worries? No, it would be a crime

14 against innocent people for me to be silent. So,

15 ultimately, I am grateful to be able to speak up at this

16 parole hearing and to say, I'm strong and powerful because

17 I spoke up with a burning conviction of the truth. I

18 still also feel sick and worried that it isn't enough.

19 Please, with all my heart, hear me at the peril of

20 innocent people who may not come into contact with a

21 sinister and deceptive person, Joseph Garcia. Please with

22 all my heart, and I promise you, I will always stand up

23 for what is true and right. I am Tyra and I have to

24 survive rape instead of feel the joy of my youth.

25   **PRESIDING COMMISSIONER SHEFFIELD:** Thank you so much

1   all for your statements. Um, and at this time we will

2   exit to deliberate. So, please remain online and we will

3   return when we conclude.

4   **[RECESS]**

5

6

7

8

9

10

11

12

13

14

15

16

17

18

19

20

21

22

23

24

25

1　　　　　**CALIFORNIA BOARD OF PAROLE HEARINGS**

2　　　　　　　　　　　**DECISION**

3　　　　**DEPUTY COMMISSIONER METTE:**　We're back on record.

4　　　　**PRESIDING COMMISSIONER SHEFFIELD:**　The time is 1:15

5　　p.m., and all parties previously identified have returned

6　　for issuance of the decision regarding Joseph Garcia, CDCR

7　　number, H-0-1-6-9-5.　Uh, this is a denial of parole.

8　　This is a five year denial.　Based on the legal standards

9　　and the record, we find you pose a current unreasonable

10　　risk to public safety and are therefore not suitable for

11　　parole.　In reviewing parole suitability, a denial of

12　　parole must be based on findings that the incarcerated

13　　person poses a current danger to society.　Also, in this

14　　case, the law does require special consideration of

15　　elderly factors as well.　Uh, the panel did consider your

16　　central file, Comprehensive Risk Assessment, documents in

17　　the 10 day file, your testimony, uh, statements from

18　　victims and victims representatives and input from the

19　　attorneys.　Uh, we did not rely on confidential

20　　information for our decision today.　So, our decision is

21　　based on the following.　Um, your static factors, those

22　　are all clearly aggravating factors.　If we look at your

23　　criminal history, it is extensive.　It started young, uh,

24　　burglary, robbery, uh, parole violations as a juvenile.

25　　**JOSEPH GARCIA　　H01695　　08/12/2025　　DECISION PAGE 1**

1 It accelerated on, uh, to continued burglaries, thefts,

2 drug use, and then onward to false imprisonment, forcible

3 rape, uh, sodomy and weapon use. Your self-control at the

4 time of your offense or offenses in this case is

5 aggravating. Um, today you did testify or, um, at least

6 affirm your prior statements that you are innocent of the

7 bulk of the crimes that you have been convicted of. Um,

8 the panel did find that you lacked sincerity and

9 credibility in that, uh, testimony and that position that

10 you took today. And we do consider the record contained

11 in the appellate documents and the court documents in your

12 file, uh, to be the facts of this case. Um, given that

13 the panel does find at the time of your commitment

14 offense, you did not control your behavior in a number of

15 ways. You have numerous violent rapes or attempted rapes

16 against many victims. Uh, these crimes often involve

17 substance use. You were drinking at the time, you were

18 very manipulative. Some of these were planned crimes that

19 were days, weeks, months. Um, these were not impulsive

20 crimes and, um, they involved sexual deviance. You've

21 been diagnosed with a paraphilic disorder, the coercive

22 type of paraphilic disorder that played into your

23 offenses, uh, just incredibly callous crimes, um,

24 targeting vulnerable victims and, uh, planning to harm

25 **JOSEPH GARCIA   H01695   08/12/2025   DECISION PAGE 2**

them and then following through. However, those are the
static factors. They are not going to change. Uh, those
unchangeable factors may no longer indicate a risk of
current danger to society when there has been a lengthy
period of rehabilitative programming. So, the next
factors are the dynamic factors, this is where you can
show rehabilitative change. Your programming, we found to
be aggravating. You really have not been involved in much
programming. Lately, we can see a real decline. Um, and
what was really significant for us is that we see no work
in the area of sex offending. Your crimes are sex
offenses. Without that, your programming is just woefully
insufficient. You need to address your primary risk
factor, um, in order to take adequate programming. Um, we
also didn't see significant victim impact, domestic
violence, healthy relationships. All of these issues are
still there, still present. You have not taken
programming in them. Um, we gave this, uh, category a
little bit less weight given some of the cognitive issues,
but ultimately, we'll, we'll explain later. Um, it, it
still did play into our decision, given what we saw and
what we believe you're capable of today. Uh, your
institutional behavior was also aggravating. Uh, you have
a number of write-ups that we spoke about during just the

JOSEPH GARCIA   H01695   08/12/2025   DECISION PAGE 3

1 last couple of years. Um, you have five disrespects
2 without potential for violence, uh, from the past two
3 years. You have disobeying an order from 2024. You have
4 two false reports of criminal offenses from 2024. So, we
5 really see this escalating, uh, you know, poor behavior in
6 prison. And so, that had to be an aggravating factor for
7 us today. Uh, your personal change, this is really the
8 crux of our decision that was aggravating. Um, again,
9 you're re -- you have all this recent misconduct. It's
10 showing -- it's not just consistent, it is accelerating,
11 disrespect, impulsivity, rule breaking, uh, all of these
12 things that have a nexus to your past criminal behavior.
13 Um, additionally, as I mentioned before, this is a case of
14 clearly implausible denials. Um, you have an extensive
15 record of predatory crimes of sexual violence or attempted
16 sexual violence, uh, most of which you deny committing.
17 You cannot internalize programming if you don't admit what
18 you did. You cannot address what you've done if you won't
19 say that you did it. Um, your denials show, you know,
20 continued criminal thinking, continued manipulation, and a
21 real lack of self-awareness. Uh, we did not talk about
22 all these crimes in detail today for a number of reasons,
23 but, you know, the panel did review the facts in the
24 record, which were extensive, and we did hear victim
25 **JOSEPH GARCIA   H01695   08/12/2025   DECISION PAGE 4**

1   statements today reiterating those facts. Um, your

2   continued denials of these crimes are frankly, somewhat

3   offensive to our intelligence, but more importantly, they

4   are offensive to the many women that you grievously

5   harmed. Um, you clearly have very little understanding of

6   victim impact, um, if you are able to come here today and

7   deny the pain that you caused these women as they sit here

8   in front of you. Um, we do thank the victims for coming

9   forward with their statements today. Um, the great

10 bravery that they showed in doing so. Um, we do

11 appreciate that, um, so that your stories can be heard

12 and, and can be added to the discussion here. They are

13 very important. Um, and Mr. Garcia, your lack of empathy

14 towards your victims, your lack of understanding of harm,

15 um, that does, um, serve as a continued risk factor as

16 well. Uh, you also continue to demonstrate disrespect and

17 mistreatment of women, uh, that you don't really seem to

18 see. Uh, I don't think that you really have any

19 cognizance that you're doing it still, uh, you have been

20 manipulative with your fiance, lying to her about your

21 very serious criminal history until just a couple months

22 ago. Uh, you spoke about objectifying and sexualizing

23 female staff members recently and your instinct to think

24 they're flirting with you. Uh, you recently engaged in

25 **JOSEPH GARCIA   H01695   08/12/2025   DECISION PAGE 5**

1 phone sex with your fiance. When you were asked what was

2 problematic about it, you said the problem was that the

3 officers could think poorly of your fiance because of it.

4 Uh, that response was telling, uh, because first you did

5 not identify that engaging in deviant sexual acts that are

6 against the rules is consistent with your past criminal

7 behavior. You are still doing it. Um, and also your

8 thought was that the officers would judge only the woman

9 in this circumstance and that, and you did not consider

10 the fact that they might be judging you as well. Uh,

11 these are all current issues with misogyny and sexual

12 deviancy that are still concerning, uh, given your record

13 and clearly connected to your commitment offense. Um, the

14 issue of cognitive decline had come up today. Uh, we

15 considered that. We did see some at times minor

16 cognitive, uh, decline, which we took into consideration.

17 But ultimately, Mr. Garcia, you have not changed your

18 position, um, on these crimes. You have consistently

19 denied that you committed these offenses. Now, you have,

20 it sounds like, become more forthcoming about, um, one or

21 two of them. But the denials have been consistent that

22 isn't something that seems to be a product of cognitive

23 decline in any way. Um, you also continue to manipulate

24 others. You tried to manipulate us today. Um, and so,

25 **JOSEPH GARCIA   H01695   08/12/2025   DECISION PAGE 6**

1   you know, you were able to answer our questions. You were

2   able to understand them. Sometimes maybe it took us, uh,

3   we had to repeat them, but you, you did clearly understand

4   what we were saying and respond to our questions in, in a

5   coherent way. Uh, so, we did not find that cognitive

6   decline, um, weighed significantly in, in mitigation for

7   you in this, in this case. Um, your release plan was also

8   aggravating. You submitted some support letters, but not

9   any plans. Uh, you did tell the clinician you didn't want

10   to go to transitional housing, which is just a very poor

11   idea. You would need the transitional housing. You'll

12   need the extra support in order to ensure a safe landing

13   in the community. Um, so, you still -- you don't have any

14   relapse plans. You know, you, you need to really think

15   about what your risk factors are. You spoke a little bit

16   about that today in terms of triggers and coping skills.

17   So, start putting that stuff down on paper and start

18   really being honest with yourself and thinking about what

19   things you need to look out for that could cause you to

20   re-offend and how you're going to manage those triggers

21   and those risks, um, in the community. Uh, we did also

22   consider your CRA. This was a recent high rating. Um, as

23   I said at the beginning of the hearing, a high risk rating

24   in your late 70s is pretty unusual. Um, but after

25   **JOSEPH GARCIA   H01695   08/12/2025   DECISION PAGE 7**

1 reviewing your record and speaking with you today, we do

2 believe that that was a well-supported rating. Um, we did

3 also give special consideration to elderly factors. And

4 certainly we took into account you are 77 years old. Uh,

5 you do have a number of health issues. You, um, again,

6 have some minor cognitive decline that seems to be

7 beginning to happen. Um, however, you have continued to

8 engage in misconduct. In some ways the clinician seems to

9 think it's actually escalating your misconduct. Um, the

10 fact that you're aging and, and becoming less in control

11 of your behaviors as a result. Uh, so, the elderly

12 considerations didn't weigh heavily again, in terms of

13 mitigation here. Um, before I discuss the denial,

14 commissioner, do you have any further comments?

15 **DEPUTY COMMISSIONER METTE:** Thank you. This is a

16 joint decision by the panel and I concur with the

17 findings. I do have a couple of comments that I want to

18 make. Um, specifically on recommendations. I can

19 obviously concur fully with comm -- what Commissioner

20 Sheffield says. I do want to include some further

21 recommendations as far as programming concerning denial

22 management, criminal thinking, continuing with mental

23 health management programming, at least through, uh, EOP

24 and substance abuse. We really didn't touch on this at

25 **JOSEPH GARCIA   H01695   08/12/2025   DECISION PAGE 8**

1 | all, but as indicated in the CRA, there are positive tests
2 | at least for methamphetamine, which is quite surprising
3 | for someone in his 70s. Um, but it's there, um, that
4 | needs to be addressed for other panels will ask you. When
5 | I was preparing for this case, and I was struck by a quote
6 | that was in the last hearing, that was from the last
7 | hearing 10 years ago, and I'm going to read that quote
8 | from the presiding commissioner from then. Um, and this
9 | was in discussing, um, institutional behavior that was
10 | close in time to that prior hearing. This is page 156 of
11 | the prior transcript starting at line 15. We know that
12 | the life crimes would appear to us to be very impulsive
13 | and for the same reason that your prior criminal history,
14 | that's impulsive. And what these 115s suggest to us is
15 | that you have a continued problem with controlling your
16 | impulsivity and particularly your actions with females.
17 | And given the fact that your exposure to your female base
18 | -- uh, the, the -- to your victim based females in prison
19 | is severely limited here. That last 115 was particularly
20 | concerning to us because it seemed to be a signal of a
21 | mindset that is yet to be abated. And that suggests to us
22 | that you still don't have the necessary skillset and
23 | coping mechanisms necessary to abate that mindset. And
24 | that would suggest to us that absent those, you're likely
25 | **JOSEPH GARCIA   H01695   08/12/2025   DECISION PAGE 9**

1 to respond as you have in the past. I'm struck by that

2 quote because besides potential minor co -- mild cognitive

3 decline, I don't know what's different. And I'll say that

4 we weighted the cognitive issues in your age heavily in

5 making the decision, but it bears the question as far as

6 if that quote still applies, something needs to be thought

7 of concerning that. We wish you the best of luck.

8 Commissioner.

9   **PRESIDING COMMISSIONER SHEFFIELD:** Thank you. So,

10 based on these findings, we do conclude you pose a current

11 unreasonable risk of danger to public safety if released

12 and are unsuitable for parole. Uh, we do find clear and

13 convincing evidence that neither a 10 or 15 year denial is

14 appropriate in consideration of victim and public safety.

15 And here is really where your age and current diagnosis,

16 uh, played a factor for us. So, uh, we did ultimately

17 find that a five year denial would be appropriate as the

18 time necessary for you to address the risk factors that we

19 have discussed. Um, additionally, we did hear statements

20 today from the victims that raised some concerns for us,

21 uh, regarding the publication of this book where you are

22 claiming innocence and people potentially reaching out and

23 harassing the victims. It sounds like this was quite

24 recent in the last few years. Uh, this is of grave

25 **JOSEPH GARCIA   H01695   08/12/2025   DECISION PAGE 10**

1 | concern if it does bear out to be true. So, prior to the
2 | next hearing, we are going to order, or at this time, we
3 | will be ordering an investigation so that the results of
4 | the investigation will be available to the next panel at
5 | your next hearing. And the investigation will be into,
6 | um, what this book is, what your participation in this
7 | book has been, Mr. Garcia, who else has participated in
8 | this book. Is this -- are these your support people, um,
9 | that are helping you claim your innocence, and who, if
10 | anyone, has reached out to the victims or other people
11 | connected with this case in connection with this book and
12 | what have they been saying to them, um, because this does
13 | raise real issues, uh, real questions around, uh, current
14 | dangerousness that are, are necessary to explore. And,
15 | um, it is gravely concerning that the victims would
16 | potentially continue to be harassed, traumatized, and
17 | harmed in this way so many years after the offense. Um --
18 | **DEPUTY DISTRICT ATTORNEY CURLEY:** Commissioner
19 | Sheffield?
20 | **PRESIDING COMMISSIONER SHEFFIELD:** Yes.
21 | **DEPUTY DISTRICT ATTORNEY CURLEY:** Um, just before we
22 | move on to the next point, if I could, um, just go ahead
23 | for the record, uh, put on the record and give that
24 | investigator a headstart on that investigation and say, I
25 | **JOSEPH GARCIA   H01695   08/12/2025   DECISION PAGE 11**

1   don't know if you can see that, I actually have a copy of

2   the book. It is entitled, um, Eye Witness, the Case of

3   the Carefully Crafted Central Coast Rapist by Lori, O --

4   L-O-R-I, Carangelo, C-A-R-A-N-G-E-L-O. Here is a copy.

5   Again, it's a little bit hard with this, um -- with the

6   way the cameras work in here, but, but this is, this is

7   the book. Um, and I know we don't usually make a video

8   record, so if there's any other records I can provide to

9   the panel via email, I'm happy to do so.

10 **PRESIDING COMMISSIONER SHEFFIELD:** Thank you. I

11 appreciate that. We'll let the investigative team know.

12 And, um, and that name -- that author's name did sound

13 like a name of a support person, uh, letter, you know,

14 that we have received in the, the file of someone who

15 intends to support you, Mr. Garcia. So, again, that's --

16 just reiterates the concerns that we have. Um, so, this

17 all being said, um, Mr. Garcia, we do hope that you start

18 really taking your programming seriously and you do take a

19 hard look at yourself, um, and begin to dig into, you

20 know, who you were, who you are, and why you have done

21 what you've done and why you continue to struggle, uh,

22 even today with many of these same issues. And, uh, we do

23 wish you luck on that. You can, uh, request an earlier

24 hearing than the denial period we issue today, if there

25 **JOSEPH GARCIA   H01695   08/12/2025   DECISION PAGE 12**

1 has been a change in circumstance or new information,

2 establishing a reasonable likelihood that you do not

3 require an additional period of incarceration. The

4 decision's not final. It will be reviewed by the board

5 for up to 120 days, and you'll be notified in writing if

6 there are any changes to the decision. So, thank you to

7 all who participated in the hearing today. The time is

8 1:32 p.m., and the hearing is adjourned.

9   **ADJOURNMENT**

10

11

12

13

14

15

16

17

18

19

20

21

22

23

24

25 **JOSEPH GARCIA   H01695   08/12/2025   DECISION PAGE 13**

THIS TRANSCRIPT CONTAINS THE PROPOSED DECISION OF THE

BOARD OF PAROLE HEARINGS (BOARD) ANNOUNCED AT YOUR RECENT

BOARD HEARING AND IS PROVIDED TO YOU IN COMPLIANCE WITH

PENAL CODE SECTION 3041.5, SUBDIVISION (A)(4), AND

CALIFORNIA CODE OF REGULATIONS, TITLE 15, SECTION 2254.

THIS PROPOSED DECISION WILL BECOME FINAL WITHIN 120 DAYS

OF THE DATE OF THE HEARING AS REQUIRED BY PENAL CODE

SECTION 3041, SUBDIVISION (B), UNLESS THE BOARD NOTIFIES

YOU IN WRITING BEFORE THEN THAT THE PROPOSED DECISION HAS

BEEN MODIFIED, VACATED OR REFERRED TO THE FULL BOARD,

SITTING EN BANC, DUE TO AN ERROR OF LAW, ERROR OF FACT OR

NEW INFORMATION PURSUANT TO CALIFORNIA CODE OF

REGULATIONS, TITLE 15, SECTION 2042.   THEREAFTER, THE

GOVERNOR HAS AUTHORITY TO REVIEW THE BOARD'S DECISION AND

AFFIRM, MODIFY, OR REVERSE IT PURSUANT TO PENAL CODE

SECTIONS 3041.1 AND 3041.2.

JOSEPH GARCIA   H01695   08/12/2025   DECISION PAGE 14

CERTIFICATE AND DECLARATION OF TRANSCRIBER

I, Peter Neubauer, am a disinterested party, and have no interest in the outcome of the hearing. Further, I certify this transcript is a true, complete, and accurate record, to the best of my ability, of the recorded material provided for transcription of proceeding for:

In the matter of the Parole   CDCR Number: **H01695**
Consideration Hearing of:

JOSEPH GARCIA

CALIFORNIA HEALTH CARE FACILITY

STOCKTON, CALIFORNIA

AUGUST 12, 2025

10:45 AM

Signed: *Peter Neubauer*

Transcribed by: Peter Neubauer

Dictate Express Transcription

Attorney Christine Veronica Morse (Fitch) warns Joe to STOP promoting "EYEWITNESS" book"

BOOKS ABOUT YOU

STOP promoting your books. Make sure no one ever reaches out to victims or their family or friends. Because the rape you admitted to is in the book as a rape that you claim to be innocent of, future commissioners are probably going to want you to set the record straight to all the readers of, and believers in, that book. That likely requires you to tell all of the people who have supported you over the years that you are *not* innocent of everything.

Part Two of Plan for Next Hearing

Once you have gone 18 months to 3 years with no violations, and you have completed significant amounts of programming, especially the sexual offender counseling and the Road to Freedom, you can submit a petition to advance your hearing.

You are only allowed to submit this petition once every three years. Therefore, if you submit it too soon, and it is denied, you have to wait 3 years to submit it again. So don't submit it too soon (like only 6-12 months from now; even 18 months is kind of soon).

When you submit your petition to advance your hearing, you list the reasons why your circumstances have *significantly changed* from when you got your denial. In your case, you will say something like the following.

I have been completely violation-free since my last hearing. I have done extensive programming, including sex offender programming. I have written detailed relapse prevention plans. I have release plans and a support network. As I am almost 80 years old, my medical conditions have worsened and my cognitive decline has increased.

If your petition to advance is approved, then the Board will schedule another parole hearing within 6 months of that approval.

This two-part plan (first, do the work, then, submit the petition) is totally doable for you. You are very smart and you achieve what you put your mind to. Remember, once you submit the petition, keep doing the work! You must stay in the programming, especially sex offender programming or therapy, and you must stay violation-free all the way up to your next hearing.

I am taken off your case at this point, and I must focus on my other cases. However, if you have questions, you can certainly write to me. I am rooting for you, Joseph. I REALLY want to see you get out of there. You shouldn't be there any longer, you've served enough.

Sincerely,

Christine Morse

If it's true that Joe Garcia suffers "mild Dementia," it is mportant to know that Dementia begins as an occasional **loss of thinking, remembering, and *reasoning* skills.** On September 15, 2025, Joe Garcia, wrote to this author that [his attorney]: "suggested to me if I didn't give the board something fresh like a confession of one of the crimes that I would most likely be denied another 10 years. I gave in out of fear and gave a false confession of the Morro Bay rape with the Black attacker [of Jaqueline Brooks]. She was at the board by way of monitor screen. I found out later that she was there because someone had informed her that I had confessed to the crime in my Parole Evaluation which I am also sending you. I was told to 'act' like an old remorseful man in front of the board members which I did. I was told I would probably get a suitability finding which turned out to be another 'circus.' Lori, I am back to my normal self. No more operating out of fear. Next time I will tell the truth and let things fall where they may." [Author's Note: In 1989, Jacqueline Brooks, then age 18, assisted creation of the police artist's composite sketch of her assailant (page 26, and on the cover of this book) who she described as "Negro," but at Joe's 2025 parole hearing, she claimed it was Joe. In 1989, Tyra Wittmeyer, then 15, identified her rapist whose voice she knew, stating *"It wasn't Joe... It was Steve"* (page 23) but that also changed at Joe's 2025 parole hearing.]

Now for an update with my attorney. It was suggested to me if I didn't give the board, something fresh like a confession of one of the crimes that I would most likely be denied another 10 years.

I gave in out of fear and gave a false confession of the Morro Bay rape, with the BLACK attacker. (She was at the board by way

2.

of monitor, the screen, I found out later that she was there because someone had informed her that I had confessed to the crime in my Parole Evaluation which I am also sending you.

I was told to "act" like an old remorseful man in front of the Board members (screen) which I did. I was told I'd probably get a suitability finding which turned out to be another "circus".

Lori, I am now back to my normal self. No more operating out of fear. Next time I will tell the truth and let things fall where they may.

www.ingramcontent.com/pod-product-compliance
Lightning Source LLC
Chambersburg PA
CBHW061425040426
42450CB00007B/911